YOUNG CHILDREN WITH SPECIAL NEEDS

A Developmentally Appropriate Approach

Michael D. Davis
Virginia Commonwealth University

Jennifer L. Kilgo
University of Alabama at Birmingham

Michael Gamel-McCormick
University of Delaware

Allyn and Bacon
Boston ■ London ■ Toronto ■ Sydney ■ Tokyo ■ Singapore

Series Editor: Ray Short
Editorial Assistant: Karin Huang
Senior Marketing Manager: Kathy Hunter
Editorial Production Administrator: Donna Simons
Editorial-Production Service: Matrix Productions Inc.
Composition Buyer: Linda Cox
Manufacturing Buyer: David Suspanic
Cover Administrator: Jenny Hart

Copyright © 1998 by Allyn & Bacon
A Viacom Company
160 Gould Street
Needham Heights, MA 02194

Internet: abacon.com
America Online: keyword: College Online

Library of Congress Cataloging-in-Publication Data

Davis, Michael D.
    Young children with special needs : a developmentally appropriate approach / Michael D. Davis, Jennifer L. Kilgo, Michael Gamel-McCormick.
        p.   cm.
    Includes bibliographical references and index.
    ISBN 0-205-18894-X
    1. Handicapped children—Education (Early childhood)   2. Inclusive education.   I. Kilgo, Jennifer Lynn.   II. Gamel-McCormick, Michael.
III. Title.
LC4019.3.D38   1998
371.9'047—DC21   97-44676
                                                              CIP

Printed in the United States of America

10 9 8 7 6 5 4 3 2 1   02 01 00 99 98 97

DEDICATIONS

To Bud, who evolved from professor to mentor to friend. To Meg and Sally, who influenced my earlier writing, and to Cassady and Crash, who influence me today; I love you, and you love me right back. And to Connie, who is always and forever the sunshine of my life. —MDD

Thank you to the many families of children with special needs who have taught me so much, especially my friend and colleague, Hansi Brittain, and her family. Hansi's influence is apparent throughout this book.

I would like to acknowledge gratefully my entire family, who provided their unwavering support throughout the writing of this manuscript. To Anna Katherine, my daughter, who is the light of my life, I thank you for always waiting patiently for me to "finish just one more paragraph." It's hard to wait when there are frogs to be caught, dolls to be fed, and games to be played. To Alan, my husband and greatest fan, I say thanks for believing in me and in the importance of my work. Finally, I dedicate my work on this project to my dear late father, James E. Kilgo, who so carefully instilled in me many years ago that the greatest joys in life come from achievement. May he know the pleasure of this accomplishment. —JLK

My thanks to the many families of children with and without disabilities with whom I have worked. It is through your experiences and willingness to share that I have learned important lessons about working with your children and methods for passing along that information to others. —MTG-M

CONTENTS

LIST OF FIGURES

LIST OF TABLES

PREFACE

Young Children with Special Needs: A Developmentally Appropriate Approach is meant to assist practioners, both preservice and inservice, in both general education and special education, in designing effective, appropriate learning programs for young children with disabilities. The book is based on the premise that classroom modifications implemented to make learning accessible for a child with a disability often improve learning for other children as well.

The approach of this text crosses two disciplines: early childhood education and early childhood special education. These fields have been distinctly separated for twenty or more years and have begun to come together during the past decade. As young children with disabilities have moved into more natural settings such as preschools, child care centers, and family day care, a need has increased to apply the special skills, knowledge, and strategies of early childhood special education in these more traditional early childhood settings. Likewise, teachers in the early segregated programs for young children with special needs have recognized that peers with typically developing skills are important models, motivators, and reinforcers for children with disabilities. The realization that each field has much to offer the other has been one of the wonderful by-products of this emerging collaboration.

Early childhood education and early childhood special education have many similarities and areas of agreement. They have a common foundation in child development. In addition, both fields value the family as the critical component in a child's background and understand the importance of building on the experiences that the child brings to the classroom.

Of late, three additional areas have shown widespread agreement across the two fields: (1) young children's need for hands-on, interactive learning; (2) a curriculum that reflects the social, emotional, physical, and cognitive growth of children; and (3) the importance of developmentally appropriate practice (DAP) as a vehicle for developing programs for all young children.

Developmentally appropriate practice reflects children's natural learning abilities and assists them in growing in all areas. Such practice is based on children's real experiences with their world and provides them with many opportunities to interact with materials, peers, and adults.

Both early childhood and early childhood special educators have begun to recognize that the foundation of interactions with materials, peers, and adults upon which DAP is grounded is also the basis of most special education strategies. The names for the interactions are different (e.g., reinforcers and peer/adult responses, motivators and children's preferences/interests, antecedents and teacher-arranged learning environments), and the methods of ensuring that those interactions occur are sometimes different. However, as professionals in each of the fields collaborate further, they are recognizing that the approaches and strategies can be blended to enhance all children's development and learning.

We have worked to incorporate the important contributions of both fields into a text that reveals not a patchwork of these contributions, but a finely woven fabric in which families, early childhood educators, and early childhood special educators all support young children with special needs.

The book contains a number of features that should assist readers in moving from theory to practice. Each chapter begins with a list of objectives designed to guide readers and concludes with a set of activities and questions that can be used to review major ideas. Three case studies of young children with disabilities are in Chapter 1. Although some modifications have been made to ensure confidentiality, the cases of Tarrel, Brad, and Tiffany are real. They reflect the children's experiential backgrounds, likes and dislikes, family concerns, and educational programs. Each of the cases is revisited throughout the book, enabling readers to reassess continuously the children's learning needs, based on information presented in subsequent chapters.

The best teachers are those who use their professional skills and knowledge to observe carefully, plan thoroughly, teach thoughtfully and systematically, and assess accurately. These teachers are sensitive to the diversity found in their classrooms and ensure that the curriculum and instructional methodologies reflect the differences in all children. It is our hope that this book will enable more professionals to join the category of "best teachers."

ACKNOWLEDGMENTS

A word of thanks is extended to our colleagues at Virginia Commonwealth University, the University of Alabama at Birmingham, and the University of Delaware. Their support and friendship are greatly appreciated.

Debbie Woodward, a friend and colleague at Virginia Commonwealth University, wrote Chapter 8. She brings a wealth of knowledge and practical, sensible ideas to guiding the behavior of young children with disabilities.

The Virginia Commonwealth University Childcare Center and Kindergarten and the University of Alabama RISE program were very gracious in allowing us to take pictures of their children and teachers. Both are fine examples of inclusive learning centers for young children.

The authors are indebted to the following people, who consented to review individual chapters during the development of the book: Amy Sue Reilly, Auburn University, and Barbara Lowenthal, Northeastern Illinois University. Their ideas helped to refine the book and make it more "user friendly."

The able assistance of Ray Short and his colleagues at Allyn and Bacon made this work a reality. Ray's continuous encouragement and subtle nudging kept us reasonably on target and in relatively good humor. Karin Huang's willingness to answer countless questions cordially and Merrill Peterson's fine editing are greatly appreciated.

Last, we proudly acknowledge the hundreds of teachers, children, and families who have touched our lives and informed this book. We have tried to give a voice to their concerns, questions, and practices.

1

EARLY CHILDHOOD EDUCATION AND EARLY CHILDHOOD SPECIAL EDUCATION: THE BEST OF BOTH WORLDS

> *Good practice in schools depends on seeing the world*
> *through each child's eyes, registering objectively*
> *their interests and existing competencies, and*
> *understanding sufficiently the principles of*
> *development to know how to help each child learn*
> *efficiently, effectively and meaningfully. Good*
> *practice does not permit asking children to learn*
> *now, with difficulty, something they will manage*
> *more easily later. Nor does it include busy work, the*
> *teaching of isolated skill development through*
> *memorization and rote, or a reliance on work sheets.*
> *—Gifford, 1992, p. 8*

OBJECTIVES

As a result of reading this chapter, readers should be able to perform the following:

- Describe the common foundation between early childhood education and early childhood special education.
- Explain the basic premises of developmentally appropriate practice.
- Describe some of the factors that limit the use of developmentally appropriate practice in the classroom.
- Justify the role of parents as partners in decision making in developmentally appropriate classrooms.

INTEGRATING EARLY CHILDHOOD EDUCATION AND EARLY CHILDHOOD SPECIAL EDUCATION

The purpose of this book is to provide early childhood education (ECE) and early childhood special education (ECSE) practitioners, those working with children from birth to age 8, with a framework for using principles of developmentally appropriate practice to design effective learning programs for young children with special needs. The book reflects ECE and ECSE perspectives on children who are in a variety of early childhood settings such as preschools, child care centers, family day care sites, and kindergartens. Of particular importance are the families and the roles they play in the growth and education of their children.

Developmentally appropriate practice is a holistic approach to the education of young children and is based on theories of child development. It is concerned with social, emotional, physical, and intellectual growth. As such, it reflects the interactions of children with materials, peers, and adults, and the integration of a child's background, culture, community, race, and familial expectations with the mission and goals of the program or school. The ap-

proach is a puzzle that makes up a unified whole. No single piece
ing, and no single piece can be dominant for all children.

Within the early childhood education reform movement, a qu
arisen on the application of principles of developmentally appropr. .c practice to populations of young children with special needs. Clearly, there are at
least three positions on the question: it is inappropriate, it is applicable some
of the time with some of the students, and it is the only way to proceed. In this
book, we present a view that argues for developmentally appropriate practice
as a vehicle for educating all young children. Guralnick (1993) suggests that
the common foundation for child development in early childhood education
and early childhood special education enables professionals to use developmental principles and processes, as well as environmental and biological influences, to understand the development of children with and without
disabilities. In addition, he feels that educational practices based on a shared
developmental framework should be applicable to widely heterogeneous
groups of children.

Although this book treats the evolution of developmentally appropriate
practice as a concept in early childhood education, it does not present a detailed discussion of developmentally appropriate practice from a founda-
tional-theoretical perspective; that is better left to other sources. Rather, the
purpose is to present a justification for developmentally appropriate practice
as a vehicle for working with young children with special needs and to explore applications of developmentally appropriate practice in a variety of
common classroom settings and occurrences.

In early childhood education and early childhood special education,
there is an understanding that the family is a critical part of a child's education. The literature is clear on the positive effects of parents' involvement with
schools. More importantly, legally and ethically, families have authority in
the decision-making process as it relates to their children's education. If we
believe in developmentally appropriate practice, we must believe in the importance of the family as a partner in learning.

Over time, developmentally appropriate practice has become accepted as
a legitimate approach to young children's learning. While some educators still
struggle with the external perception that children are only playing, others
have seen that the relationships constructed in developmentally appropriate
classrooms are necessary building blocks for later learning. However, classrooms that favor academic instruction, teacher-directed learning, and rote
memorization are still in the majority and may be for the foreseeable future because the resources that support curriculum change, such as library books for
children to read, manipulatives for math experiences, and materials for creative play experiences, are in short supply (Horsch, 1992). Developmentally
appropriate practice cannot take place without adequate materials for children
to manipulate. It cannot exist in classrooms with too many children or in classrooms that are too small for ease of movement.

Teachers of young children are in the enviable position of having the opportunity to advance children's understanding of their world. Developmentally appropriate practice is a vehicle that enables teachers to realize the best in all children by providing activities that focus on social, emotional, physical, and intellectual growth. Teachers use the children's needs and interests as the basis for assessing, planning, and implementing activities that reflect the differences inherent in all groups of children.

CASE STUDIES

For practice in using children's needs and interests as the basis for designing appropriate programs for young children, three case studies are included for readers to analyze and interpret. Each case is based on a real child and family; however, modifications have been made so that the children cannot be identified. The cases are revisited throughout the book to allow readers to focus on them, using continually more complex information.

Tiffany is an 18-month-old child with cerebral palsy. She lives with her mother and sister and attends a family child care center. Brad has Down syndrome, is 40 months old, and lives with his mother, father, and two brothers. He attends a child care center and is in a room with fifteen other children and two teachers. Tarrel is a 69-month-old child with a developmental delay. He attends a team-taught kindergarten with thirty-two other children. Tarrel lives with his parents and three siblings. Tiffany, Brad, and Tarrel present different challenges to teachers, and each of them can be successful in a developmentally appropriate program.

Case Study 1: Tiffany

Age: 18 months (1 year, 6 months)
Disability: Cerebral palsy

Tiffany is an 18-month-old girl who lives with her mother and has a 5-year-old sister, Sara, who also has cerebral palsy. Tiffany's mother had a normal pregnancy and delivery with both of her children. Sara's cerebral palsy was diagnosed when she was 2 years of age and is generally considered mild. Her doctors could not determine what caused the cerebral palsy and felt that it was safe for her mother to have additional children. After Tiffany's birth, it was determined that both she and Sara have an enzyme imbalance that generated calcium deposits during gestation, causing damage that resulted in cerebral palsy. This enzyme imbalance means that Tiffany must limit her carbohydrate intake and eat more foods with high fiber and protein content.

The girls' father left the family shortly after Tiffany's birth. Although he has minimal contact with her, he does visit Sara, sometimes taking her for short afternoon visits on weekends. In the eyes of her mother, Tiffany's father has not acknowledged her birth or anything connected with her disability. Since leaving the household, he has provided minimal financial support; however, he does bring clothing for Sara and food for the family. Tiffany's mother works as a clerical assistant in a law office. She is an hourly employee who does not have benefits. She qualifies for Medicaid, and both Tiffany and her sister have been able to obtain necessary medical care.

Tiffany's cerebral palsy is primarily the diplegic type, causing her to have very little control over her legs. She must wear braces to keep her ankles, knees, and hips from overextending. The cerebral palsy also affects her speech and some use of her hands. Tiffany's cognitive skills seem to be normal, but it has been difficult to determine this because of the heavy reliance on motor movements to measure cognitive abilities at her age. She seeks out interactions with adults and children and indicates her desires through grunts and eye gaze.

Tiffany has been receiving early intervention services since she was 6 months old. She receives physical therapy, occupational therapy, and speech therapy treatments weekly and is seen by an early interventionist, who assists her day care providers. Tiffany spends nine hours a day at a large family child care center that serves twelve children between the ages of 12 months and 6 years. In addition to the homeowner, two other caregivers work with the children. Tiffany is the only child with a disability. The center is in a large home in which three rooms are dedicated to the children's needs. The home is a split-level. Two of the children's rooms are on a lower level, and one room, usually used for eating and naps, is on street level. The lower level leads to a backyard that is used for a playground.

On traditional, standardized, norm-referenced assessment instruments, Tiffany appears to have an overall developmental delay of approximately 50 percent. Her age equivalency skills according to the *Bayley Scales of Infant Development* (Bayley, 1994) and *The Infant Scale of Communicative Intent* (Sacks & Young, 1982) indicate the following:

Mental skills:	9 months
Motor skills:	6 months
Social/behavioral skills:	11 months
Receptive language:	13 months
Expressive language:	8 months

Assessment Information

Through observations, communication samples, criterion checklists, parent reports, and anecdotal records, Tiffany has displayed the following skills and behaviors during the past four months:

- She likes playful interactions with her mother and sister and her many relatives; playing peek-a-boo or language games holds her attention for up to thirty minutes.
- She is able to wedge a bottle between her hands and hold it in her mouth but is not able to grasp the bottle. When sucking, she sometimes chokes on liquids of thin consistency.
- She enjoys watching brightly colored objects and can track balls rolling across the floor for up to twenty feet. Tiffany can predict the path of an object, even when it disappears behind a piece of furniture.
- Tiffany bats at towers or other tall structures created by other children.
- She can wait her turn when in a small group of two or three children but becomes cranky and fussy when tired.
- Tiffany does not like to be touched by stuffed animals, bristle blocks, or other "spiny" toys or objects.
- Tiffany enjoys sitting with an adult and looking at books or listening as children and adults sing. She sways back and forth to the rhythm of the music.
- She also likes to swing with an adult or to sit in a rocking chair.
- Tiffany tries to turn to the person who calls her name.
- She consistently uses the same sounds to indicate her sister and grandmother and to request cereal. She approximates the word "Mama."
- Tiffany tries to roll herself toward other children who are playing on the floor in the same area, and she attempts to pull herself up against furniture but does not have the arm strength to do so.
- When another child takes a toy away from her, Tiffany screams and thrashes.
- Tiffany tries to bat at music boxes and "roller" jack-in-the-boxes in an attempt to activate them.
- Tiffany sometimes holds objects in her mouth in order to wedge another object between her two hands.
- Tiffany enjoys being in water and water play.
- Tiffany generally eats only food that is the consistency of pudding or yogurt. At times she tolerates foods such as applesauce or partially ground vegetables and meats.
- Her favorite foods include vanilla pudding, lemon yogurt, fried chicken, soft breads, and Cheerios. She generally does not try new foods.
- She recognizes sounds that indicate when routines are changing. For example, she knows that a bell indicates that children at the family day care center must clean up and that soft music means that it is time to nap.
- She grunts or points with her arms or sometimes her head to indicate what she wants, and she has a tantrum if she does not get what she wants.
- She has great difficulty falling asleep and often becomes overtired and fussy.
- She likes to ride on the backs of her mother, relatives, and caregivers.
- Tiffany dislikes going to the doctor or hospital and often bites and screams when she knows that she is going for a visit.

Family Preferences for Outcomes for Tiffany
- Tiffany will begin to learn to eat other foods that are high in fiber and protein and will begin to feed herself.
- Tiffany will be able to communicate what she wants to her mother, her relatives, and her caregivers.
- Tiffany will be able to communicate with other children her age.
- Tiffany's intellectual development will continue and be enhanced as much as possible.
- Tiffany's limbs will remain flexible, and she will begin to be able to stand and eventually to move around.

Environmental Considerations
- Tiffany awakes at 6:00 A.M. Her mother drops her off at her caregiver's house at 7:30. She is picked up at 5:30 and arrives home at 6:30 P.M.
- Tiffany takes two naps of approximately ninety minutes, one in the morning and one in the afternoon.
- The eleven other children at Tiffany's family child care center are very active and noisy.
- Tiffany's caregivers serve breakfast, a morning snack, lunch, and an afternoon snack.
- Tiffany goes outside to play each day with the other children.
- Tiffany accompanies the group on all trips, including visits to the grocery store, post office, fast-food restaurants, and on other weekly routine visits.
- Tiffany is usually carried around her family's house and her child care provider's house.
- Tiffany's mother often has visiting relatives such as cousins, Tiffany's grandmother, and many aunts.

Tiffany's Daily Weekday Schedule
A typical daily schedule for Tiffany is as follows:

5:30 A.M.	Mother wakes her and puts her in her high chair with a bottle.
6:00 A.M.	Mother feeds Tiffany breakfast.
6:30 A.M.	Mother bathes and dresses Tiffany.
7:00 A.M.	Mother drives Tiffany and her sister to family day care.
7:30 A.M.	Tiffany and her sister arrive at child care; Tiffany is placed on the floor next to music boxes, jack-in-the-boxes, and other preferred toys.
8:00 A.M.	Tiffany is placed in a high chair and given a second breakfast.
8:30 A.M.	Tiffany is placed on the floor with other children; dolls, blocks, and other toys are placed within her reach.
9:30 A.M.	Tiffany naps.

11:00 A.M.	Tiffany and all other children go outside. Tiffany usually spends time in the swing or at the sandbox.
11:30 A.M.	All children come inside and clean up.
11:45 A.M.	The children eat lunch.
12:30 P.M.	Tiffany plays on the floor with simple toys (e.g., ball, stuffed animals, noise makers).
1:30 P.M.	Tiffany takes a second nap (all other children have gone to sleep at 12:30).
3:00 P.M.	Tiffany wakes up and gets a snack.
3:30 P.M.	The children play outside.
4:00 P.M.	The children play on the floor.
5:30 P.M.	Mother picks up Tiffany and her sister.
6:30 P.M.	Tiffany has dinner, a bath, and listens to stories.
7:00 P.M.	Tiffany goes to bed.

Summary

Although Tiffany has significant physical limitations due to her disability, most of her daily routine is similar to that of toddlers without disabilities. She spends a large portion of her day with toddlers and preschool-age children, she experiences high levels of social interaction at both her child care and home settings, and she shows interest in activities and materials common to all children her age. Tiffany's family wants her to participate in a daily routine that is as normal as possible. They hold as a high priority her continued normal development in all areas not affected by her disability. Most importantly, Tiffany is showing normal levels of cognitive, social, and communication skills despite her physical limitations. Her family and child care providers will have to ensure that adaptations allow her to experience her environments maximally and they must support her interactions with adults and peers to facilitate her overall development.

Case Study 2: Brad

Age:	42 months (3 years, 6 months)
Disability:	Down syndrome

Brad is a 42-month-old who lives with his mother and father and his older brothers, Todd (10 years) and Charles (8 years). Brad was born with Down syndrome and a congenital heart anomaly. He is a playful, gregarious boy who likes others. At 18 months of age, he had surgery to repair his heart. He continues to have relatively complex medical needs related to his heart, vision, and hearing. An ophthalmologist has determined that Brad is far-sighted and needs to wear glasses for almost all short-range tasks such as painting, writing, or building. Brad has glasses but does not like to wear them. Unless engaged in an activity that he highly enjoys, he removes his glasses.

Brad also has been diagnosed with a moderate hearing loss. He is able to respond to some commands, especially those made by adults. He often cannot hear what his peers are saying and becomes confused in noisy, active settings. His overall expressive language seems to be at the level expected of a 2- to 2½-year-old (e.g., uses two- and three-word sentences and can tell you what he wants or point to things). Brad's parents have begun to discuss his use of sign language but are not sure that it is the best approach for him.

Brad's family has experienced financial and interpersonal stress due to Brad's disabilities. Although the family does have medical insurance, they must pay a portion of each doctor visit and surgery, causing them to fall behind in paying their medical bills. The interpersonal stress has resulted in the inability of Brad's parents to agree on the appropriate mode of communication or on strategies for helping Brad to keep his glasses on while playing. Both parents feel that their older children are suffering because of the time and money spent on Brad. Although they do not want to decrease the family resources that go to Brad, they are frustrated that they cannot spend the same amount of time and money on their other two sons.

Brad spends seven hours a day at a child care center, in a room with fifteen other children his age. There are two teachers in the room and one other child with a disability. The other children are between the ages of 36 and 48 months. Brad's mother drops him off at approximately 8:30 A.M. and his father picks him up between 3:30 and 4:00 P.M.

Brad's developmental skills vary greatly and are dependent upon the setting, the situation, and the people around him. As measured by traditional, standardized, norm-referenced instruments such as the *Bayley Scales of Infant Development* (Bayley, 1994) and the *Battelle Developmental Inventory* (Newborg, Stock & Wnek 1994), Brad has overall delays of 40 percent to 50 percent. His age equivalency scores are as follows:

Cognitive skills:	2 years, 1 month
Expressive language:	1 year, 9 months
Receptive language:	1 year, 6 months
Gross motor:	2 years, 4 months
Fine motor:	2 years, 8 months
Self-care:	2 years, 1 month
Social:	1 year, 10 months

Assessment Information

Through observation, language samples, criterion-referenced checklists, work samples, parent reports, and anecdotal records, Brad has displayed the following skills and behaviors during the past six months:

- Brad matches objects of different colors, shapes, and sizes. He has begun to be able to categorize by two different characteristics (e.g., shape and color).
- He can sequence stories and events that have three or four discrete phases.
- Brad greatly enjoys being in a group with other children but sometimes hits or has tantrums, especially in open-ended, free-play situations.
- He has difficulty expressing what he wants in large-group and open-ended situations.
- He enjoys dramatic play activities and plays in front of a mirror by himself, putting on clothes such as shawls, ties, and hats.
- Brad has difficulty with buttons and zippers and cannot put on a shirt or coat by himself.
- Brad enjoys outdoor play and any tactile play (e.g., sand, water, Play Doh, pudding). He sometimes becomes so excited by water or sand play that he throws objects or even hits others.
- Brad is not yet toilet trained and does not tell his parents or other adults when he is wet or has had a bowel movement.
- He does not like to put on his own clothes and prefers that his mother or father help him.
- At his child care setting, Brad has a tantrum or hits when adults try to help him move from a free-play situation to a group situation while he is working on something he likes.
- Brad seems to have a vocabulary of approximately fifty words, which he uses infrequently.
- Brad often points to things that he wants or pushes an adult toward something that he wants.
- When Brad does not get what he wants from his peers, he sometimes hits or bites.
- Brad has begun to use some simple sign language that his teachers have taught him. These signs are primarily for functional activities such as wanting something to eat or drink.
- Brad can walk anywhere but has difficulty on surfaces that have an uneven grade (such as a playground covered with mulch or pea gravel). He tires easily and sits down when he does not want to walk further.
- When working with small objects, such as pegs, Leggos®, or other manipulatives, Brad often becomes frustrated and scatters the materials.
- He can use a spoon and a fork to feed himself but often tires of these and reverts to using his hands, even with food such as pudding.

- When drinking, Brad drips liquids down his chin and often spills from an open cup.

Family Preferences for Outcomes for Brad

- Brad will become more independent and take more responsibility for self-care, including feeding and dressing.
- Brad will become toilet trained.
- Brad will interact with his peers without hitting or biting.
- Brad will be able to communicate verbally to his mother, father, and older brothers what he wants.
- Brad will be able to make a smooth transition from one activity to another.

Environmental Considerations

Brad's family feels that he should be given the same opportunities as any other child his age and would like to see him experience life in as normal a manner as possible. Because he is eligible for early childhood special education services in his local school district, they are happy for him to participate. However, they do not want him to be part of a segregated classroom that serves only children with disabilities. They would like to see Brad receive services in the child care center where he has been for the past year. His parents feel that the center allows Brad to be with children his own age and that the activities in the center allow him to work on skills and behaviors that other children his age are acquiring. Brad's child care center has the following attributes:

- There are sixteen children, including Brad, and two teachers in his classroom.
- The room is very active and noisy. The noise is usually produced by the children while they are engaged in active learning. To an outsider, the room can appear somewhat chaotic.
- All of the children arrive at the center between 7:30 and 10:00 A.M. and leave between 2:30 and 5:30 P.M.
- During the time Brad is in the room, morning snack, lunch, and afternoon snack are served.
- There are two long free-play periods from 9:30 to 11:00 and from 1:55 to 3:25.
- The class has an outside play period from 11:10 to 11:40.
- There is a ninety-minute nap/rest period from 12:10 to 1:40.
- Most groups are full-class groups, and activities occur at 9:15, 11:00, 1:40, and 3:25. Few, if any, small groups are held during the daily routine.
- The classroom has eight activity areas, and there is a heavy emphasis on manipulatives and art. The materials in these areas change every four to six weeks.

Brad's Daily Child Care Schedule

8:30	Arrival/Greeting Brad is dropped off by his mother; he enters the classroom, greets his teachers, and is allowed to choose his activities.
8:30 - 9:15	Limited free-play Simple activities in four or five interest areas are available for the children (e.g., puzzles, Leggos and bristle blocks, and markers).
9:15 - 9:30	Morning circle All children join in morning routines such as the "Good Morning" song, selection of daily helpers, and discussion of the day's activities.
9:30 - 11:00	Free-play Eight different interest centers are available to the children: blocks, housekeeping, manipulatives, art, sand, books, writing center, and computer. The activities at these centers change every four to six weeks.
11:00 - 11:10	Song circle The children gather in a large group to sing the class's repertoire of songs.
11:10 - 11:40	Outside time The children go to the playground, where swings, a sand box, and riding toys are available. During inclement weather, the children go to a gym where riding toys, mats, and climbing structures are available.
11:40 - 12:10	Lunch The children eat in the classroom, family style.
12:10 - 1:40	Rest time All children take a nap or rest on their cots.
1:40 - 1:55	Story group All children gather around the teacher to listen to a picture book story.
1:55 - 3:25	Free play The eight activity areas offered in the morning are again available.
3:25 - 3:40	Movement group All children participate in a music and movement activity lead by the teachers.
3:40 - 4:00	Dismissal

Summary

Brad has a number of developmental concerns that are associated with his disability, Down syndrome. He has low muscle tone, which has affected his fine motor skills and his ability to use tools and utensils. His muscle tone also makes it difficult for him to sustain high levels of physical activity for long periods. Brad's sensory impairments also have affected his skill development. His communication skills are significantly behind those of peers who are nondisabled. In addition to these developmental delays, Brad has some challenging behaviors that may be related to his disability.

Despite all of Brad's needs, he is a happy three-year-old who enjoys being with other children and adults. His demeanor has led his parents to believe that Brad needs to be with children his own age. Although his child care setting is sometimes not ideal, the setting enables him to experience activities and routines that other children his age experience. The combination of Brad's developmental delays, his challenging behaviors, and his family's desire for him to participate in the experiences of a nondisabled preschooler requires a program that is individually appropriate.

Case Study 3: Tarrel

Age: 69 months (5 years, 9 months)
Disability: Developmental delay

Tarrel is a 5-year, 9-month-old boy who lives with his mother and father and his three siblings, Jarrel (10 years), Sarrel (8 years), and Darrel (4 years). Tarrel's mother had a normal pregnancy and delivery. At 1 year of age, Tarrel's parent began to think that his development might be different from their other children's. They were concerned that he could not yet play with pop beads, sorting box shapes, and other toys. They were also concerned that Tarrel was not babbling as much as their other children did at his age. After consulting with various professionals, they decided to wait to see whether Tarrel's development would change.

When Tarrel was 2 years old, his parents and doctor decided to have him tested for possible delays in development. It was determined that Tarrel did have developmental delays in his fine motor, communication, and cognitive skills. He began early intervention services at 2½ years of age and continued to attend a child care center for eight hours a day while his parents worked. Tarrel remained in early intervention services until his placement in a kindergarten this year.

Tarrel's kindergarten class has thirty-two children between the ages of 4 years, 5 months and 6 years, 3 months. It is a team-taught class with one teacher who is trained in early childhood education and another who is trained in early childhood special education. The class has six children with individual education programs (IEPs). For three hours during the morning, a paraprofessional is also present in the classroom.

On traditional, standardized, norm-referenced assessment instruments, Tarrel appears to have an overall developmental delay of approximately 30 percent to 35 percent. His age equivalency skills according to the *Battelle Developmental Inventory* (Newborg, Stock, & Wnek, 1994) and the *Test for Early Language Development* (Hresko, Reid, & Hammill, 1991) indicate the following:

Cognitive skills:	4 years, 1 month
Expressive language:	3 years, 10 months
Receptive language:	4 years, 5 months
Gross motor:	4 years, 6 months
Fine motor:	3 years, 9 months
Self-care:	3 years, 10 months
Social:	3 years, 8 months

Assessment Information

Through observations, language samples, work samples, criterion checklists, parent reports, and anecdotal records, Tarrel has displayed the following skills and behaviors during the past six months:

- Tarrel likes to play in the block corner, building simple structures and using props such as animal figures, people, cars, and other objects. He participates in this type of activity for twenty-five to forty minutes.
- He does not like to play with table toys such as puzzles, Leggos, and bristle blocks.
- He enjoys sitting with an adult and one or two other children to look at and listen to a book for short periods of time.
- He can recognize his name in primary print and also the words "mommy," "daddy," and "dog."
- Tarrel generally participates in parallel or associative play. When he wants something from another child he sometimes pushes or shoves to get it.
- He walks away when confronted by another child who wants materials or a piece of equipment he is using.
- He has difficulty using scissors to cut paper but tries when others are doing the same task. Tarrel generally avoids art projects unless there is a group process associated with it (e.g., a mural, a "stuffed" figure of an animal or person, decorations for the room).
- One art/writing activity that he likes is using markers to create pictures of himself, his family, and his pets. He places his drawings in homemade books that the class constructs.
- He enjoys being at the water and sand table and, if permitted, spends an entire period at those centers.
- He likes to blow through a straw at the water table to create bubbles.

- He can use a fork to stab food and a spoon to scoop foods like yogurt or apple sauce. Sometimes, however, the utensils slip through his fingers.
- Tarrel has a vocabulary of more than 250 words, including names of all common items in his house, family members, and classmates. He rarely uses these words when communicating with others; he usually points to things that he wants.
- He enjoys small-group interactions with one or two other children.
- He likes to roll, jump, and hop when in the gym or on the playground.
- He likes to swing and slide.
- Tarrel's favorite foods include crunchy cheese snacks, french fries, bread, pudding, and peanut butter and jelly sandwiches.
- He will sit in a group for about ten minutes.
- He loves to be held and rocked.
- He enjoys high-energy interactions with adults (e.g., horse rides).

Family Preferences for Outcomes for Tarrel
- Tarrel will learn to use utensils to feed himself without spilling.
- Tarrel will be able to sit and pay attention for at least fifteen minutes and occupy himself at home for at least twenty minutes.
- Tarrel will be able to tell his parents and siblings what he wants using his vocabulary, and he will expand his receptive and expressive vocabulary.
- Tarrel will get along with other children and develop friendships with them.
- Tarrel will begin to recognize more written words and use written language functionally.

Environmental Considerations
- Tarrel attends child care one hour before school and two hours after school.
- Tarrel's kindergarten day is five and one-half hours long (9:00 A.M. to 2:30 P.M.).
- Tarrel is in a group of thirty-two children, with five other children in the group having disabilities. These disabilities include hearing impairments, vision impairments, Down syndrome, cerebral palsy, and fragile X syndrome.
- Tarrel's kindergarten has five small groups (morning circle, story circle, review group, music and movement group, and closing group) daily, with each lasting approximately fifteen minutes. Except for the morning circle, these groups usually consist of ten to twelve children.
- Tarrel's kindergarten serves a morning snack and lunch; his child care setting serves breakfast and an afternoon snack.
- Tarrel has an opportunity for "free-play" once a day in kindergarten for thirty minutes. He has the opportunity to participate in "free-play" for an hour during his afternoon child care time.

- Tarrel's kindergarten class goes outside once each day (weather permitting) for thirty minutes. His child care group goes outside for an hour at the end of the day.
- Tarrel's kindergarten class must move between the classroom, the cafeteria, and the outside playground. These transitions take place at least six times a day and include walking at least fifty yards each time.
- All students in Tarrel's class are expected to use words to solve problems or conflicts.

Tarrel's Kindergarten Schedule
A typical daily schedule for Tarrel's kindergarten class is as follows:

8:45 - 9:00	Arrival/Greeting
	All children arrive on buses, greet teachers, hang up coats and other belongings, return notes from home, and move to their desks.
9:00 - 9:15	Opening morning circle
	The children gather in a group on a rug and listen to an opening session led by the teacher.
9:15 - 10:15	Center time
	Students have the opportunity to choose among five centers (art, manipulatives, dramatic play, blocks, and listening/reading) related to the opening session and the theme unit currently being studied. Children can move freely among the centers.
10:15 - 10:30	Cleanup
	All children assist in cleaning up materials and putting away equipment.
10:30 - 10:45	Story circle
	The children gather in a large group to listen to a story, watch a puppet show, hear a flannel board story, or participate in some other language and literature group activity.
10:45 - 11:30	Work tables
	The children circulate among three work tables, where they must complete a task related to the lesson introduced at the beginning of the day. The tasks are usually prereading and writing related, art oriented, or problem solving in nature.
11:30 - Noon	Outside
	All children play outside on large muscle equipment, in a sand area, or with balls.

Noon - 12:10	Bathroom Children use the bathroom, if necessary, and wash their hands.
12:10 - 12:30	Lunch All children eat in a large cafeteria that accommodates 200 students. Nine kindergarten, first-grade, and second-grade classes eat together for twenty minutes.
12:30 - 12:45	Review group All children meet in a large group to review the activities of the morning and to share what they have done during the day.
12:45 - 1:30	Rest time All children rest on mats, quietly work with puzzles and other manipulatives, or look at/read books.
1:30 - 1:45	Music and movement group The children join in a large group. The teacher sings songs and leads them in movement activities.
1:45 - 2:15	Free play Children can choose among five activity areas (art, dramatic play, blocks, water/sand table, books).
2:15 - 2:30	Closing group The closing song is sung, the children are given notes to take home to their families, and the day is reviewed.
2:30	Dismissal

Summary

This year, Tarrel has moved from a segregated early intervention program to a child care program for a large group of children with and without disabilities. The kindergarten curriculum is flexible, and staffing in the classroom is adequate to address the needs of the wide variety of children. Tarrel has excellent relationships and interactions with adults and small groups of children. These skills can be used to help him address some of his areas of delays, such as attention to task and fine motor skills. It is still important for Tarrel to work on developmental tasks that will enhance his ability to work with symbols and written language. This is a priority for his family, so it will be an important part of the curriculum for him during the coming months.

Because Tarrel is in an inclusive setting geared toward meeting the needs of a very diverse group of students, there are opportunities to group him with peers who are working on the same skills as he. Peer models will be able to display skills and behaviors that Tarrel can emulate. Designing classroom experiences so that he has the opportunity to observe and practice skills with peers functioning at or near the same developmental level is an important goal for developmentally appropriate programming.

ACTIVITIES AND RESOURCES

Activities

1. With a partner, choose one of the cases and complete each of the following tasks:
   a. List five things the child can do in a classroom without any modifications.
   b. List five things the child can do in a classroom with minor modifications.
   c. List five things the child can do in a classroom with major modifications.
   d. Generate three questions that you would like to ask the child's parent(s).
   e. Generate three concerns that you would have if the child were placed in your classroom.
2. Choose a different case and share it with a practicing teacher. Ask the teacher how he or she would go about preparing the children and the classroom for the new child. Characterize the responses as positive, neutral, or negative.
3. Observe a segregated classroom that has only children with special needs and an integrated classroom that has a diverse population, including children with special needs. Describe the differences.

REFERENCES

Bayley, N. (1994). *Bayley scales of infant development* (2nd ed.). San Antonio, TX: Psychological Corporation.

Gifford, J. (1992). A stitch in time: Strengthening the first years of school. Compulsory Years of Schooling Project. Project paper no. 3. Commissioned Report no. 16, National Board of Employment, Education and Training. Canberra (Australia) Schools Council.

Guralnick, M. (1993). Developmentally appropriate practice in the assessment and intervention of children's peer relations. *Topics in Early Childhood Special Education, 13*(3), 344–371.

Horsch, P. (1992). School change: A partnership approach. *Early Education and Development, 3*(2), 128–138.

Hresko, W.P., Reid, D.K., & Hammill, D.D. (1991). *Test for early language development.* Austin, TX: Pro-Ed, Inc.

Newborg, J., Stock, J., & Wnek, L. (1984). *Battelle developmental inventory.* Chicago, IL: Riverside Publishing.

Sacks, G.K., & Young, E.C. (1982). *The infant scale of communicative intent.* Philadelphia, PA: St. Christopher's Hospital for Children.

2

DEVELOPMENTALLY APPROPRIATE PRACTICE: WHAT IT IS AND HOW IT WORKS

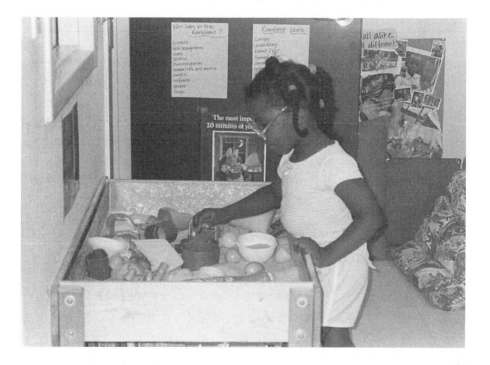

The principal goal of education is to create men who
are capable of doing new things, not simply
repeating what other generations have done—men
who are creative, inventive, and discoverers. The
second goal of education is to form minds which can
be critical, can verify, and not accept everything that
is offered. So we need pupils who are active, who
learn early to find out by themselves, partly by their
own spontaneous activity and partly through
material we set up for them, who learn early what is
verifiable and what is simply the first idea to come to
them.
                    —Piaget, as cited in Elkind, 1989, p. 115

OBJECTIVES

As a result of reading this chapter, readers should be able to perform the following:

- Define developmentally appropriate practice and describe the differences between age appropriate and individually appropriate practice.
- Explain the events that led to developmentally appropriate practice as a favored way to educate young children.
- Justify the use of theme-based units in programs for young children.
- Describe how cultural diversity is reflected in individual appropriateness and explain how teachers can include diversity in the curriculum.
- Explain why real objects and/or experiences are important for young children's learning.
- Refute the myths that surround developmentally appropriate practice.

HISTORICAL BACKGROUND

The field of early childhood education has experienced enormous growth in terms of both size and recognition. Early childhood education, while having a long history, is seen as a relatively new entity in the arena of "serious" teaching and learning. For years early childhood education was seen as playtime, and early childhood educators were seen as surrogate parents who were there to provide socialization experiences but not necessarily educational ones. In fact, many thought that real school did not begin until first grade, hence the term *preschool* was adopted. State policies added to the perception by mandating child care regulations related to fire, safety, and health standards but not to educational programs or teacher licensure.

For a variety of reasons, the role of early childhood education began to change. Child day care was no longer for only a select few, but was a necessity for many families. Head Start, Follow Through, and other programs provided evidence that good early childhood education was beneficial to children and did not undermine the role of parents.

In the late 1950s, the quality of education in the United States of America was called into question as the result of Sputnik and the perception that the Union of Soviet Socialist Republics was educationally superior. This translated into curriculum revisions that focused on having children do more sophisticated work earlier in their school careers. Second-grade information was pushed down into the first grade, and first-grade information into kindergarten. Moreover, instructional methods used with older children found their way into programs for young children. Dittos, workbooks, rote memorization, almost exclusive use of teacher-directed, highly structured large group lessons, lack of opportunities to move about the room and make choices, teaching isolated skills, and over-reliance on extrinsic reward systems replaced circle time, sand, water and dramatic play, child-written stories, and small-group activities as instructional methods. Standardized tests, behavioral objectives, and passing scores replaced anecdotal records, student projects, and informal interviews as methods of choice to be used for evaluating learning.

Of particular concern in the field of early childhood education has been the overuse of standardized tests because they tend to give an incomplete picture of children's accomplishments and foster the use of inappropriate curricula. The National Association for the Education of Young Children's (NAEYC) *Position statement on standardized testing of young children 3 through 8 years of age* (1988) suggests that standardized tests should be used only when there is a clear benefit to the children and when the tests will be only one part of an overall assessment of the child. Further, NAEYC believes that the most important consideration in using standardized tests is the utility criterion: the purpose of testing must be to improve services for children and to ensure that children benefit from their educational experiences. In the case of children with special needs, standardized tests can help to ensure that accurate screening occurs and that eligibility determination is unbiased. However, as is the case for their nondisabled peers, program planning best occurs with flexible, child-sensitive assessment procedures (Bricker and Cripe, 1992; Campbell, 1991).

Ultimately, children were promoted based on their ability to meet preordained, arbitrary academic objectives rather than on their social, emotional, physical and intellectual growth. Some programs whose creators prided themselves on developing the "whole child" became programs that prized the memorization of facts related to reading and mathematics. In other words, early childhood programs ceased to reflect the things that historically made them appropriate for young children, and hands-on, experientially based learning was no longer seen as a valid way for children to learn. Meeting arbitrary objectives became more important than meeting the needs of children.

Decisions about curriculum and instruction were made for expediency's sake; things that were easily counted were more important than those that could not be machine scored. One right answer was easier to record than multiple interpretations of a problem. Objectives were either mastered or not mastered. In addition, some teachers were disenfranchised. They were not involved in the curriculum or instructional decision-making process and did not have the opportunity to influence practice. Decisions were made by individuals with little knowledge of young children's learning.

In some cases, teachers lacked the in-depth knowledge in child development, learning theory, language acquisition, instructional techniques, appropriate materials, classroom management, assessment, working with parents, and so on, needed to influence others about the nature of successful programs. They found themselves in the position of having a "gut-level" feeling about appropriate practice but not the formal knowledge to convince others.

Teachers were designing programs for young children that did not reflect what we knew, either historically or through research, as necessary for young children to grow and develop as learners or as individuals. Elkind (1986) suggested that we were guilty of "miseducating children." Elkind's view was that we knew a great deal about the education of young children; however, we were guilty of ignoring much of what research and experience had taught us about best practices. Professionals had allowed the field to be shaped by individuals who had little knowledge of young children.

When prespecified objectives become the focus of a program, children who meet the objectives are viewed as being successful and those who do not are seen as having problems. It was never the case that the teacher or the program was to blame; rather, if a child did not succeed, it was the child's fault. Scoring well on a test was more important than understanding concepts; getting a "smiley face" on a ditto was more important than drawing a picture of a field trip. Children who met objectives received positive strokes, and those who did not do well were told that they were failures. The messages sent to parents often convinced them that satisfaction, happiness, and conceptual learning were less important than meeting the designated number of objectives for kindergarten. As a result, some parents became more concerned with scores and "achievement" than they were with their child's becoming a successful learner. "Do your best" was replaced with "You did not do well enough."

Children were pushed into learning in ways that may have been appropriate for older children but were inappropriate for younger ones. Unfortunately, the more narrow the expectations in a classroom, the more likely children are to exhibit inappropriate behavior. The more flexible the expectations, the less likely inappropriate behaviors are to be seen. The more rigid we became, the more apparent the children's problems became. These inappropriate programs resulted in a variety of outcomes.

- Stress: Some children began exhibiting symptoms of stress, including nail biting, hair twirling, and antisocial behavior.
- Unhappiness: School ceased to be a place where children wanted to be. A feeling of joy was replaced with a feeling of resentment.
- Growth in one of four areas of development—social, emotional, physical, intellectual: Although some children did very well in an academic setting, many of the same children did not have opportunities to grow socially, emotionally, or physically. Their bookwork was fine, but eye-hand coordination, social skills and self-esteem were lacking.
- Higher retention rates: In some areas of the country, kindergarten retention rates were as high as 20 percent. Children who did not meet the objectives were required to go through the same instructional program a second time.
- Earlier labeling of children: Some schools labeled children who did not meet the required number of objectives as developmentally delayed.
- Unrealistic expectations for children and teachers: Some programs demanded results that were simply not possible for children, no matter how hard the teachers tried.

An exploratory study by Burts and others (1989) found that children attending less developmentally appropriate kindergarten programs exhibited more stress-related behaviors in the classroom (e.g., fidgeting, lip biting, the use of disfluent speech) than did those in more developmentally appropriate programs. Children displayed more stress behaviors during whole group and workbook and worksheet activities than did children in developmentally appropriate programs. The authors felt that their findings supported the position of Elkind (1986).

DEVELOPMENTALLY APPROPRIATE PRACTICE

NAEYC, in an attempt to influence public school kindergartens and programs for 4-year-olds, created the Commission on Appropriate Education for 4- and 5-Year-Olds to develop a position paper. The commission, chaired by Bernard Spodek, submitted a final report and at least two minority reports that did not reflect a consensus of the members but did, however, describe the differing perspectives that existed on the question of what constituted developmentally appropriate practice (Bredekamp, 1991). As a result, NAEYC, in conjunction with a consultant, Bess-Gene Holt, developed a document that defined developmentally appropriate practice, from birth through age 8. The resulting document, *Developmentally Appropriate Practice in Early Childhood Programs Serving Children from Birth Through Age Eight, Extended Edition* (Bredekamp, 1987[1]), has become a well-received, often quoted guide to developmentally appropriate practices for young children. As Bredekamp (1991) suggests, although there are a variety of other ways to consider appropriateness, including ethically, financially, or educationally, developmentally appropriate seems to reflect the consensus position of early childhood professionals.

By definition, developmentally appropriate programs are those that reflect children's natural learning abilities and interests, and assist them in growing socially, emotionally, physically, and intellectually. Such programs are based on children's real experiences with their world and provide them with many opportunities to interact with materials, peers, and adults.

It is helpful to consider each part of the definition in terms of what it means for teachers and children. First, developmentally appropriate practice is based on children's natural learning abilities and interests. If children are presented with challenging and intriguing activities, they will want to participate and will continue their involvement as long as they find meaning and challenge in their work.

Second, children do not focus on one domain at a time. Social, emotional, physical, and intellectual growth are related, and, in fact, an activity that leads to physical growth may also foster new vocabulary, group skills, and self-esteem.

Next, programs are based on children's real experiences with their world. Pets, families, neighborhoods, trips, and special celebrations are all part of their world. They provide the basis for dramatic play, artistic representations, stories, and explorations that help children learn more about an area of interest.

Professionals support developmentally appropriate practices as those that build skills and knowledge within the context of children's real needs and interests. The instructional program reflects the children; however, it is child centered rather than child directed. Developmentally appropriate practice is not laissez-faire education as some have suggested. Children do not do whatever they like.

Teachers provide a variety of activities that have the potential to enhance children's learning. Materials, room arrangement, rules, centers, and schedules are all designed to assist learning. Teachers already know the parameters of the activities and what children may learn from them. They also know that each child learns different things and that some need more time than others to explore the materials fully. Children make independent decisions to operate within an environment that is designed to foster learning.

---

[1]As this book was being completed, NAEYC published a revised copy of *Developmentally Appropriate Practice in Early Childhood Programs: Revised Edition* by Sue Bredekamp and Carol Copple (1997).

Skills are taught within the context of integrated theme-based units that include goals and objectives from a number of content areas. For example, an urban kindergarten class may be studying transportation and focus on buses. They may listen to stories; discuss where people go on the bus; graph the numbers of children who walk to school, take the bus, or are driven by a family member; take a bus trip; write stories with accompanying representations; interview a bus driver; make up a group poem; and discuss the meanings of traffic signs.

Children from a rural area might also study transportation, focusing on cars and trucks. Those who live on the shore may focus on boats. Such units would be designed around familiar ideas and concepts and would provide opportunities for children to extend their knowledge.

Developmentally appropriate practice does not prohibit children from learning reading, writing, and mathematics. Those who are ready to read are provided with opportunities to move ahead; those who are not ready are not pushed. In one classroom, some children may be reading books on their own, some reading with assistance, some listening to a tape and following the pictures in a book, and some listening to a volunteer read a story. They are all involved with print, and they are all participating in activities that foster language development. However, no child is forced to participate in an activity that will result in failure.

In each case, the teacher decided on the book and related activity most appropriate for the individual child. The activities provided for learning but did not lead to frustration. They were social opportunities because children worked in groups, intellectual activities because children were dealing with new vocabulary and concepts, and emotional activities because children experienced success, which enhanced self-esteem.

TEACHING THE WHOLE CHILD

The concept of the whole child means that the program focuses on social, emotional, intellectual, and physical growth. None of the four growth areas stands alone. Social growth affects emotional growth. Physical growth affects intellectual growth. A child playing at the water table is developing eye-hand coordination as well as learning the physical attributes of water. If the child is part of a group of children who are playing at the water table, social development is taking place as they learn to participate in a cooperative situation. Language development is improving as they learn new words to describe how the water feels, looks, and smells.

Although teachers often plan for lessons that are primarily for one type of growth (e.g., providing a dramatic play center fostering social growth), they recognize that other areas are also being developed as a result of the activity. A child playing house is learning how to work with others and developing social skills, he or she is feeling the satisfaction of being an accepted part of a group. Guralnick (1993) feels that a child development perspective supports the notion that the ability to establish appropriate and effective relationships with one's peers is a critical task for children during the preschool years. These relationships have important implications for cognitive, communicative, and overall social development.

Fostering Independence

Developmentally appropriate classrooms are designed to foster independence. Through room arrangement, materials, rules, accessibility, and philosophy, the teacher provides children with multiple opportunities for both making decisions and carrying them out. The more ways that children can operate in a classroom without teacher direction, the greater the likelihood that they will become independent learners who will not have to wait for the teacher in order to participate in learning activities.

However, it is important to remember that children are making choices within a classroom designed and equipped by a teacher who understands the parameters of learning and what children will learn from various materials. Again, it is not laissez-faire. The choices that children make are controlled by the teacher because the teacher controls what is in the room. Gifford (1992) cautions that although young children need structure, they do not need rigidity. Children need opportunities to become thoroughly involved in engaging activities, to work on projects until they are finished, and to think and reflect on what they have done or would like to do.

Age Appropriateness and Individual Appropriateness

Developmentally appropriate practice has two components, age appropriateness and individual appropriateness. They are defined as follows:

> *Age Appropriateness: Knowledge of the typical development of children within the age span served by the program provides a framework from which teachers prepare the learning environment and plan appropriate experiences.*
>
> *Individual Appropriateness: Each child is a unique person with an individual pattern and timing of growth as well as an individual personality, learning style and family background. The program should be responsive to these individual differences. (Bredekamp, 1987, p.2)*

Age appropriateness is the umbrella that enables teachers to make gross decisions regarding furniture, materials, schedule, unit topics, pacing, and room arrangement. Because teachers have a wealth of information about what children are like at various ages, we can use that accumulated wisdom as a basis for initial decision making regarding the context of the environment. Children with disabilities, even those whose development may not be on age level, function effectively within the context of an age-appropriate classroom because of modifications that reflect the nature of individual appropriateness.

Individual appropriateness requires that teachers collect information about the children and use that information to develop a learning environment that is reflective of what the children need and also of their prior experiences. For example, all classrooms for young children have some type of reading center. Age appropriateness enables teachers to select tables, chairs, pillows, stuffed animals and plants to make the center attractive and welcoming for children. Individual appropriateness requires that they equip the center with books that are reflective of the children's interests. A classroom in a rural area may have a variety of materials about farm animals, and one in a city may have books on domestic pets. In addition, individual appropriateness requires that a classroom with a child in a wheelchair be modified to allow for wider aisles, lower placement of materials, and built-up easels that allow the wheelchair to fit underneath them. The basic furniture, materials, and arrangement are still age appropriate, but the modifications made to reflect individual children are a reflection of individual appropriateness.

Developmentally appropriate practice and traditional academic practice have different approaches to teaching and learning. The purposes are different, as are the outcomes in terms of what children experience and learn. Table 2.1 indicates some of those differences.

Cultural Diversity

An important consideration in developmentally appropriate practice is the emphasis on cultural diversity as an integral part of the program. Certainly part of individual appropriateness is reflecting the cultures that children bring to the class. Racial, cultural, ethnic, familial, and religious diversity can be found in any class of young children. The key is to include diversity in all aspects of the curriculum. Derman-Sparks (1993) refers to this approach as "authentic multiculturalism." She feels that in order for children to understand and appreciate the differences in others, they have to deal with them as part of day-to-day living. Focusing on diversity only as part of a holiday celebration reduces the true importance of the differing values that we hold as individuals.

Any classroom of young children may include members from different neighborhoods, races, religions, and family structures (one-parent, two-parent, blended, foster). There may be children who do not eat pork for health reasons and others who do not eat it for religious reasons. Some children may celebrate Christmas while others celebrate Kwanza or Hanukkah. There may be children who see their mother as the head of the family and others who

TABLE 2.1   Developmentally Appropriate Practice versus Traditional Academic Practice

DAP	Academic
Child-centered	Skill-centered
Active	Passive
Generates knowledge	Uses knowledge
Concrete	Abstract
Individualized	Group
Independent	Dependent

live in a three-generation household. Some children may have lived their whole lives in the same house and others may have lived in a number of different countries. Teachers who believe in the importance of diversity make it their business to know their children and to incorporate individual differences into the daily activities of the school. Further, they are sensitive to the differences in children and do not present material that misrepresents or ignores what others believe.

How Young Children Learn

Real objects and experiences form the basis of children's learning. Things that they experience firsthand are understood at a level of complexity that can not be matched by second- and thirdhand experiences. For example, through a picture a child may know what a cow looks like but little else. Many children come away from a farm story that is read to them with the idea that cows are about the same size as dogs. They learn that cows moo and eat hay. They do not have any sense of real size, smell, feel, or sound. Saying "moo" and hearing a cow moo are very different experiences.

A child who has visited a farm knows cows in ways that cannot be communicated in a picture book. Because learning is a sensory experience for young children, a child who has visited a farm knows the feel, smell, sound, and size of cows. Often children respond with "They stink," when asked about cows. (If you have had experience with cows, you may have said the same thing.) However, although such an experience is important, it is not enough, in and of itself, to provide children with a complete understanding of the world. The critical factor is what teachers do after the trip to ensure that children have the opportunity to use the experience in a variety of ways to improve their vocabulary, increase their understanding, represent their learning, hear what others learned, and to generally refine everything they have learned about the farm, integrating the new knowledge with their existing knowledge. What they have experienced is what they talk about, think about, and play out.

According to Piaget (1962), play is the way children manipulate the outside world so that it fits their organizational schema. His view is interactional: children's cognitive structures develop from infancy as a result of hands-on interactions with their physical world. These developmental changes are cumulative; thus the way a child solves a problem depends on a cognitive structure that is the result of earlier interactions. The growth of intelligence is an equilibration process involving adaptation. When equilibrium is upset, there is a tendency to restore it using two complimentary processes: (1) assimilation, the incorporation of new data into one's own framework; and (2) accommodation, the modification of the existing framework to incorporate the newly assimilated data.

Progressive assimilation and accommodation over time lead to successive refinements in knowledge and in thought. For example, Susie is a 4-year-old playing in the outdoor sandbox. She is an experienced sandbox player who has used shovels, pails, sifters, tractors, and trucks for about eighteen months. This morning Susie is sifting sand by taking a shovelful, dropping it in the sifter, and shaking it until the sand is gone. Jimmy walks by the sandbox and accidentally spills a bucket of water. Susie's next shovelful is taken from the wet sand. When she tries to sift it, nothing happens. Disequilibrium is created. After two additional attempts, she gets deep enough so that the sand is dry and again it sifts. Initially, her cognitive scheme allowed that sand would sift. Disequilibrium was created when the wet sand would not sift. She assimilated the new information and accommodated her cognitive structure to include the new piece of information. Now she knows that dry sand sifts and wet sand does not. This piece of information is a direct result of an encounter with her environment. It will always be a part of her understanding of the world and will be used to help her understand how similar materials, such as flour and dirt, behave as she encounters them through physical interactions.

In addition to child–material interactions, two other types of interactions that are important in developmentally appropriate classrooms: child–child and child–adult. Child–material interactions enable children to explore the world, learning about the physical nature of things and expanding their motor and cognitive skills. Child–child interactions help children learn about social rules and roles and enable them to hear and see how other children solve problems. Child–adult interactions enable teachers to better understand the processes children use as they interact with the world. Teachers provide opportunities to enrich children's thinking by asking questions or by adding new materials to the activity. Child–adult interactions lead to increased self-esteem as a result of children's receiving positive feedback regarding the quality of their work.

UNDERSTANDING DEVELOPMENTALLY APPROPRIATE PRACTICE

Gronlund (1995) offers three key elements that can assist adults in understanding and justifying developmentally appropriate practice. The first key element is that children learn through active engagement. Their level of interest is greater when they are intrigued by a situation and are curious about why it happened. Second is the importance of the concept of play with a specific intent and purpose. Children in developmentally appropriate programs are not wasting time or "only playing." They are involved in open-ended activities that enable children with different needs to benefit in different ways. The teacher knows the parameters of the materials and observes the children to determine what they are learning. The third key element is that classroom activities should move from simple to complex. Children's understanding moves along a continuum in terms of complexity; therefore teachers must provide activities and materials that enable children to grow over time.

Developmentally appropriate practice has been accepted by a number of professional associations as the recommended approach for working with young children. In addition to the National Association for the Education of Young Children (1988), the National Association of State Boards of Education (1988) and the National Association of Elementary School Principals (1990), among others, have all endorsed the use of developmentally appropriate practice. Of particular importance is the broad constituencies the groups represent. School boards and principals, as well as early childhood educators, recognize the efficacy of developmentally appropriate practice.

Issues and Concerns

Early childhood professionals are always interested in the "bottom line" in terms of how children benefit from differing programs. One of the authors conducted an informal poll of teachers who believe and practice in a developmentally appropriate fashion. A number of common characteristics of children emerged from the poll. Although there is no scientific validity to the results, it is interesting to note the descriptions. Teachers tend to describe the children as being very independent and able to follow directions without continual reminders. The children are curious and ask a great number of "why" questions because they are interested in finding out how things work.

Communication is a major part of who children are. They write, read, listen, act, draw, lead, follow, and discuss all day, every day. As a result, they have become comfortable with the importance of sharing their knowledge with others. Children see reading and mathematics as tools to be used to gain information rather than as ends in and of themselves. The children are adept at cooperative learning and are willing to participate in large-group, small-group, and individualized activities.

TABLE 2.2   Teacher Views on the Characteristics of Children Who Have Participated in Developmentally Appropriate Programs

Independent
Curious
Good communication skills
Reading and mathematics as tools for learning
Adept at cooperative learning
Respect for others
Healthy self-esteem

Lastly, they have respect for others and, because they have had many more successes than failures, they have a healthy level of self-esteem. Table 2.2 lists the characteristics of children who have participated in developmentally appropriate classrooms as seen by their teachers.

IMPLEMENTING DEVELOPMENTALLY APPROPRIATE PRACTICE

Teachers are often concerned with the difficulty of implementing a new approach. Like almost everyone else, early childhood teachers resist change. Part of the problem of implementing developmentally appropriate practice is that many individuals are not aware of the true complexity of the approach and the nature of the knowledge base needed for success. At first some thought that reading the Bredekamp (1987) book was enough to guarantee success. Eventually, professionals in the field came to realize that implementing developmentally appropriate practice was a very involved initiative.

Davis (1989) suggested that a number of variables must be addressed as teachers of young children move toward developmentally appropriate practice. First, teachers need a knowledge base that reflects the nature of developmentally appropriate practice and the nature of child development in terms of what they mean for curriculum, instruction, assessment, classroom management, and working with families. Moving to developmentally appropriate practice means a major change in the way many teachers operate.

Second, teachers of young children must be able to convince others of the efficacy of developmentally appropriate practice. At the very least, principals, parents, and colleagues must be brought on board as supporters. It is very difficult to be successful if others in the environment are working against you. Kostelnik (1992) described some of the myths about developmentally appropriate practice that evolved because of misinformation about what really transpires as a result of moving toward the new approach (see Table 2.3). The myths are particularly helpful because they provide a framework for early childhood professionals to use in designing staff development sessions for

TABLE 2.3   Myths Associated with Developmentally Appropriate Programs

1. There is one right way to implement a developmentally appropriate program.
2. Developmentally appropriate practice requires that teachers abandon all of their prior knowledge and experience. Nothing they have learned in the past is acceptable in the new philosophy.
3. Developmentally appropriate classrooms are unstructured classrooms.
4. In developmentally appropriate classrooms, teachers don't teach.
5. To be developmentally appropriate, elementary teachers and administrators must "water down" the traditional curriculum. Children learn less than they have in the past.
6. Developmentally appropriate programs can be defined according to dichotomous positions. One position is always right, the other position is always wrong.
7. Academics have no place in developmentally appropriate programs.
8. Developmentally appropriate programs are suitable for only certain kinds of children.
9. Developmental appropriateness is just a fad, soon to be replaced by another, perhaps opposite trend.

Source: Kostelnik 1992, pp. 17–23.

nonbelievers. They also help teachers understand that the key to developmentally appropriate practice is to make decisions that reflect the needs and interests of the children in their room at that time. Slavishly adhering to a set of standards does not result in a developmentally appropriate program.

Third, moving to developmentally appropriate practice costs money. It is true that many early childhood teachers can do almost anything with nothing because they have become adept at scavenging, but it is also true that developmentally appropriate practice cannot be successful with thirty children in one room, seated at desks, with no space or materials for centers. Reasonable class sizes, appropriate furniture and materials, and space for centers and displays are all necessary. In addition, funds are needed for staff development so that teachers can gain knowledge and share their frustrations and successes with others who are in the implementation process.

Next, the implementation of developmentally appropriate practice does not occur in a single day. Rather, it is evolutionary. Teachers may start with one center or activity that is developmentally appropriate and expand to the whole day over a three- to six-month period of time. The important consideration is teacher comfort; teachers should not move faster than they are ready or they will not experience success.

Last, and most important, teachers must have faith that developmentally appropriate practice is the most effective approach for all young children. This belief is most important on days when nothing goes right and it almost seems easier to go back to the old ways of operating.

One common misunderstanding about developmentally appropriate programs is the assumption that because blocks, paints, dress-up clothes, and other similar materials are found in the classrooms of both 4-year-olds and 8-year-olds, both groups are doing the same thing and there is no progression of skills or thinking as children get older. A close inspection of both classrooms would reveal that although the basic materials may be the same, as children become more capable, the related props change. Four-year-olds may have only blocks, while 8-year-olds have blocks, cars, trucks, road signs, backdrops, road maps, markers, and pictures. As children's thinking becomes more complex, teachers modify the environment to extend their understanding further. Four-year-olds may verbally share the structure with their classmates; 8-year-olds may share by reading a story they wrote about the block-building experience.

For example, the guidelines for developmentally appropriate practice in the primary grades serving 5- through 8-year-olds (see Table 2.4) contain many of the same standards for younger children but also add new criteria that reflect the changing nature of children.

TABLE 2.4   Relevant Principles for Developmentally Appropriate Practice in the Primary Grades Serving 5- through 8-Year-Olds

1. Teachers must always be cognizant of the whole child.
2. The curriculum should be integrated.
3. Children should be engaged in active, rather than passive activities.
4. The curriculum should provide many developmentally appropriate materials for children to explore and think about, and opportunities for interaction and communication with other children and adults.
5. The content of the curriculum must be relevant, engaging, and meaningful to the children themselves.
6. Primary age children should be provided opportunities to work in small groups on projects that provide rich content for conversation. Teachers facilitate discussion among children by making comments and soliciting children's opinions and ideas.
7. Teachers should recognize the importance of developing positive peer group relationships and provide opportunities and support for cooperative small group projects that not only develop cognitive ability but promote peer interaction.
8. To develop a sense of industry or sense of competence, primary age children need to acquire the knowledge and skills recognized by our culture as important, foremost among which are the abilities to read and write and to calculate numerically.
9. The younger the children and the more diverse their backgrounds, the wider the variety of teaching materials required.
10. Curriculum and teaching methods should be designed so that children not only acquire knowledge and skills, but they also acquire the disposition or inclination to use them.

Source: Bredekamp 1987, pp. 62–66.

Of particular importance is the concern of parents and teachers for reading, writing, and mathematical competence. If third grader Johnny is happy, content, and well liked but still cannot read, parents will begin doubting that developmentally appropriate practice is serving Johnny's needs.

SUMMARY

No one way of teaching can meet the needs of all children, and no one set of guidelines can be applied strictly, without interpretation based on a teacher's experience and knowledge. Developmentally appropriate practice provides teachers with a framework that helps them make informed decisions about what to do with children. When teachers insist on only one way of doing something in a developmentally appropriate classroom, they are guilty of being as rigid as someone who advocates an academic approach. Bredekamp (1991) suggests that one purpose of developmentally appropriate guidelines is to "open up" curriculum and teaching practices and move them away from traditional approaches. Kostelnik (1993) agrees that there is no single set of guidelines that provides everything one needs to know about early childhood education. She further states that guidelines cannot be applied unthinkingly. Professional teachers with appropriate knowledge and experience interpret events and make judgements that reflect the interaction of guidelines with the particular needs of individual children. Teachers of all young children will find that the developmentally appropriate guidelines work best when they are utilized within the context of a specific classroom and unique children.

ACTIVITIES AND RESOURCES

Activities

1. Read *Stone Soup* (Brown, 1947) to children and talk about the story. Another time read the story, make the soup, and then discuss what children have learned. How do their responses differ? What other modifications could you make to the storytelling experience that might heighten children's level of engagement?
2. Observe the block centers in a classroom of 4-year-olds and one of 6-year-olds. How do the children's behaviors differ? Record your observations according to whether the behaviors are indicative of social growth, physical growth, intellectual growth, or emotional growth.
3. Interview a teacher in a developmentally appropriate classroom, and then interview one in an academic classroom. How do their goals for children differ? If you were a parent which would you prefer for your child? Why?
4. Describe the process you would follow to change from an academic program to a developmentally appropriate one.

5. Choose a partner. Pretend that he or she is the parent of one of your children and is not pleased with what the child is learning. Present to the parent the reasons you have for using developmentally appropriate practice.

Class Discussion Questions

1. As a teacher, what would be your greatest misgiving about implementing developmentally appropriate practice?
2. What are the characteristics of an activity that is real, relevant, and engaging for a classroom of kindergarten children?
3. How can blocks be a creative, intriguing medium for both 5- and 8-year-olds?
4. Why is there always more to children's involvement in developmentally appropriate classrooms than meets the eye?
5. Developmentally appropriate practice is an appropriate approach for all children. Do you agree or disagree? Why?

REFERENCES

Bredekamp, S. (1987). *Developmentally appropriate practice in early childhood programs serving children from birth through age eight*. Washington, DC: National Association for the Education of Young Children.

Bredekamp, S. (1991). Redeveloping early childhood education: A response to Kessler. *Early Childhood Research Quarterly, 6*(2), 199–209.

Bricker, D. & Cripe, J. (1992). *An activity-based approach to early intervention*. Baltimore, MD: Paul H. Brookes.

Burts, D.C. and others, (1989, March). *A comparison of stress behaviors observed in kindergarten children in classrooms with developmentally appropriate vs. developmentally inappropriate instructional practices*. Paper presented at the annual meeting of the American Educational Research Association, San Francisco, CA.

Campbell, P. (1991). Evaluation and assessment in early intervention for infants and toddlers. *Journal of Early Intervention, 15*(1), 36–45.

Davis, M.D. (1989). Preparing teachers for developmentally appropriate kindergarten classrooms. *Dimensions, 17*(3), 4–7.

Derman-Sparks, L. (1993). Revisiting multicultural education: What children need to live in a diverse society. *Dimensions, 21*(2), 6–10.

Elkind, D. (1986). Formal education and early childhood education: An essential difference. *Phi Delta Kappan, 67*(9), 631–636.

Elkind, D. (1989). Developmentally appropriate practice: Philosophical and practical implications. *Phi Delta Kappan, 71*(2), 113–117.

Gifford, J. (1992). A stitch in time: Strengthening the first years of school. Compulsory Years of Schooling Project. Project paper no. 3. Commissioned Report no. 16, National Board of Employment, Education and Training. Canberra (Australia) Schools Council.

Gronlund, G. (1995). Bringing the DAP message to kindergarten and primary teachers. *Young Children, 50*(5), 4–13.

Guralnick, M. (1993). Developmentally appropriate practice in the assessment and intervention of children's peer relations. *Topics in Early Childhood Special Education, 13*(3), pp. 344–371.

Kostelnik, M.J. (1992). Myths associated with developmentally appropriate programs. *Young Children, 47*(4), 17–23.

Kostelnik, M.J. (1993). Recognizing the essentials of developmentally appropriate practice. *Childcare Information Exchange,* 73–77.

National Association for the Education of Young Children. (1988). NAEYC position statement on standardized testing of young children 3 through 8 years of age. *Young Children, 43*(3), 42–47.

National Association of Elementary School Principals. (1990). *Early childhood education and the elementary school principal: standards for quality programs for young children.* Alexandria, VA: Author.

National Association of State Boards of Education. (1988). *Right from the start: The report of the ASBE task force on early childhood education.* Alexandria, VA: Author.

Piaget, J. (1962). *Plays, dreams and imitation in children.* New York: Norton.

3

PRINCIPLES OF DEVELOPMENTALLY APPROPRIATE PRACTICE APPLIED TO YOUNG CHILDREN WITH SPECIAL NEEDS

OBJECTIVES

As a result of studying this chapter, readers should be able to perform the following:

- Describe the many influences on the development of early childhood special education as a discipline.
- Discuss the major goals and practices of early childhood special education and how they are compatible with the developmentally appropriate practices (DAP) guidelines.
- Describe a framework and recommendations for blending practices from the disciplines of early childhood special education (ECSE) and early childhood education (ECE).

The intent of this chapter is to provide an overview of early childhood special education, a relatively young field that focuses on the needs of infants and young children with disabilities and their families.

THE EVOLUTION OF ECSE AS A DYNAMIC FIELD

ECSE as a Blend of Three Parent Fields

In a discussion of early childhood special education, it is important to understand the many forces that have shaped the field. A number of studies conducted over the past fifty years have supported the concept of early intervention and education. For an in-depth review of this research, see Peterson (1987), Bailey and Wolery (1992), or Bruder (in press).

Rather than developing as a single entity, ECSE is a blend of three primary educational movements or "parent fields" whose merger began in the sixties and culminated in the new discipline of ECSE in the seventies. The three parent fields that had a significant impact on ECSE were (1) special education, which was designed for school-age children with disabilities; (2) early childhood education, which focused on the educational and care needs of children from birth through age 8; and (3) the compensatory education movement, which included programs for children who were at risk for school success (Peterson, 1987). Figure 3.1 represents the three fields that have been blended over time to result in ECSE.

The question that emerges is how each of these parallel educational movements has contributed to the field of ECSE. The special education movement established the assumption that children with disabilities were entitled

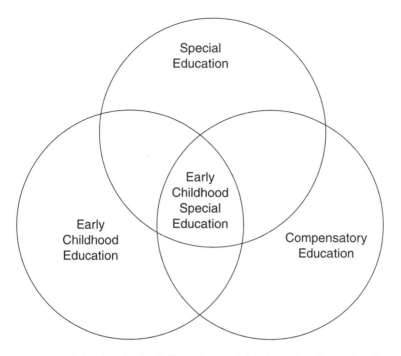

FIGURE 3.1   Early Childhood Special Education Is a Blend of Three Parent Fields

to a free, appropriate education with their nondisabled peers. The early childhood education movement brought acceptance to preschool education and child care as beneficial experiences for young children. The compensatory education movement initiated programs, such as Head Start, designed to prevent disadvantaged children from failing in educational environments. More importantly, the compensatory education movement demonstrated that early intervention and education are cost-effective means of benefiting young children and their families. Had these important milestones not been achieved in each of the parent fields, professionals probably would not have turned their attention to the needs of young children with disabilities (Peterson, 1987; Noonan & McCormick, 1993).

ECSE has drawn heavily from a number of other discipline perspectives such as psychology, social work, human development, health care disciplines, and speech and hearing sciences. As professionals from ECSE interact with those from other disciplines, viewpoints become broadened and blended, resulting in new perspectives on the provision of services for young children with disabilities and their families.

LEGISLATIVE INFLUENCES

In addition to the influences of various educational movements on the development of ECSE, a number of federal laws and their subsequent amendments and regulations, and also state laws, have shaped the way in which early childhood services have been provided to young children with disabilities. Legislation from special education, general early childhood education, and compensatory education has had a significant influence on the current status of ECSE. Table 3.1 provides a list of the major federal legislation that has affected services for young children with disabilities.

TABLE 3.1   Major Federal Legislation in Early Childhood Special Education

1965	The *Economic Opportunity Act* established Project Head Start to provide services to preschool children living in poverty. Services included day care, education, medical/dental, and family support.
1968	P.L. 90-538, the *Handicapped Children's Early Education Assistance Act* (HCEEAA), formed the Handicapped Children's Early Education Program (HCEEP), with the purpose of establishing and demonstrating the feasibility of various models and programs for young children with disabilities. (Note: It is now called the Early Education Program for Children with Disabilities (EEPCD).
1972	P.L. 92-424, the *Economic Opportunity Act Amendments*, required Head Start programs to reserve at least 10% of their enrollments for young children with disabilities.
1975	P.L. 94-142, the *Education of the Handicapped Act* (EHA), mandated a free and appropriate public education for all children with disabilities (optional services for 3–5 year olds), individualized planning, placements in the least restrictive environment, and procedural safeguards/due process.
1986	P.L. 99-457 amended P.L. 94-142 by extending the full-service mandate to preschoolers ages 3–5 years (Part B) and starting a new voluntary program for infants, toddlers, and their families (Part H).
1988	Technology-Related Assistance for Individuals with Disabilities established assistive and adaptive technology among the related services that may be needed for a child to benefit from special education.
1990	P.L. 101-376, the *Americans with Disabilities Act* (ADA), was a landmark civil rights law that banned the discrimination of individuals with disabilities in public and private services.
1990	P.L. 101-476 reauthorized P.L. 94-142 and renamed the title of EHA as the *Individuals with Disabilities Education Act* (IDEA). (Note: The "person first" language was added and the term *disabilities* replaced *handicapped* in the legislation).
1991	P.L. 102-119, the *Individuals with Disabilities Education Act Amendments*, reauthorized Part H of P.L. 99-457 and revised some sections of P.L. 99-457.

Head Start Legislation

Head Start programs began in 1965. Head Start, the largest federally funded early childhood program, was founded to give low-income preschoolers an advantage in the early years. Services were comprehensive and included day care, education, health services, and family support. The program was based on research demonstrating the positive effects of early intervention on the development of disadvantaged children, particularly in the areas of language and cognitive development. Although the original legislation did not address children with disabilities, the 1972 *Economic Opportunity Act Amendments* (P.L. 92-424) established the requirement that Head Start programs reserve at least 10 percent of their enrollments for preschoolers with disabilities. Thus, the focus of Head Start was expanded to include young children with disabilities and their families. In 1993 the federal regulations that govern the provision of services to children with disabilities in Head Start programs were revised to meet the needs of this population more appropriately.

P.L. 90-538

The *Handicapped Children's Early Education Assistance Act* (HCEEAA) of 1968 provided federal funds to support the identification of effective procedures and the development of model demonstration programs for young children with disabilities and their families. Initially these projects were referred to as the Handicapped Children's Early Education Program (HCEEP); they are now called the Early Education Program for Children with Disabilities (EEPCD). These projects have demonstrated the effectiveness of numerous models and practices and have provided much needed data to extend the knowledge base for services for young children with disabilities and their families. A system for identifying validated models was implemented, and funds were provided for disseminating information about the projects. These model projects have had a tremendous impact on early intervention programs throughout the United States. Some of the best-known projects, which have provided various models of home-based and center-based services for others to replicate, include the Portage Project in Wisconsin, Project PEECH (The Precise Early Education of Children with Handicaps) at the University of Illinois, and the Model Preschool Program at the University of Washington.

Technology-Related Assistance Act

This act, passed in 1988, has been particularly important for individuals with disabilities in that it established assistive and adaptive technology among the related services a student may need in order to benefit from special education.

Technological advances have had a significant impact on all aspects of the lives of individuals with disabilities.

P.L. 94-142

The *Education of the Handicapped Act* (EHA), P.L. 94-142, is the landmark federal law that first established a national policy for the education of children with disabilities from ages 3 to 21. The law mandated that all school-age children with disabilities receive a free appropriate public education. Its major impact was on children 6 years of age and older because it relieved states from providing education for children with disabilities from ages 3 through 5 if normal children in these age ranges were not served by the state's public schools. However, P.L. 94-142 has been instrumental in shaping several current early childhood special education practices including parental participation, due process, and the use of the Individualized Education Program (IEP).

P.L. 99-457

A major achievement for early childhood special education was the passage of P.L. 99-457 in October of 1986, amending and reauthorizing P.L. 94-142. Under P.L. 99-457, the provisions of P.L. 94-142 were extended downward and mandated for preschoolers (ages 3 through 5). This part of the law was referred to as Part B (the Preschool Grant Program).

Part H of the law (the Handicapped Infants and Toddlers Program) was a voluntary program for each state, providing monetary incentives to states to serve infants and toddlers at risk for and with disabilities (from birth through age 2) and their families. It encouraged states to establish a system of coordinated, comprehensive, multidisciplinary, interagency programs. Inherent in the provisions of Part H was the need for interagency collaboration in order to provide a more coordinated system of services and to prevent the costly duplication and overlapping of services. Another important dimension of Part H was the emphasis on families. Part H requires that services for infants and toddlers and their families be based upon an Individualized Family Service Plan (IFSP).

P.L. 101-476

In 1990, P.L. 101-476 reauthorized P.L. 94-142 and changed the name of the *Education of the Handicapped Act* (EHA) to the *Individuals with Disabilities Education Act* (IDEA). Throughout the act, the term *handicapped* was replaced with *disabilities* and the "person first" language was used (e.g., child with a disability versus handicapped child). The notion behind the changes was to demonstrate greater respect and sensitivity toward individuals with disabilities and their families by recognizing the person before his disability.

Americans with Disabilities Act *(ADA), P.L. 101-376*

Due to the recent passage of the landmark civil rights legislation, ADA, all individuals with disabilities are protected from discrimination and have the right to equal access and reasonable accommodations in public and private services. The provisions of ADA include equal access for young children with disabilities to enrollment in early childhood programs, a requirement that has far-reaching effects for young children with disabilities and their families.

In addition to the legislation highlighted in this section, other significant legislation has recognized the importance of the early years on the development of young children. Such legislation has included the *Family Support Act* of 1988 and the *Child Care and Development Block Grant* of 1991. States are authorized to coordinate programs such as Head Start and child care to ensure accessibility to families in need of services.

This body of legislation has been a major force in the evolution of the field of early childhood special education. It provides the foundation on which early intervention services are built and removes young children with disabilities and their families from second-class citizenship. Table 3.2 provides

---

TABLE 3.2   Legal Requirements of Early Childhood Special Education

- Children (ages 3 through 8) with disabilities are entitled to a free, appropriate public education.
- The assessment procedures used to identify, classify, and place children with disabilities in early childhood special education programs must be nondiscriminatory.
- Every child with a disability must have an Individualized Education Program (IEP) (ages 3 through 8) or an Individualized Family Service Plan (IFSP) (birth through 3).
- Children with disabilities must be placed in the least restrictive appropriate environment. This means that services should be provided to the greatest extent possible in settings with nondisabled children.
- Children with disabilities have equal access to enrollment in early childhood programs for nondisabled children. In Head Start programs, 10 percent of the enrollment must be reserved for children with disabilities.
- Parents of children with disabilities have the right to be involved in planning and developing the state and local educational policies and in developing and implementing their child's IEP or IFSP.
- Parents of children with disabilities have a right to question and challenge any actions taken by the school in relation to their child's education.

Source: Adapted from Wolery & Wilbers (1994). *Including children with special needs in early childhood programs.* Washington, DC: NAEYC, pp. 19-20. Copyright 1994 by NAEYC. All rights reserved.

TABLE 3.3   Comparison of the Required Components of the IFSP and the IEP

Individualized Family Service Plan (IFSP)	Individual Education Plan (IEP)
1. A statement of the child's present levels of functioning in cognitive, communication, social/emotional, and adaptive skill development	1. A statement of the child's present levels of educational performance, including academic achievement, social adaptation, prevocational and vocational skills, psychomotor skills, and self-help skills
2. A statement of the family's resources, priorities, and concerns related to enhancing the child's development	2. A statement of annual goals that describes the educational performance to be achieved in all areas in which the child needs specially designed instruction
3. A statement of the expected intervention (for the infant or toddler and the family), including the criteria, procedures, and timelines used to determine progress	3. A statement of short-term instructional objectives with criteria, evaluation procedures, and schedules for determining (at least once a year) whether instructional objectives are being met
4. A description of specific early intervention services necessary to meet the unique needs of the child and family (e.g., frequency, intensity, and method of delivering services)	4. A statement of specific educational services needed by the child, including all special education and related services and any special instructional media and materials needed
5. The projected dates for initiation of services and expected duration of services	5. The projected date for the initiation of those services and the anticipated duration given
6. The name of the service coordinator from the profession most immediately relevant to the child's or family's needs who will be responsible for carrying out the plan and coordinating with other agencies and persons	6. A list of the individuals responsible for implementing the IEP
7. Procedures to support the transition of the child to services provided under Part B	7. A justification of the type of educational placement that the child will have
8. A statement of natural environments in which early intervention services will be provided	8. A description of the extent of classroom participation in regular education

a summary of the legal requirements for early childhood special education that are a result of the legislation.

Legislation has forced many developments in the field of early childhood education. For example, the IFSP is required by Part H of IDEA and the IEP is required by Section 619 of Part B of IDEA. The IFSP is a written document, developed in collaboration with families, outlining services for infants and toddlers and their families. IFSPs require a statement of an infant's or toddler's present level of development in five domains (physical, cognitive, communication, social or emotional, and adaptive development); family information, including a statement of the family's resources, priorities, and concerns related to enhancing the development of the child; outcomes to be achieved for the child and family, as well as the criteria, procedures, and timelines used to monitor progress; specific services the child and family will receive, and similar information; the name of the service coordinator; a statement of the natural environments in which services are to be delivered; and a plan to support the transition of the child at age 3 to preschool services or other services.

The IEP, a written plan required for children with disabilities from ages 3–21, is developed by a team that must include the child's parent(s), the child's teacher, an agency representative, and other representatives deemed appropriate by the parents or school district. The IEP contains a statement of the child's present level of educational performance in each of the domains (adaptive, cognitive, communication, physical, and social or emotional); the child's annual goals and short-term objectives; the special education and related services to be provided; the extent to which the child will participate in the regular education program; the way in which the child's progress will be determined; and the date of initiation and projected duration of services. In addition, the IEP can include transition services if the IEP team finds it appropriate. For example, parents may request information and assistance in determining the most appropriate next environment for their child. The IFSP and the IEP have similarities as well as differences. Table 3.3 provides a comparison of the IEP and IFSP components.

MAJOR PREMISES OF EARLY CHILDHOOD SPECIAL EDUCATION

To provide a holistic view of the field of ECSE, a brief description of the major premises of ECSE is provided in Table 3.4. These premises are based on research that has demonstrated the effectiveness of various practices and models of early intervention. The ECSE premises are adapted from the work of a number of professionals in the field of ECSE. They are evolutionary and are

TABLE 3.4   Basic Premises of Early Childhood Special Education

1. Assessment of young children should be dynamic; include multimeasures, multi-informants, and multisettings; and be linked to programming.
2. Services should be designed around an individualized teaching plan (IEP or IFSP) consisting of goals and outcomes based on the family's concerns, priorities, and resources; the child's strengths and needs; and the skills required for future school and nonschool settings.
3. Programs serving young children with special needs must offer a range of services that vary in intensity and structure, based on the needs of the children they serve.
4. Programs should promote the child's development through instruction tailored to the child's development in key domains (adaptive, cognitive, communication, physical, and social or emotional).
5. Programs serving young children with special needs should be family centered, with particular emphasis placed on the family as the primary decision maker in their child's program.
6. Programs should promote the child's optimal development through instruction that is tailored to the child and produces the highest possible levels of engagement, independence, and mastery.
7. Specific instruction aimed at developing children's skills should be embedded in daily activities.
8. Methods of instruction and intervention should be effective, efficient, and functional.
9. Programs should provide for and prepare children for normalized life experiences.
10. Programs and instruction should be designed to prevent the emergence of future problems or disabilities.

based on legislation, research, and recommended practices. Each is described briefly in the following section.

An underlying premise of ECSE is that assessment should be dynamic rather than static; include multimeasures, multisettings, and multi-informants; and be linked to programming. This means that the assessment process should be flexible, and should occur on an ongoing basis in the natural environment. Multiple culturally and linguistically appropriate measures are recommended. Family members, as well as early care and education providers, can be helpful in providing information concerning the abilities of the child in multiple settings. Family members should be an integral part of all phases of the assessment process: screening, eligibility, program planning, and evaluation.

It is important to remember that the overall purpose of assessment is to discover how an individual child's development is proceeding in the various domains of development. It is important first to decide what questions need to be asked in order to know what types of assessment information should be collected. When determining a child's eligibility for services, the assessment information will be different than when designing the individual teaching plan or monitoring educational progress. Regardless of the specific question that assessment information is designed to answer, the tests and measures must be used for the purpose they were intended and administered by appropriately trained professionals.

A second premise of ECSE is that services must be designed around an individualized teaching plan (an IEP or IFSP), as required in the *Individuals with Disabilities Education Act*, consisting of goals and outcomes based on the family's priorities and resources, the child's strengths and needs, and the skills required for future school and nonschool settings. The IEP and IFSP are statements of individualized goals or outcomes for a child with a disability and his or her family, with a plan for implementation and evaluation. Because children who receive ECSE services have disabilities, delays, or deviations in development, which may interfere with their success in future settings, the IEP or IFSP must often focus on skills that the children will need in the next environment. In other words, the goals or outcomes should emphasize skills that have both present and future utility.

A third premise of ECSE is that programs serving young children with special needs must offer a range of services that vary in intensity and structure, based on the needs of the children they serve. The abilities of young children are so diverse that services must be provided in an individualized manner. The kinds of programs, range of services, and the amounts of services required can vary tremendously. For example, placement can range from home-based to center-based programs, consist of a variety of related services, and be offered from one day to five days per week for varying amounts of time. In addition, service delivery can be provided in self-contained, inclusive, or other settings designed to meet the identified needs of the child.

A fourth assumption of ECSE is that programs should promote the child's development through instruction tailored to the child's development in key domains. The key domains of development emphasized in ECSE include adaptive, communication, cognition, physical, and social or emotional skills. Of course, the key domains are interrelated; as a result, activities for young children with disabilities usually foster development in several domains concurrently.

For ECSE, a fifth premise is that programs serving young children with special needs should be family centered, with particular emphasis placed on the family as the primary decision maker in the child's program. Some professionals choose to use the term *family driven* to emphasize the belief that families should actually drive services so that they are specifically designed to meet the family's individual needs. In the past, terms used included *parent involvement*, indicating that families should be involved in their children's programs, and *family focused*, meaning that services should focus on the family rather than only the child.

A family-centered approach is one in which the family unit, rather than the child, is considered to be the center of the service delivery system. A family-centered approach reflects the growing awareness that decisions made about educational services for young children affect not only the child, but most often the rest of the family as well. Further, it is assumed that interventions that strengthen the family will indirectly influence the development of the child. Professionals are encouraged to work closely with families; help them in identifying their concerns, priorities, and resources; respect their values and opinions; and support them in achieving goals and outcomes important to the family. Certainly an important dimension of family-centered services is respect for diversity (e.g., cultural, linguistic, economic, and geographic) among families.

The sixth premise of ECSE is that programs should promote the child's optimal development through instruction that is tailored to the child and produces the highest possible levels of engagement, independence, and mastery. Instruction for young children with disabilities often varies in terms of intensity, based on the needs, abilities, and learning styles of individual children. Engagement has been defined as "the involvement of situationally appropriate interactions with the physical environment, materials, or other persons" (Bailey & Wolery, 1992, p. 37). Young children with disabilities should be involved in meaningful activities for extended periods of time. They must develop the ability to function with as little help as possible from other people. Various types of assistive and adaptive technology can enable young children with disabilities to move around their environments, communicate with others, and participate in developmentally appropriate activities that might otherwise not be possible. As a result of individualized instruction and adaptations, young children with disabilities should be able to acquire new skills or knowledge and should become reasonably successful in mastering the demands of the environments in which they most frequently live and play.

In ECSE, a seventh factor is that specific instruction aimed at developing children's skills should be embedded in daily activities. Activity-based intervention (ABI) has been described by Bricker and Cripe (1992) as ". . . a child-directed, transactional approach that embeds intervention in individual goals and objectives in routine, planned, or child-initiated activities" (p. 40). This approach capitalizes on "child-initiated" as well as "routine and planned . . . activities that children choose or enjoy" (p. 27). Although instructional objectives are established in ABI, they are stated in more general terms and are addressed in planned activities within the natural environment. ABI actively links assessment, intervention, and evaluation, which is critical to effective programming in ECSE.

An eighth premise of ECSE is that methods of instruction and intervention should be effective, efficient, and functional. The effectiveness of programming for young children with disabilities is very much a product of the instructional strategies employed. The instructional strategies must be individualized and multifaceted because there is no one strategy that works for all children nor is there a single strategy that always works for a given child. Much emphasis must be placed on the selection of the best methods to meet the needs of each child in the most efficient manner possible. A functional approach to instruction is used with young children with disabilities. In a functional approach, targeted skills are those needed frequently within the context of routines that occur in the natural environment (e.g., dressing, eating, and greeting others). As one parent described it, "During circle time at school, my child learned to indicate on the weather chart that it was raining outside, but he never learned to go get his raincoat and umbrella and use them on a rainy day."

A ninth premise of ECSE is that programs should provide for and prepare children for normalized life experiences. The concept of normalized life experiences is reflected in IDEA, with one of the provisions being that children with disabilities must be placed in the least restrictive appropriate environment. While still addressing the specific goals and objectives of children with disabilities, programming for young children with disabilities must be viewed from an ecological, naturalistic, normalized approach (Bailey & McWilliam, 1990). The ultimate goal is for young children with disabilities to have the same opportunities as their normal peers to participate in all of life's communities.

A final consideration in ECSE is that programs and instruction should be designed to prevent the emergence of future problems or disabilities. A major focus is the remediation of current problems and the prevention of future developmental problems. By intervening early, parents and professionals may ameliorate the effect of a disability on young children. Through early intervention services, a young child with cerebral palsy, for example, may receive therapeutic services (e.g., physical and/or occupational therapy) that foster motor development and prevent the emergence of contractures and deformities.

The premises described in this chapter are related to services provided in ECSE programs. Although a number of other variable aspects of ECSE are discussed in subsequent chapters, the ones in this section are featured throughout the book.

TRENDS AND ISSUES IN EARLY CHILDHOOD SPECIAL EDUCATION

The field of ECSE faces tremendous issues and challenges. A number of trends are prominent in ECSE today and, as a result, have significantly influenced the field's development. Trends that have had the greatest impact include the movement toward inclusion and the movement to blend recommended practices from ECE and ECSE. These two movements are discussed in the following section. In addition, old versus new recommended practices in ECSE are described.

The Influence of the Inclusion Movement

Aided by legislative actions, the movement toward serving children with disabilities in educational settings designed for nondisabled children has gained momentum. America's Goals 2000 and the *Improving America's Schools Act* of 1993 call for an inclusive approach to achieving higher educational outcomes for all students, including those with disabilities. These federal initiatives have had a tremendous impact on ECSE in recent years.

There is also considerable support for inclusion in the literature. Findings of a recent survey conducted by the National Center on Educational Restructuring and Inclusion (NCERI) revealed the following: the number of school districts with inclusive educational programs has increased dramatically since 1994; the outcomes for students with and without disabilities in inclusive programs are positive; and students with a wider range of disabilities are in inclusive education programs (NCERI 1995). As Baker, Wang, and Walberg (1995) noted, evidence from the last fifteen years suggests that the segregation of students with disabilities in separate classrooms "is actually deleterious to their academic performance and social adjustment, and that special students generally perform better on average in regular classrooms" (p. 34). More research is needed, however, on the effectiveness of various aspects of inclusion.

It is important to understand the varying terminology used to describe the inclusion process: integration, mainstreaming, least restrictive environment, and full inclusion. *Integration* is a broad term describing any enrollment of children with and without disabilities in the same program. *Mainstreaming* is the placement of children with disabilities in programs having a majority of children who are not disabled. *Least restrictive environment* describes a setting among other settings that is appropriate for the child and provides the most contact possible with nondisabled children. *Full inclusion*, on the other hand, is an approach in which children with disabilities are placed in the same programs or classrooms and receive individualized and appropriate services alongside their nondisabled peers. The assumption underlying full inclusion is that all children belong together and children with disabilities should be served in the same programs they would have attended if they did not have a disability. Although full inclusion has been targeted as an element of exemplary practice in both ECE and ECSE, the placement of young children with disabilities in inclusive settings has emerged as one of the most important, complex, and controversial practices in the field of early childhood education today (Peck, Odom, & Bricker, 1993). For children between the ages of birth and 6 years, the biggest problem is that many states do not provide public education to nondisabled children of these ages. Although many people support the concept of inclusion, others have been concerned that inclusion of students in the mainstream could result in exclusion from remedial assistance for these students. They fear that the location of services will be emphasized over the appropriateness of services. One of the most controversial issues has been the appropriate placement of young children who are deaf. Central to this issue is the very individualized communication need of this population. However, even with the potential problems and differing opinions, many professionals from a number of organizations support inclusion. These groups include the International Council for Exceptional Children (CEC), the Learning Disabilities Association of America (LDA), United Cerebral Palsy Associations, Inc. (UCPA), and others. In 1993, the Division for Early Childhood (DEC) of CEC issued a position statement that offered guidance regarding inclusion (see Figure 3.2).

The DEC position statement on inclusion has served several important functions. It states the values that DEC, as a professional organization, holds regarding inclusion. In addition, it informs professionals and families of what

---

Inclusion, as a value, supports the right of all children, regardless of their diverse abilities, to participate actively in natural settings within their communities. A natural setting is one in which the child would spend time if he or she had not had a disability. Such settings include, but are not limited to, home and family, play groups, child care, nursery schools, Head Start programs, kindergartens, and neighborhood school classrooms.

DEC believes in and supports full and successful access to health, social services, education, and other supports and services for young children and their families that promote full participation in community life. DEC values the diversity of families and supports a family guided process for determining services that are based on the needs and preferences of individual families and children.

To implement inclusive practices, DEC supports: (a) the continued development, evaluation, and dissemination of full inclusion supports, services, and systems; (b) the development of preservice and inservice training programs that prepare families, administrators, and service providers to develop and work within inclusive settings; (c) collaboration among all key stakeholders to implement flexible fiscal and administrative procedures in support of inclusion; (d) research that contributes to our knowledge of state-of-the-art services; and (e) the restructuring and unification of social, education, health, and intervention supports and services to make them more responsive to the needs of all children and families."

FIGURE 3.2 DEC Position Statement on Inclusion

DEC considers to be recommended practice and clarifies some of the issues surrounding inclusion.

The movement toward inclusion, characterized by the increased number of young children with disabilities who attend community child care or education programs along with their nondisabled peers, has created a need for stronger collaboration between professionals from ECE and ECSE. In fact, as Guralnick (1990) predicted, inclusive programs have become the "setting of choice for the vast majority of children with special needs." He also suggested that "the decade of the 1990s [would] test the commitment and depth of the partnership between special education and the general early childhood community" (p. 4). The legislation has forced many developments in the field of early childhood. For example, the IFSP is required by Part H of IDEA and the IEP is required by Section 619. Now that early childhood programs are serving more children with disabilities, professionals from ECE and ECSE have confronted many new challenges and opportunities and have become more aware of the need to communicate and collaborate.

It has become increasingly important for professionals from ECE and ECSE to examine and discuss the goals and practices of their respective disciplines so that commonalties can be enhanced and differences resolved. Time to talk and plan together are critical elements of successful inclusion.

From a family's perspective, inclusion is important because it affords children the opportunity to receive their education alongside their nondisabled peers. Through inclusion, children with and without disabilities are able to benefit from the same learning environments, participate in the same activities, and develop friendships. For parents of children with disabilities, inclusion is usually a more desirable option than having them excluded from educational opportunities as they were in the past. As a parent of a child with a disability described, "It is difficult to imagine how it feels to call an early childhood program and rather than inquiring about what kind of curriculum they have or types of activities, you first have to ask them if they accept children with disabilities. Because of inclusion, the dream of my child having the opportunity to go to the same early childhood program and to develop friendships with her normally developing peers has finally been realized."

The need for ECE professionals, ECSE professionals, and families to work together becomes even more apparent when addressing issues of inclusion. Often parents struggle with making decisions about the "most appropriate" services for their children versus the "highest quality" services. For example, parents may realize the many potential benefits of their children's being included with their nondisabled peers and may feel that this would be the most appropriate placement. On the other hand, they may feel secure with the special education teacher's expertise and the low student-to-teacher ratio found in a self-contained early childhood special education classroom. Parents may feel that the specific services are of a somewhat higher quality. The challenge becomes how to make the most appropriate services become the highest quality services. Families and professionals from across disciplines (e.g., general early childhood, early childhood special education, and related services) must collaborate in developing inclusive services that best serve children with disabilities. By involving families, the chances of providing inclusive services that respond to the child's needs and the family's priorities are enhanced.

THE MOVEMENT TO BLEND RECOMMENDED ECE AND ECSE PRACTICES

As described in Chapter 1, the guidelines for developmentally appropriate practice were developed by professionals from the National Association for the Education of Young Children (NAEYC) (Bredekamp, 1987) to specify contemporary practices that reflect state-of-the-art practices in ECE. It is important to note that the guidelines are for practice within a single discipline—that discipline being ECE. One should also understand that until recently, early childhood special education did not have a set of guidelines parallel to those of DAP. The Division for Early Childhood (DEC) of the Council for Exceptional Children established a task force to develop a document for ECSE that would be similar to the DAP guidelines but would be reflective of the best practices in ECSE. The task force drew upon the expertise of the DEC membership and family members of young children with disabilities, drafted an initial set of recommended practices, and then incorporated them into a validation questionnaire that was distributed to eight hundred respondents. The findings of the task force centered around practices that reflect quality in ECSE and culminated in *DEC Recommended Practices: Indicators of Quality in Programs for Infants and Young Children with Special Needs and Their Families* (DEC Task Force on Recommended Practices, 1993).

As a follow-up to the previous study, McLean and Odom (1993) compared accepted practices identified by DEC and NAEYC in terms of the similarities and differences in emphasis that existed in the areas of inclusion, family involvement, assessment, program planning, curriculum, intervention strategies, service delivery models, and transition. They concluded that the practices recommended in both the NAEYC and DEC documents were indicative of the differing needs of children and families served by the two fields; however, no major areas of direct disagreement or conflict existed between the practices recommended by NAEYC and DEC. In fact, many professionals from both fields felt that the similarities far outweighed the differences. As a result, a dialogue has emerged regarding the usefulness of developmentally appropriate practices for young children with disabilities (Carta, Schwartz, Atwater, & McConnell, 1991; Johnson & Johnson, 1992). These discussions between ECE and ECSE professionals have served to raise issues, clarify misconceptions, and increase the respect that one field has for the other.

Additional Trends in ECSE

ECSE has evolved as a result of legislation, funded research, and demonstration projects that have led to a refinement in the undertaking of the best practices for working with young children with disabilities. Some of the major ways in which the field of ECSE has changed over the last several years are shown in Table 3.5. These currently recommended practices will be discussed in the following section and highlighted throughout the text.

Consultation and Collaboration

The role of the ECSE teacher has changed in recent years from the traditional classroom teacher role to a collaborative consultation role. As a result of the inclusion movement, an increasing number of young children with disabilities receive special instruction while enrolled in community-based programs for nondisabled children (e.g., general education programs and child care programs). All teachers are potential teachers of children with disabilities, and ECSE teachers spend more time serving as team teachers, resource teachers, or collaborative consultants.

ECSE and ECE teachers are now required to work together more closely than ever before. Professionals from ECSE must possess a clear understanding of what constitutes recommended practice in their respective disciplines and must be able to share that knowledge with others in a collaborative manner. The ECSE teacher may need to acquire knowledge regarding curriculum

TABLE 3.5   Old versus New Recommended Practices in ECSE

Old Practices	New Practices
1. Special education orientation	1. Blending of DAP and ECSE practices
2. Segregated services	2. Inclusive services
3. Classroom teacher role	3. Collaborative consultation role
4. Traditional assessment	4. Naturalistic assessment
5. Academic orientation	5. Play-based orientation
6. One-to-one instruction	6. Individualized, small-group instruction
7. Mass trial instruction	7. Activity-based intervention
8. Isolated tasks	8. Naturalistic/functional curriculum
9. Focus on skills and products	9. Focus on interactions and processes
10. Adult directed	10. Child initiated, adult supported
11. Child-focused services	11. Family-centered services
12. Monocultural practices	12. Multicultural responsiveness
13. Interdisciplinary or multidisciplinary team approach	13. Transdisciplinary team approach
14. Focus on the present	14. Transition planning (future focus)

content in ECE and develop strategies to share with the ECE teacher for embedding IEP objectives into ongoing activities and monitoring progress.

Assessment

In recent years, traditional assessment procedures that have relied on norm-referenced or criterion-referenced instruments have been replaced by assessment practices that are ecologically based, functional, and linked to programming. In addition, a greater emphasis has been placed on the central role families play in the assessment process. *Authentic assessment*, a term that is becoming more widely used in ECSE, has been defined as the "process of observing, recording, and otherwise documenting what children do and how they do it as a basis for making educational decisions" (Pucket & Black, 1994). Authentic assessment is appropriate in ECSE for the following reasons: (1) it is a flexible process, (2) it provides qualitative information, (3) it provides relevant and useful information, (4) it occurs in the natural environment, and (5) it is collected over time.

Curriculum and Instructional Methods

According to Fox, Hanline, Vail, and Galant (1994), "there appears to be a trend in ECSE, with a growing empirical base, to move towards interventions that reflect the practices articulated by NAEYC and away from a narrow, remedial approach to early intervention" (p. 253). When instruction is rigid and controlled, young children with disabilities often have difficulty generalizing newly acquired skills. An increased emphasis is now being placed on the generalization of skills through the use of general case instruction. As Noonan and McCormick (1993) point out, there has been "a shift over the last decade away from rigid and controlled instructional practices to more naturalistic teaching methods" (p. 22) in ECSE, such as (1) a play-based orientation rather than an academic orientation; (2) individualized, small-group instruction preferred over one-to-one instruction; (3) activity-based intervention (with objectives embedded into daily activities) versus mass trial instruction; (4) naturalistic/functional curriculum versus isolated skills or tasks; (5) a focus on interactions and processes rather than on skills and products; and (6) child-centered and adult-supported learning rather than adult-directed learning.

Family-Centered Practices

Another major change in ECSE is that the focus of services has moved from a child-focused approach to one in which the child is considered within the context of the family. The focus of ECSE is on strengthening and supporting the family system as it adjusts to the requirements of a member with special needs. Family-centered services are designed to empower the family so that it functions more effectively in meeting the needs of the child with a disability. The family-centered movement has had a significant impact on early intervention methods by encouraging families to enter into a partnership with professionals in all aspects of early intervention and education. Families are acknowledged as being unique, able to participate as decision makers, and able to serve as partners in planning, implementing, and evaluating the service delivery process.

Multicultural Emphasis

Closely tied to the family-centered movement has been the multicultural movement. Because of the family-centered emphasis in ECSE, sensitivity to cultural diversity has become particularly important. Practices in ECSE have moved from a monocultural to a multicultural emphasis in the curriculum, as well as in the day-to-day interactions with children and families. This multicultural emphasis requires that practices be "adapted for use with children or families who hold values or identify themselves as members of ethnic groups that differ from the mainstream in American society" (DEC Task Force on Recommended Practices, 1993).

Transdisciplinary Services

Another dimension of ECSE that has changed in recent years is the manner in which professionals from across disciplines work together and the way related services are delivered. A transdisciplinary team approach has become the recommended model, versus a multidisciplinary or interdisciplinary approach.

In a multidisciplinary team approach, the professionals represent their own disciplines and provide assessment and intervention in an isolated manner (e.g., individual report writing, individual goal setting, and discipline-specific direct intervention with the child and/or family). There is very little integration across disciplines, making it very difficult to develop coordinated, comprehensive programs for children and their families. In comparison, an interdisciplinary team approach is one in which the professionals carry out specific disciplinary assessments and interventions; however, there is a formal commitment to the sharing of information throughout the process of assessment, planning, and intervention.

The transdisciplinary team approach, which has become the recommended model in ECSE, is a type of team organization for assessment and intervention that requires the team members to share roles and systematically cross discipline boundaries. Possibly the greatest advantage of this approach (over the multidisciplinary or interdisciplinary approaches) is that it requires the combined expertise of team members to promote a more integrated approach to assessment and intervention. In a transdisciplinary approach, the team members function as a unit, sharing their discipline-specific information and skills to accomplish a common set of intervention goals for a child and family.

A transdisciplinary model lends itself to integrated therapeutic services in the natural environment. Integrated therapy is recommended over a "pull-out" model in which children are removed from the natural environment to receive physical, occupational, or speech and language therapy. Integrated therapy is designed to be conducted during functional activities, an approach that teaches children the purpose of skills and enhances the generalization of skills.

Transition Planning

Transition planning has become a central component of appropriate services for young children with disabilities and their families. The early childhood period is a time of many transitions for young children with disabilities and for their families as the children move from infant to preschool services and preschool to school-age services. Each transition includes a number of significant changes that families and children experience in terms of who receives services, what services are received, where services are received, how they are delivered, and by whom they are delivered. Planning for these changes becomes the critical component of successful transition. Thus, transitions in the early years should involve a series of well-planned steps that result in the successful placement of the child and family into another program. Noonan and Kilgo (1987) stress the comprehensiveness of transition planning and define transition as (1) a longitudinal plan; (2) a goal of smooth and efficient movement from one program to the next; (3) a process including preparation, implementation, and follow-up; and (4) the philosophy that movement to the next environment implies movement to a program that is less restrictive than the previous program.

RATIONALE FOR APPLYING THE DAP GUIDELINES TO YOUNG CHILDREN WITH DISABILITIES

Notwithstanding the substantial similarities and congruence in the fields of ECE and ECSE regarding what constitutes recommended practice, the usefulness of DAP as an intervention model for young children with disabilities has continued to be a topic of much discussion among professionals from both fields. Many have endorsed DAP as a useful intervention model for young children with disabilities (Burton, Higgins-Hains, Hanline, McLean, & McCormick, 1992; Finger, 1991; Fox et al., 1994; Johnson & Johnson, 1992). When providing a rationale for the applicability of DAP for young children with disabilities, the proponents of this approach have pointed out that young children with disabilities should be thought of as children first and as children with special needs second. They have been quick to emphasize that children with disabilities are far more similar to than different from their nondisabled peers; moreover, they often share common interests and enjoy similar activities. For example, a young child with a disability is likely to be

TABLE 3.6   List of Commonalities between DAP and ECSE Practices

- Both DAP and ECSE practices recognize the importance of individualization and building early educational experiences on development.
- Both DAP and ECSE practices de-emphasize reliance on and use of standardized assessments and emphasize authentic assessment procedures.
- Both DAP and ECSE practices encourage the integration of assessment activities and curricular decisions and actions.
- Both DAP and ECSE practices recognize the importance and value of child-initiated activities and of using contextually relevant experiences.
- Both DAP and ECSE practices recognize the importance of active engagement and participation.
- Both DAP and ECSE practices emphasize social interactions with others and the development of social competence.
- Both DAP and ECSE practices value teachers' responsiveness to children's behavior and patterns of interaction; however, in ECSE practice, the teacher may well take more directive roles.
- Both DAP and ECSE practices are designed to promote learning and development; however, in ECSE practice, interventions may focus more directly on specific, identified, and defined outcomes or goals.
- Both DAP and ECSE practices recognize the importance of children's families; however, in ECSE practice, the early educator's role in relation to families is much broader.
- Both DAP and ECSE practices recognize the need for professionals to be highly competent and skilled; however, in ECSE practice, more disciplines will be involved in planning, implementing, monitoring, adjusting, and evaluating the program.
- Both DAP and ECSE practices recognize the need to address children's transitions from one program to another.

Adapted from Wolery 1993.

interested in many of the same theme topics (e.g., the circus, farm animals, and transportation) and enjoy many of the same activities (e.g., various centers, outdoor play, field trips, and art). Although young children with disabilities may not function on the same developmental level as their same-age peers in all developmental areas and may require adaptations, they still develop in a similar manner and learn by interacting with their environment. Table 3.6 contains a list of the commonalties between developmentally appropriate practices and ECSE practices as generated by Wolery (1993).

DAP AS THE FOUNDATION IN PROGRAMS FOR YOUNG CHILDREN WITH DISABILITIES

For programs serving young children with disabilities, many professionals have suggested an approach that blends recommended practices from ECE and ECSE. Although research supporting this approach is limited (Carta et al.,

1991), many professionals feel that the developmentally appropriate practice (DAP) guidelines should be the basis for all programs serving young children, including children with disabilities, and that practices from ECSE should be applied as needed in designing programs for young children with disabilities.

Central to the tenets of developmentally appropriate practices is that all individuals should have the opportunity to develop as "whole" children. Both ECSE and ECE focus on various domains of development in young children. The *Individuals with Disabilities Education Act* recognizes five developmental domains: adaptive, cognitive, communication, physical, and social or emotional. In ECE, the domains typically emphasized are intellectual, physical, social, and emotional. Although the domains are defined somewhat differently, the notion is that integrated learning experiences should be designed to help children develop multiple skills from several domains at the same time rather than learning isolated skills.

A basic belief held in developmentally appropriate practice is that all young children should have equal opportunities to experience their environment, make their own choices, engage in exploratory play, develop independence, and move beyond their current skills and ability levels. This approach represents a radical departure from a traditional academic orientation that often resulted in a teacher-directed, structured curriculum with a specific set of objectives established for all children.

As teachers strive to blend DAP and ECSE practices, it is important to consider closely the two primary dimensions of DAP: age appropriateness and individual appropriateness. In applying principles of developmentally appropriate practices in their classrooms, teachers use their knowledge of child development (age appropriateness) as the framework for providing learning experiences that meet the unique needs of each child (individual appropriateness). Although the concept of age appropriateness suggests that it is desirable for young children to learn in groups with experiential, hands-on activities, it does not rule out the application of ECSE strategies. The individual appropriateness dimension of DAP indicates that the techniques and strategies that are effective for each child should be used. Balancing these two principles in day-to-day practice with young children with disabilities will ensure that programs are developmentally appropriate. After the developmental levels, skills, interests, and unique strengths and needs of each child are identified, practices that are both age appropriate and individually appropriate can be implemented in programs serving children with disabilities.

The DAP guidelines are based on the assumption that if children are allowed to explore their interests, their interests will guide them to choose and learn content that they are developmentally "ready" to learn. Young children with known or suspected disabilities may not always be "ready" to learn the same skills as their nondisabled peers of the same age. To support the inclusion of young children with disabilities, activities should be age appropriate, even when they do not correspond to the children's readiness levels. The activities should serve as the context of instruction. Specific objectives, or the way in which children with disabilities participate in activities, should be individualized to address their unique needs. Allowing for different types and levels of participation in curriculum activities is consistent with the basic tenets of DAP: curriculum should be age appropriate and individualized.

For children with disabilities, adaptations may be required in the age-appropriate content to enable them to make choices and participate in activities based on individual interests. For a child with a physical disability who wants to paint a picture using water colors, adaptations may be required regarding the implement used to apply the paint and the method of stabilizing the paper. With the necessary adaptations, young children with special needs can be afforded the chance to develop creativity, confidence, and independence as they interact and socialize with their nondisabled peers.

A model describing this blended approach was developed through a federally-funded project in Monmouth, Oregon. In Figure 3.3, elements of DAP are listed in the right column and those of ECSE are listed in the left column. The dilemma presented in this illustration is how to include all of the elements in designing an educational program for a young child with a disability. Figure 3.4 shows that DAP elements can serve as the foundation in an

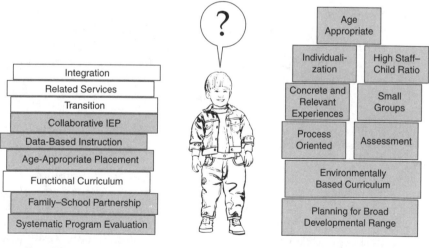

FIGURE 3.3   ECSE versus DAP

Teaching Research Models, Teaching Research Training and Early Childhood Department, Western Oregon State College, Monmonth, OR 1992.

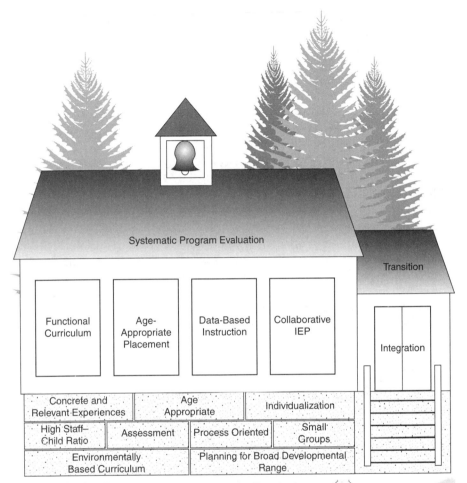

FIGURE 3.4   DAP and ECSE

Teaching Research Models, Teaching Research Training and Early Childhood Department, Western Oregon State College, Monmonth, OR 1992.

educational program and the ECSE practices can be applied as needed in constructing the program.

Many early childhood programs across the country have incorporated the strategies, techniques, and equipment of early childhood special education into developmentally appropriate programs. The results have been warm, stimulating, child-centered environments that meet the needs of young children with disabilities and also children without disabilities.

ISSUES AND CONCERNS REGARDING THE APPLICABILITY OF DAP GUIDELINES TO YOUNG CHILDREN WITH DISABILITIES

Although there are many potential benefits of applying the DAP guidelines to ECSE programming, there are also a number of concerns. Wolery, Strain, and Bailey (1992) stated that "a program based on the guidelines alone is not likely to be sufficient for many children with special needs" (p. 106). In other words, many professionals feel that the DAP guidelines are indeed necessary for young children with disabilities but are not sufficient or comprehensive enough to meet all of their unique needs. They have also struggled with how recommended practices in ECSE can be blended with the DAP guidelines.

A major concern is that the movement to a DAP model will encourage those in ECSE to disregard what has been learned about effective programming for young children with disabilities. Because ECSE professionals have spent many years establishing a knowledge base and developing recommended practices, it is only right that any suggested changes be considered fully. Following are some of the more commonly asked questions and some thoughts regarding those questions.

Discussion of Commonly Asked Questions

- Are developmentally appropriate practices compatible with what we know to be effective practices in early childhood special education?

Although some differences in philosophy serve as a foundation for ECE and ECSE practices, the DAP guidelines do appear to be compatible with ECSE practices. As reported by McLean and Odom (1993) after reviewing the NAEYC and DEC recommended practice documents, there appear to be no major areas of direct disagreement or conflict between the two sets of recommended practices. In some areas, there are differences such as the IEP and IFSP requirement, the emphasis placed on working with families, and the number of professionals involved from across disciplines. These differences, however, appear to be a matter of degree of emphasis rather than incompatible practices.

- Can we realistically blend best practices in ECSE with developmentally appropriate practices?

Although research supporting this approach is limited (Carta et al., 1991), many professionals have suggested that the developmentally appropriate practice (DAP) guidelines can be applied to all children. Further, many professionals contend that the DAP guidelines should provide the foundation for programs serving young children with disabilities. On an as-needed basis, strategies and adaptations from ECSE can then be applied for individual children with disabilities.

- Will the movement to a developmentally appropriate practice model encourage professionals to disregard what has been learned about effective programming in ECSE?

Applying a DAP model will not negate the ECSE practices used with young children with special needs over the years. None of the ECSE strategies developed to meet ECSE best practice guidelines and regulatory requirements would be ruled out by the application of the DAP framework. In fact, the DAP guidelines do not require particular strategies. Instead, the guidelines suggest that teachers should choose the strategies that meet the needs, interests, and abilities of their children. Certainly, for young children who have more severe disabilities, more intrusive instructional methods may be needed if less intrusive methods have been unsuccessful.

- Are developmentally appropriate practices comprehensive enough to address the individual needs of young children with disabilities?

The DAP guidelines endorse heterogeneous groupings and promote curriculum content that meets a wide range of abilities. "The curriculum is flexible so teachers can adapt to individual children or groups" (NAEYC & NAECS/SDE, 1991, p. 137). Within a DAP curriculum framework, children are allowed to work at different levels on different activities rather than being required to do the same thing at the same time as all other children. It seems that the individual appropriateness dimension of DAP allows for flexibility and adaptations to meet the needs of individual children.

- Does the developmentally appropriate practice model allow for the precise individual programming necessary to carry out IFSPs and IEPs?

Programming for young children with disabilities is determined by individual goals and objectives identified on the IEP or the outcomes and strategies on the IFSP. As Bowe (1995) described, IEPs and IFSPs are an "ordered arrangement of individually selected learning experiences that responds to children's particular needs" (p. 73). Although the DAP framework does not articulate precisely what should be addressed in programs for young children, realistic curriculum goals and plans are based on regular assessment of individual needs, strengths, and interests.

- Does the developmentally appropriate practice model work with young children with disabilities who are low responders or unable to access materials?

DAP's emphasis on child-initiated interaction with the environment has been a concern to some professionals in ECSE. DAP guidelines usually describe classrooms that do not "push" children to learn specific skills (Carta et al., 1991). The reason that young children are eligible for ECSE programs is that they have a disability resulting in a problem or delay in their development. Some children with specific disabilities of a physical nature, for example, may have difficulty initiating an activity or may not have accessibility to an activity. ECSE programs are designed, therefore, to increase that child's skills or to provide strategies to circumvent the disability so that the child can function as normally as possible across environments. This goal, therefore, necessitates that ECSE programs focus more directly on teaching specific skills, adapting activities, and providing support in order for low responders or children who are more challenged to participate in learning activities. This also can be true in ECE programs when children who are developing normally are taught specific skills to help them access learning activities or when they are assisted or guided during child-choice activities. In developmentally appropriate programs, the degree of support needed by young children with disabilities may be greater than that for normally developing children.

- Although developmentally appropriate practices meet the needs of normalization for young children with disabilities, will the most effective, efficient, and functional methods of teaching be employed?

There is some concern that, although DAP programs certainly meet the criteria of a normalized setting and in some instances provide an effective setting for acquiring skills, they may not meet the other two criteria for ECSE programming: efficiency and functionality (Carta et al., 1991). DAP programs usually do not emphasize direct, one-to-one instruction for children; however, it is consistent with the DAP guidelines to do so. In some cases, this may be the most efficient way to teach a skill to a child with a disability. Likewise, DAP programs do not always address the functionality of skill development, particularly of skills needed for the next environment. In fact, a DAP approach often discourages considering the next environment and encourages skill development at the child's present level. When normally developing children enter kindergarten or first grade, it may be more realistic to expect the environment to conform to the needs of the child. However, for young children with disabilities, being successfully included in a normalized setting will occur only when functional skills needed for the next environment are targeted (Kilgo, Richard, & Noonan, 1989).

- Will a developmentally appropriate practice model allow for the continuous measurement of children in order to monitor progress within a curriculum?

In ECSE, accountability is a fundamental concern because of the mandated IEPs and IFSPs for young children with disabilities. Thus, ECSE places primary importance on the development of measurable and observable skills in young children with disabilities so that their progress can be tracked. The need for setting specific goals and objectives, along with clear procedures for acquiring those goals and criteria for determining whether the goals have been met, are not stated in the DAP guidelines (Carta et al., 1991). ECSE programs must have documentation showing that they are carrying out the programming necessary to help young children with disabilities and their families meet their goals. Although a DAP approach does not emphasize individual outcomes or discuss strategies such as quantitative data collection to the degree that ECSE has or must, it does address outcomes and underscore the importance of regular assessment of individual strengths, needs, and interests. "Information about each child's growth, development, and learning is systematically collected and recorded at regular intervals" (NAEYC & NAECS/SDE, 1991, p. 139). It seems that DAP programs may need to be expanded for young children with disabilities in order to include more individualized goals and continuous monitoring that determines success in meeting the goals.

- Do developmentally appropriate practice guidelines stress parent involvement to the degree that they become decision makers in the planning of services?

In ECSE programs, family participation is highly valued. ECSE programs, in addition to fostering the involvement of families in their children's programming, work to empower families to be involved to the degree that they desire (Carta et al., 1991; Dunst, Trivette, & Deal, 1988). Although a DAP approach does not rule out fostering these types of skills and involvement with families, this philosophy is not explicitly stated in the DAP philosophy or guidelines. DAP guidelines state that "parents have both the right and responsibility to share in decisions about their children's care and education" (Bredekamp, 1987, p. 12). Although the philosophy of empowerment and allowing parents to take control of their children's services may not be included in the DAP statements, the guidelines do not rule out such a perspective. In fact, one ethic in ECE is that teachers have the responsibility to educate parents in order to help them understand, work with, and make decisions about their children.

Addressing the Issues and Concerns

Although there are a number of important questions and concerns regarding the "carte blanche" use of DAP in ECSE programming, a DAP approach can be expanded and successfully used in many ways to serve young children with disabilities and their families. Most importantly, the DAP guidelines do not rule out the use of strategies that meet ECSE best practice guidelines and regulatory requirements.

Moving toward a Blended Approach

In order for DAP to serve as the foundation of programs serving young children with disabilities, a number of steps must be taken. First and foremost, ECE and ECSE professionals need a clear understanding of what is considered to be recommended practice in their respective fields. These professionals must also understand the congruence between ECSE and DAP practices. The emphasis has to be placed on DAP as a framework upon which programming for any child can be built. Further, it must be clear that DAP practices do not rule out any programming that would be appropriate for a specific child (individual appropriateness). Strategies for blending the recommended practices of ECSE and ECE include the following:

1. Educating ECSE and ECE professionals about the recommended practices of ECE and ECSE and the commonalties these philosophies have in terms of programming.
2. Implementing a model that emphasizes that DAP is a framework upon which programming for any child can be built; this would not rule out any programming appropriate for a specific child.
3. Educating ECSE and ECE staff regarding the ease with which using the DAP framework allows young children with disabilities to be integrated into ECE settings.

SUMMARY

Early Childhood Special Education (ECSE) is an evolving young field that focuses on serving infants and young children with known or suspected disabilities and their families. The field of ECSE as we know it today has been influenced by other educational movements, ongoing research efforts, and legislative actions. This chapter provided a holistic view of ECSE with an emphasis on the major premises underlying recommended practices that have emerged in ECSE in recent years.

The major trends or movements that are prominent in early childhood education today are: (a) inclusion, and (b) the blending of practices from ECSE and general early childhood education (ECE). Thus, recommended practices for serving young children with disabilities and their families have changed dramatically in recent years and are continuing to evolve. In this chapter, old ECSE practices were contrasted with newer recommended practices. The compatibility of ECSE recommended practices with Developmentally Appropriate Practices (DAP) was discussed highlighting their similarities and differences. Finally, a model was presented for blending practices from ECE and ECSE in order to provide appropriate experiences for young children with disabilities and their families.

These recommended practices and trends in the field of ECSE are discussed throughout the remaining chapters of this book. Emphasis is placed on how ECSE components translate into practice and how they can be blended with practices and trends in ECE.

ACTIVITIES AND RESOURCES

Activities

1. Observe an inclusive classroom in which developmentally appropriate practice guidelines are being followed. Identify at least three activities in which age-appropriate content is being adapted to meet the needs and abilities of a child with a disability.
2. Observe two preschool classrooms, one in which children with and without disabilities are being served together, and one in which children with disabilities only are being served. Identify the major differences in the two settings. Suggest ways in which the disparities in the two settings could be reduced.
3. Interview the parent(s) of a young child with a disability who is being served in an inclusive setting. Ask the parent(s) to explain why an inclusive setting was chosen for the child, any reservations the parent(s) had, and the benefits of the placement.

Discussion Questions

1. Identify 3 landmark pieces of legislation, and describe the impact they have had on services for young children with disabilities and their families.
2. Describe the recent major changes that have occurred in ECSE in terms of recommended practices.
3. Describe the congruencies that exist in the recommended practices of ECE and ECSE. Explain the major differences that exist and the degree of difference.
4. Provide a rationale for applying the developmentally appropriate practice guidelines to young children with disabilities.
5. Do you agree or disagree with the following statement? "Developmentally appropriate practice is a necessary but not sufficient condition for working with young children with disabilities." Provide a rationale for your position.
6. Explain how practices from ECE and ECSE can be blended. Provide strategies for moving to a blended approach.
7. List three common concerns that have been raised regarding the applicability of DAP to young children with disabilities. Provide a response to these concerns.

Readings

See Smith (1988), Turnbull (1990), or Garwood and Sheehan (1989) for more information regarding ECSE laws and regulations. See Hebbeler, Smith, and Black (1991) for an in-depth review that traces the history of federal policy in ECSE from 1965 to the nineties.

For an in-depth analysis of the appropriateness of a DAP framework for young children with disabilities, see Burton, Higgins-Hains, Hanline, McLean, and McCormick (1992); Carta, Schwartz, Atwater, and McConnell (1991); Fox, Hanline, Vail, and Galant (1994); Mahoney, Robinson, and Powell (1992); and Wolery, Strain, and Bailey (1992).

Resources

Activity-Based Intervention. Bricker, D., Veltman, P. & Munkres, A. (1995). Baltimore, MD: Brookes Publishing Company.
    This fourteen-minute video presents strategies that foster learning within natural contexts. The strategies include tips on promoting functional skill development; facilitating routine, planned, and child-initiated activities; and fostering learning through natural consequences and reinforcements.

REFERENCES

Bailey, D., & McWilliam, R. (1990). Normalizing early intervention. *Topics in Early Childhood Special Education, 10*(2), 33–47.
Bailey, D., & Wolery, M. (1992). *Teaching infants and preschoolers with disabilities* (2nd ed.). New York: Macmillan.

Baker, E. Wang, M., & Walberg, H. (1995). The effects of inclusion on learning. *Educational Leadership, 52*(4), 33–35.

Bowe, F. (1995). *Birth to five: Early childhood special education.* Albany, NY: Delmar Publishers.

Bredekamp, S. (Ed.). (1987). *Developmentally appropriate practice in early childhood programs serving children from birth to age 8* (exp. ed.). Washington, DC: NAEYC.

Bricker, D., & Cripe, J. (1992). *An activity-based approach to early intervention.* Baltimore: Paul H. Brookes.

Bruder, M.B. (in press). Early childhood intervention. In J. Wood & A. Lazzari (Eds.), *Exceeding boundaries: Understanding exceptional lives.* Ft. Worth, TX: Harcourt-Brace College Publishing.

Burton, C., Higgins-Hains, A., Hanline, M., McLean, M., & McCormick, K. (1992). Early childhood intervention and education: The urgency of professional unification. *Topics in Early Childhood Special Education, 11*(4), 53–69.

Carta, J., Schwartz, I., Atwater, J., & McConnell, S. (1991). Developmentally appropriate practice: Appraising its usefulness for young children with disabilities. *Topics in Early Childhood Special Education, 11*(1), 1–20.

DEC Task Force on Recommended Practices. (1993). *DEC recommended practices: Indicators of quality in programs for infants and young children with special needs and their families.* Reston, VA: Council for Exceptional Children.

Dunst, C., Trivette, C., & Deal, A. (1988). *Enabling and empowering families: Principles and guidelines for practice.* Cambridge, MA: Brookline Books.

Finger, W. (1991). *Developmentally appropriate practice for young children with special needs: The whats/whys and hows.* Paper presented at the meeting of the National Early Childhood Conference on Children with Special Needs, St. Louis, MO.

Fox, L., Hanline, M., Vail, C., & Galant, K. (1994). Developmentally appropriate practices: Applications for young children with disabilities. *Journal of Early Intervention, 18*(3), 243–257.

Garwood, S., & Sheehan, S. (1989). *Designing a comprehensive early intervention system: The challenge of public law 99-457.* Austin, TX: Pro-Ed, Inc.

Guralnick, M. (1990). Major accomplishments and future directions in early childhood mainstreaming. *Topics in Early Childhood Special Education, 10*(2), 1–17.

Hebbeler, K., Smith, B., & Black, T. (1991). Federal early childhood special education policy: A model for the improvement of services for children with disabilities. *Exceptional Children, 58*(2), 104–111.

Johnson, J., & Johnson, K. (1992). Clarifying the developmental perspective in response to Carta, Schwartz, Atwater, and McConnell. *Topics in Early Childhood Special Education, 12*(4), 439–457.

Kilgo, J., Richard, N., & Noonan, M. (1989). Integrating future planning with transdisciplinary services for infants and their families. *Infants and Young Children, 2*(2), 37–48.

Mahoney, G., Robinson, C., & Powell, A. (1992). Focusing on parent–child interaction: The bridge to developmentally appropriate practices. *Topics in Early Childhood Special Education, 12,* 105–120.

McLean, M., & Odom, S. (1993). Practices of young children with and without disabilities: A comparison of DEC and NAEYC identified practices. *Topics in Early Childhood Special Education, 13*(3), 274–292.

National Center on Educational Restructuring and Inclusion (NCERI). (1995). *National Study on Inclusion.* New York: City University of New York.

National Association for the Education of Young Children (NAEYC), & National Association of Early Childhood Specialists in State Departments of Education (NAECS/SDE). (1991). Guidelines for appropriate curriculum content and assessment in programs serving children ages 3 through 8. *Young Children, 46*(3), 21–38.

Noonan, M. & McCormick, L. (1993). *Early intervention in natural environments: Methods and procedures.* Pacific Grove, CA: Brooks/Cole Publishing Co.

Noonan, M. & Kilgo, J. (1987). Transition services for early age individuals with severe mental retardation. In R. Ianacone & R. Stodden (Eds.), *Transition issues and directions* (pp. 25–37). Reston, VA: Council for Exceptional Children.

Peck, C., Odom, S., & Bricker, D. (Eds.). (1993). *Integrating young children with disabilities into community programs.* Baltimore, MD: Paul H. Brookes.

Peterson, N. (1987). *Early intervention for handicapped and at-risk children: An introduction to early childhood-special education.* Denver: Love Publishing Company.

Pucket, M. & Black, J. (1994). *Authentic assessment of the young child: Celebrating development and learning.* New York: Merrill.

Smith, B. (1988). Early intervention public policy: Past, present, and future. In J. B. Jordon, J. J. Gallagher, P. L. Hutinger, & M. B. Karnes (Eds.), *Early childhood special education: Birth to three* (pp. 213–28). Reston, VA: Council for Exceptional Children.

Turnbull, H. (1990). *Free appropriate public education: The law and children with disabilities* (3rd ed.). Denver: Love.

Wolery, M. (1993). Presentation at International DEC, St. Louis, MO.

Wolery, M., Strain, P., & Bailey, D. (1992). Reaching potential of children with special needs. In S. Bredekamp & T. Rosegrant (Eds.), *Reaching potentials: Appropriate curriculum and assessment for young children* (Vol. 1) (pp. 92-111). Washington, DC: National Association for the Education of Young Children (NAEYC).

Wolery, M. & Wilbers, J. (1994). *Including children with special needs in early childhood programs.* Washington, DC: National Association for the Education of Young Children (NAEYC).

4

ASSESSMENT OF DEVELOPMENTALLY APPROPRIATE CURRICULUM PROGRAMS FOR YOUNG CHILDREN WITH DISABILITIES

OBJECTIVES

As a result of studying and reviewing the concepts in this chapter, readers should be able to perform the following:

- Describe the difference between assessment for programming purposes and assessment for diagnostic or eligibility purposes.
- Identify the recommended practice characteristics of assessment procedures for young children with disabilities.
- Discuss the procedures for collecting pertinent information about young children with disabilities in order to develop long-range program plans.

Exemplary developmentally appropriate programs for young children, whether they are family child care settings, first grade classrooms or something in between, rely on a continuous assessment process to ensure that the individual and developmental needs of each child are addressed (Bailey & Wolery, 1989; Hills, 1993). Only through constant assessment of children's skill levels, needs, backgrounds, experiences, and interests can superlative early childhood programming be made available for all children. This chapter explores the process of continuous assessment as a basis for constructing and implementing developmentally appropriate programs for all students, those with disabilities, without disabilities, or at risk for delayed development. The importance of considering family preferences and the nature of the settings in which each child spends time are addressed throughout the chapter.

DIAGNOSTIC AND PROGRAMMING ASSESSMENT PROCEDURES

Assessment is the process of gathering information so that teaching and program staff can make decisions regarding children (Bailey & Wolery, 1989). Sometimes those decisions relate to whether or not a child is eligible for a specific program. Other times they have to do with what type of activities and curricula would best enhance a child's development. Still other times the decisions might center on whether or not to continue a specific curriculum approach with one child or a group of children. These decisions made by teachers and other program staff can be categorized into three groups: eligibility decisions, formative programming decisions, and summative programming decisions (see Table 4.1).

Eligibility, formative, and summative assessment decisions are made for all children in all early childhood education programs. For example, eligibility decisions are made at the beginning of a kindergarten school year to place some children in smaller learning groups for the purpose of capitalizing on

TABLE 4.1   Types of Assessment Decisions

	Types of Assessment Decisions		
Decision Type	Type of Assessment Information Gathered	Decision(s) Usually Made	When Information Is Usually Gathered
Eligibility Decisions	Standardized, norm-referenced, comparative information.	Whether or not a child is eligible for a program or services.	Prior to entry into a program.
Formative Programming Decisions	Evidence of the child's developmental skills and behaviors; family preferences and priorities for the child; family resources and strengths; settings in which the child spends time and demands of those settings.	What type of routines, activities, materials, and equipment to use with the individual child. What style(s) of learning to use with the child. What adult and peer interactions may work best with the child.	Intensively at the beginning of a program year; during the first several weeks a child is in a program; during and immediately after any major changes in a child's life. This is an on-going process.
Summative Programming Decisions	Evidence of the child's developmental skills and behaviors in comparison to those skills at the beginning of the child's entry into the program; family satisfaction and perception of whether their priorities have been met; child's ability to be successful in the settings in which he or she spends time.	Whether or not to continue a curricular approach; to determine the effectiveness of programming for an individual child or group of children; to determine the change in a child's skills and behaviors; to evaluate a program's overall effectiveness.	Periodically as needed to determine whether or not a curricular approach is effective; at the end of a program year or cycle; when dictated by administrative policy and funding sources.

their skills or addressing their specific needs. All teachers make formative assessment decisions regarding the equipment they will have in their classrooms, the materials they will make available to their students, and the activities to plan for a specific day or week. Summative assessment decisions are made periodically by all teachers. When parent/teacher conferences are held, teachers often collect examples of children's work and communicate examples of children's behaviors to share with their parents. This type of summative assessment is designed to document changes or advancements that may have occurred with the children.

As stated, formative assessment is the process of collecting information in order to make program decisions for young children. To decide upon the most appropriate content and methods for an early childhood student with disabilities, teachers and support personnel need information about the children, their families, their backgrounds, and the settings in which they spend time. This type of information helps professionals determine which skills and knowledge are important for the child to acquire and how best to structure the classroom, schedule, and other aspects of the learning environment to allow those skills to develop. The information that enables early childhood educators to plan programming for a child with a disability is qualitatively different from the information that helps them determine whether a child has a disability or is eligible for a program that serves at-risk children or those with developmental delays. For eligibility assessment decisions, educators, therapists, and administrators need information that compares a child's skills and development with the skills and development of a large group of children from the general population, to determine whether the child is significantly different from his or her peers.

ASSESSMENT FOR DIAGNOSTIC AND ELIGIBILITY PURPOSES

To decide whether a young child has a developmental delay or is eligible for a special education or at-risk program, assessment procedures are usually conducted to determine whether the child's skills are significantly different from those of a large group of children whose development falls within the range considered normal. To achieve this comparison, norm-referenced, standardized testing instruments are often used as the backbone of the assessment process. For young children, the *Bayley Scales of Infant Development-II* (BSID-II) (Bayley, 1993), the *Weschler Preschool and Primary Scale of Intelligence-Revised* (WPPSI-R) (Weschler, 1989), the *Battelle Developmental Inventory* (BDI) (Newborg, Stock, & Wnek, 1984), or one of many other instruments are appropriate. All of these instruments strive to measure a child's skills and development and to compare him or her to a large group of children who have previously taken the test. This normative or "norm" group of children is the touchstone to which teachers and other professionals can compare the child. If the child's test scores fall significantly below the scores of the children in the norm group, it may be a sign that the child has a developmental delay and is eligible for special services.

Although standardized, norm-referenced assessment instruments can provide a comparison of a child to a large norm group, this does not guarantee that the tester will be able to determine whether the child has a delay or is at risk for developing a delay. By collecting additional information from the child's family and other caregivers and by observing the child's behavior in natural settings, the tester can determine whether the child has a developmental delay or is developing at a significantly different rate from his or her same-age peers (Bredekamp, 1987; Meisels, 1985). Factors that influence the child's performance on a standardized, norm-referenced instrument must also be considered in order to interpret his or her scores appropriately. For instance, on the *Denver Developmental Screening Test* (DDST) (Frankenburg, Dodds, & Fandal, 1976) one of the items asks 4- to 6- year-old children to identify "what a shoe is made of." "Leather" is the acceptable answer, which earns the child a point. For the child whose only experience with shoes may be sneakers or sandals, "plastic," "cloth," or "rubber" are also reasonable answers. Likewise, the DDST asks 5- and 6-year-olds to define or describe items such as a "hedge" and "pavement." For young children who have lived in a rural area all of their lives and have not experienced hedges or pavement, their incorrect answers reflect the settings in which they have been raised.

The use of assessment procedures with young children and the appropriate use of assessment instruments and the information they yield have been topics of much interest for the past decade. Professional organizations of teachers and administrators recognize that standardized, norm-referenced testing of children in the early childhood years is often inappropriate (National Association of State Boards of Education (NASBE), 1991; National Association of Elementary School Principals (NAESP), 1990; National Association for the Education of Young Children (NAEYC), 1988; Southern Association for Children Under Six (SACUS), 1990). Although the instruments can provide valuable information to early childhood professionals, they can also be misused. Standardized, norm-referenced tests are best used for screening, diagnostic, and eligibility purposes. The National Association for the Education of Young Children, however, recommends that no major decisions about children's lives be made based solely upon the results of a single instrument but that observation and other assessment procedures be used to support and corroborate screening, diagnostic, and eligibility decisions (Bredekamp, 1987). (See Table 4.2.) In addition, Meisels and Provence (1989) have outlined

TABLE 4.2   NAEYC Guidelines for the Developmental Evaluation of Children

1. Decisions that have a major impact on children...are not made on the basis of a single developmental assessment or screening device but consider other relevant information, particularly observations by teachers and parents. Developmental assessment of children's progress and achievements is used to adapt curriculum to match the developmental needs of children, to communicate with the child's family, and to evaluate the program's effectiveness.

2. Developmental assessments and observations are used to identify children who have special needs and/or who are at risk and to plan appropriate curriculum for them.

3. Developmental expectations based on standardized measurements and norms should compare any child or group of children only to normative information that is not only age-matched, but also gender-, culture-, and socioeconomically appropriate.

4. In public schools, there should be a developmentally appropriate placement for every child of legal entry age.

From Bredekamp, S. (1987). *Developmentally appropriate practice in early childhood programs serving children from birth through age 8*. Washington, DC: NAEYC. Copyright 1987 by NAEYC. All rights reserved.

cautions for professionals using instruments for the purpose of screening and identifying children with possible disabilities (see Table 4.3).

In addition to the concerns regarding screening, diagnostic, and eligibility decisions, there are also issues related to standardized tests and programming. In 1990, the Southern Early Childhood Association (SECA, formerly the Southern Association for Children Under Six [SACUS]) issued a position paper detailing appropriate assessment procedures during the early childhood years (see Table 4.4). The paper states that appropriate assessment procedures for young children in early childhood programs must be related to the goals and objectives of the program and should not include the use of standardized tests that use a group approach (SACUS, 1990).

In order for effective, efficient, individualized services to be provided to young children, the procedures of assessment and curriculum implementation must be linked (Bagnato & Neisworth, 1990; Bricker & Cripe, 1992). As Bredekamp (1987) states, "Appropriate curriculum planning is based on the teacher's observations and recordings of each child's special interests and developmental progress" (p. 3). These observations should include detailed information about what skills the child has, how the child uses them, and under what circumstances they are used.

TABLE 4.3   Recommended Guidelines for Developmentally Appropriate Screening

1. Screening should be viewed as a service—as part of the intervention—and not only as a means of identification and measurement.

2. Processes, procedures, and instruments intended for screening should only be used for their specified purposes.

3. Multiple sources of information should be included in screening.

4. Developmental screening should take place on a recurrent or periodic basis. It is inappropriate to screen young children only once during their early years of life. Similarly, provisions should be made for reevaluation or reassessment after services have been initiated.

5. Developmental screening should be viewed as only one path to more in-depth assessment. Failure to qualify for services based on a single source of screening information should not become a barrier to further evaluation for intervention services if other risk factors (e.g., environmental, medical, familial) are present.

6. Screening procedures should be reliable and valid.

7. Family members should be an integral part of the screening process. Information provided by family members is critical for determining whether or not to initiate more in-depth assessment and for designing appropriate intervention strategies. Parents should be accorded complete informed consent at all stages of the screening and assessment process.

8. During screening of developmental strengths and concerns, the more relevant and familiar the tasks and the setting are to the child and the child's family, the more likely it is that the results will be valid.

9. All tests, procedures, and processes intended for screening must be culturally sensitive and unbiased.

10. Extensive and comprehensive training is needed by those who screen very young children.

Adapted from Meisels, S. J., & Provence, S. (1989). *Screening and Assessment: Guidelines for Identifying Young Disabled and Developmentally Vulnerable Children and Their Families.* Washington, DC: National Center for Clinical Infant Programs.

For all young children, but especially for those with disabilities, it is essential for educators to know what skills and knowledge they possess, under what circumstances they use the skills and knowledge, and what support they may need to acquire additional skills. This type of information, in addition to norm-referenced, standardized assessment information, provides a better understanding of the individual child and his or her specific strengths and needs. An individualized formative assessment approach permits the teacher and other professionals to plan and adapt services to fit the child's needs.

TABLE 4.4   Southern Early Childhood Association Criteria for Appropriate Early Childhood Assessment

Assessment must be valid. It must provide information related to the goals and objectives of each program.

Assessment should not include standardized tests, which are group administered, pencil and paper, multiple choice, and claim to measure achievement.

Assessment must deal with the whole child. Programs must have goals and assessment processes which related to children's physical, social, emotional, and mental development.

Assessments involve repeated observations. Many observations help teachers find patterns of behavior and avoid quick decisions which may be based on unusual behavior by children.

Assessment must be continuous over time. Each child should be compared to his or her own individual course of development over time rather than to average behavior for a group.

Assessment must use a variety of methods. Gathering a wide variety of information from different sources enables informed and professional decisions.

Assessment information must be used to change the curriculum to meet the individual needs of the children in the program.

From Southern Association for Children Under Six. (1990). *Developmentally appropriate assessment: A position paper*. Little Rock, AR: SACUS.

FORMATIVE ASSESSMENT FOR PROGRAM AND CURRICULUM DEVELOPMENT

Although knowing that a young child is similar to or very different from his or her peers is a valuable piece of information, it is not sufficient information from which to develop programming objectives, curricula, or activities to enhance that child's development or meet individual needs. Formative assessment for program and curriculum development is necessary for all teachers to help them determine the level at which a child is currently functioning; the skills, behavior, and knowledge that should be fostered; and the curriculum units and themes, equipment and materials, and daily activities that will nurture the development of the skills, behavior, and knowledge. Formative assessment information allows teachers to decide the type and number of props to place in a dramatic play center, the frequency with which to offer tactile materials in the classroom, and the amount of support children need when making decisions during free-play. Teachers make these choices in order to develop individual children's skills and the skills of the group.

To determine the skill objectives important for a child with a known or suspected disability, assessment information that is qualitatively different from eligibility information is needed. This information is sometimes referred to as *functional* or *ecological assessment information.*

Functional assessment information helps us to understand the skills a child uses in the settings in which he or she spends time (Bailey & Wolery, 1992). For instance, the results of a developmental assessment instrument given to a 4-year-old may tell you that the child can use four-word sentences. This does not, however, tell the teacher how the child uses those words. Functional assessment information provides teachers and support personnel with information such as which words the child uses, with whom the child uses the words, under what circumstances, and for what purpose. Table 4.5 compares

TABLE 4.5   Comparison of Traditional and Functional Assessment Information for a Particular Child

Comparison of Traditional and Functional Assessment Information for Tarrel

Traditional Assessment Information (According to the Battelle Developmental Inventory)	Functional Assessment Information (According to observations, anecdotal records, and communication samples)
Tarrel can use four word sentences.	Tarrel has a vocabulary of over 250 words, including names of all common items in his house, family members, and classmates. He rarely uses these words when communicating with others, usually pointing to things that he wants. When encouraged to, he will construct simple four word sentences such as "Play blocks with me."
Tarrel can build a 10 piece block tower with 1" cubes.	Tarrel likes to play in the block corner, building simple structures and using props such as animal figures, people, cars and other objects. He will participate in this type of activity for 25–40 minutes.
Tarrel can put together six piece puzzles.	Tarrel does not like to sit with puzzles, Leggos, bristle blocks, or other table toys. When he works with puzzles he uses his left hand to stabilize the puzzle frame and his right hand to move the pieces around; in six observations, he has never self-selected puzzles and when encouraged to work with them he only selects puzzles that have Sesame Street characters.
Tarrel uses a spoon and fork.	Tarrel can use a fork to stab food and a spoon to scoop foods such as yogurt or apple sauce. Sometimes, however, the utensils slip through his fingers and he becomes frustrated and may eventually stop using them. When he is frustrated, he reverts to finger feeding.

traditional and functional assessment information for Tarrel, who was described in Chapter 1.

In the example, Tarrel's fine motor and language skills are assessed. The traditional assessment information describes four skills that Tarrel possesses. The functional assessment information provides more detailed information from which a teacher or other professional can begin to understand how Tarrel uses his skills during everyday activities. The functional assessment information is child, setting, and task specific. It is collected from the settings in which the child spends most of his or her time (usually the classroom and home) and provides rich, detailed information about the child and his or her specific abilities in those settings.

THE DIFFICULTY OF MAKING ELIGIBILITY AND PROGRAMMING DECISIONS FROM THE SAME SET OF ASSESSMENT INFORMATION

Collecting information simultaneously to make eligibility and programming decisions for children is difficult and at times impossible because the information necessary to make the two decisions is inherently different. Eligibility information is primarily comparison information; comparison of the child's skills and behaviors to those of other children of similar age and to those of other children in his or her family and the settings in which the child spends time. The procedures for collecting this type of information usually call for standardization and the use of norm groups.

On the other hand, information used to determine programming goals and objectives and to plan for curriculum and daily activity plans is child, family, and situation specific. Because the information will be used to determine the interests and motivations of the child, the skills important to the child and her family, and the procedures to which the child seems to be most responsive, the information and the collection process are both highly individualized (see Table 4.6).

Like developmentally appropriate programming, for which general knowledge of child development (age-appropriate information) and child-specific knowledge (individually appropriate information) are necessary, comprehensive assessment collects two kinds of information: eligibility and formative. Problems occur when one or the other is used for an inappropriate purpose.

One problem arises when schools or programs try to combine the process of assessment for eligibility with assessment for programming. If the assessment process has collected standardized, norm-referenced information, a decision about program eligibility can usually be made. Using this

TABLE 4.6 Comparison of Assessment for Eligibility and Programming Decisions

Differences in Assessment for Eligibility and Assessment for Programming	
Assessment for Eligibility	Assessment for Programming
1. Compares a single child to a large group of children.	1. Identifies the child's current levels of developmental skills, behaviors, and knowledge.
2. Uses instruments, observations, and checklists.	2. Determines the skills and behaviors necessary for a child to function in the settings where he or she spends time.
3. Assessment information is used to determine if a child's skills or behaviors fall below a specified cut-off level.	3. Determines those skills, behaviors, and knowledge that the child's family and primary caregivers have set as priorities for the child to learn.
4. Assessment collection procedures are designed to differentiate children from one another.	4. Assessment collection procedures focus on determining the individual child's strengths and styles of learning.
5. Assessment instrument items do not necessarily have significance in the the everyday lives of young children.	5. Assessment instrument items are usually criterion-based skills that that may have importance in the everyday lives of young children.

same information to determine program objectives and teaching procedures for a child may result in inappropriate objectives and ineffective teaching strategies.

In the example of Tarrel, the standardized, norm-referenced assessment information indicated that Tarrel can use four-word sentences. If programming decisions were being made from this information, a teacher might determine that an appropriate objective for Tarrel is to use six-word or compound sentences. Using the information collected for eligibility decisions to determine an objective for Tarrel might result in frustration for both him and the staff. It is essential to have information about when, how, with whom, and under what circumstances Tarrel is using four-word sentences and whether it is his preferred mode of communicating. Because it is possible to form inappropriate goals and objectives without functional assessment information, it is recommended that the assessment process for eligibility and program planning be kept separate.

PROGRAMMING ASSESSMENT PROCEDURES: ASSESSMENT FOR ESTABLISHING PROGRAMMING GOALS AND OBJECTIVES

Typical Early Childhood Programs

Assessment to establish goals and objectives for children is a necessary and continuous task in all early childhood programs (Hills, 1993; Wortham, 1994). Assessment usually includes determining the experiences and backgrounds of the children and their families, observing the skills and behaviors the children presently possess, attending to their individual interests, and being aware of their learning styles and preferences. This individually appropriate information is then used in conjunction with the staff's knowledge of the developmental sequences of children (age-appropriate information) to determine the curriculum for the program (see Table 4.7). The curriculum reflects the goals and objectives, materials and experiences, units and field trips, and assessment procedures for all children in the program.

For example, with a classroom of 3-year-olds from an inner city, urban area, the teacher's procedures for introducing a unit on transportation vehicles may be very different from those of a teacher whose classroom is composed of 3-year-olds living in a farming community. The urban teacher may

TABLE 4.7   Process for Determining Curriculum and Daily Activities in an Early Childhood Program

Step 1:
Determine children's current level of skills and behavior.

Step 2:
Determine children's interests and experiences.

Step 3:
Determine children's families' backgrounds, cultures, traditions, and norms.

Step 4:
Determine children's styles of learning and activity preferences.

Step 5:
Compare to knowledge of typical development of children and typical developmental tasks at their age(s).

Result:
Knowledge that can be used to make decisions about general curriculum and daily activities.

decide to introduce the unit by taking a ride on a bus or subway. The vehicles she presents to the class may include streetsweepers, trash trucks, trolleys, and delivery trucks. The rural teacher may go for a hayride to introduce the unit and may present tractors, hay balers, milk tankers, and pickup trucks. Although the two teachers have chosen the same unit topic, the backgrounds, existing knowledge, and interests of the two groups of children determine the specific content and methods used.

EARLY CHILDHOOD PROGRAMS: WORKING   •
WITH CHILDREN WITH DISABILITIES

The process for determining goals and objectives for early childhood programs for children with disabilities is similar to the one used in programs for children without disabilities. However, an additional required component is the legal responsibility to determine appropriate goals and objectives and to ensure that programming is in place to support their acquisition. According to Public Laws 94-142, 99-457, and 101-476, the contractual and legal responsibilities for these activities lies with the local educational authority (LEA), which is usually the local public school (Congressional Record, 1977; Congressional Record, 1991; Congressional Record, 1996). (See Chapter 5). Personnel in each program that serves young children with special needs should be aware of the legal requirements of assessment regarding young children with disabilities (see Table 4.8).

TABLE 4.8   Legal Requirements for Assessment of Children with Disabilities

Assessment procedures used to identify and develop programming for young children with disabilities must:

- be culturally and ethnically non-biased;
- be conducted in the child's native language;
- use multiple measures;
- use multiple sources of information;
- be conducted by trained professionals;
- be conducted to ensure the best possible results from the child;
- only use instruments that are designed for their stated purpose; and
- only be conducted after consent of the child's parents or legal guardian is obtained.

Summarized from regulations for P.L. 94-142 and P.L. 101-476.

ESTABLISHING GOALS AND OBJECTIVES
FOR YOUNG CHILDREN WITH DISABILITIES

To establish the goals and objectives of students with disabilities in early childhood programs, it is necessary to collect and use three types of assessment information: child skills and behavior information; family concerns, priorities, and preferences information; and environmental information. The sum total of these provides the teacher with the profile necessary to begin designing the curriculum for young children with disabilities.

Child Skills and Behavior Information

Child skills and behavior information relates to the child's developmental skills, styles of interaction and learning, activity preferences, and temperament, and includes the following.

Communication skills: This term refers to the way the child communicates with others about wants, desires, feelings, ideas, and preferences. Communication is a complex process that may include vocalizations, gestures, formal and informal sign language, and behavior that communicates thoughts and desires. Some children with disabilities rely on augmentative communication devices, which might be as simple as a piece of paper with pictures on it or as complex as a portable computer that produces digital speech when a button or series of buttons are pressed by the child.

Cognitive skills: This term refers to the way children collect, store, categorize, integrate, and use knowledge about their worlds. This category includes skills such as short-term and long-term memory, the ability to sequence activities, the ability to detect differences among objects or events, and the capacity to predict occurrences. Cognitive skills are as simple as a baby's knowledge that if she looks at her mother and coos, her mother will respond with a smile, to a 6-year-old's ability to remember and describe the procedure for making butter from milk.

Social skills: This term refers to the way children interact with adults and/or peers in one-on-one, small-group, and large-group interactions. This category includes whether and how children initiate interactions, respond to being approached by others, and respond in group situations.

Emotional skills: These skills include children's abilities to identify and communicate feelings, and their capacity to act on emotions while respecting the rights of others.

Physical skills: Included in this skill area are a child's vision, hearing, touch, taste, and smell; his or her ability to move and get around in the environment (gross motor skills); and the ability to use his or her hands (fine motor skills).

Self-care skills: These skills are often very important to the family and include eating, grooming, toileting, and dressing. Assessment in this area is concerned with the level of independence that a child exhibits in accomplishing these skills.

Coping skills: These skills include the way a child responds to stressful situations and the behaviors used to cope with those situations. For example, when left with a new caregiver for the first time, what is the child's response and how does she cope?

Learning styles: This category focuses on children's preferences in selecting learning activities. Would the child rather watch an activity, talk about an activity, or participate in the activity?

Materials and setting preferences: This category provides information about the child's preferences for equipment, media, toys, and settings. Some children enjoy using modeling media such as clay, dough, and putty. Others prefer tactile materials such as sand, wood chips, water, or Jello. Still others prefer to work with paper and writing or marking utensils.

Using Child Skills and Behavior Information in Program Planning

The importance of child skills and behavior information is twofold. First, the developmental skill information (e.g., cognitive and social) apprises professionals of the developmental level a child has reached. This allows the teacher and other professionals to set goals at the appropriate age level and prevents the setting of goals that are too difficult for the child. Parents, teachers, and other staff may have an understanding of the normal development of a 5-year-old, but the pattern or rate of development may be different if a child has a disability. A 5-year-old with normal vision can collect information visually as well as through other senses and can use that information to promote and enhance cognitive skills. A 5-year-old who is blind does not have visual information and, therefore, must depend on other senses for collecting information about the world to increase knowledge and cognitive skills.

Child skills and behavior information is important also because all educators need to know what motivates children. By being aware of a child's preferences for materials and settings, knowing what media is most attractive and easy to access, and understanding how the child best copes with difficult situations, the teacher can design learning activities that are more likely to be interesting and hold his or her attention.

Family Concerns, Priorities, and Preferences Information

Family concerns, priorities, and preferences information comes from the child's family and/or primary caregivers and addresses their priorities for the child's development, skill acquisition, and behavior. This information reflects the family's traditions, desire for involvement, culture, family roles, and interactional styles. Finally, this category of information includes the family's needs for itself which might include knowledge about child development, information about a specific disability, or advice on behavior management or teaching skills at home.

Family Priorities for the Child

This category of information tells professionals what the family wants the child to achieve. Because teachers, therapists, administrators, and other early childhood professionals are invariably well trained in child development, they tend to focus their goals and objectives on developmental skills. Families, on the other hand, are usually concerned about both developmental issues and the acquisition of skills that will allow their children to flourish in all settings in which they spend time. For example, a parent of a 3-year-old may be concerned that her child with a language delay learn to articulate specific sounds that are developmentally appropriate. She might also be concerned that her daughter have a method to indicate that she is tired or hungry, needs to go to the bathroom, or wants to play with another child.

Family Traditions and Culture

This category of assessment information includes family experiences, structure, traditions, and roles. A traditionally matriarchal family may feel that the most important skills for a female child to learn include a strong sense of self-worth, independence, and the skills necessary to be responsible for those in her family. Just as important, the family's experience and customs regarding disabilities may play a large role in determining the goals established for the child and the methods used to ensure that the goals are achieved (Lynch & Hanson, 1992).

In the case of Tarrel, his family's priorities, traditions, and culture influence what they want his program to emphasize. They want Tarrel to develop better eating skills, pay attention to activities for longer periods of time, and use more words to express his desires. His family's culture places great value on social interactions and friendships; therefore they want him to get along with others and have the skills to make friends. His family's tradition of high levels of education and an emphasis on writing make it important to them that he learn to use written language. These priorities, family culture, and tradition influence what the family wants and expects from his early childhood education program.

In some cases a family's concerns, priorities, and preferences and the professionals' views of the child's developmental needs may not be in agreement (Bailey, 1987). When this situation occurs, it is important to negotiate a consensus regarding the child's program. It is crucial, however, to elicit each family's concerns and priorities. Ignoring their interests leads to less effective programming and may be a waste of valuable educational, developmental, and family support resources.

Environmental Information

Environmental information is data about the number and types of settings in which the child spends time. In addition to descriptions of settings, this category includes expectations and the behaviors and skills necessary for success in those environments.

Three-year-old Brad may spend time in numerous settings; however, five of those places may be crucial to him and his family. They might be the family home, his family day care provider's home, shopping trips, the church nursery, and the doctor's office. Although he spends most of his time at home and at child care, the other three settings may make demands on him and his family that are different and also very important to the family. For example, if spending time in the church nursery is important because the remainder of his family would like to participate in the church service, the behaviors and skills he needs to remain in the nursery become highly valued to the family. Although the ability to stay in the nursery is an interactive relationship between Brad's abilities and the church nursery staff's ability to care for him, Brad must learn coping skills that allow him to settle into the nursery and permit his parents to go to services. Part of this process may be having consistent staff who know Brad's preferences and having familiar toys, food, and equipment in the nursery. Also, the staff may have to assure Brad that his parents will return, show him what he can do while they are gone, and help him settle himself if he is upset. Table 4.9 provides examples of child, family, and environmental information.

The Interrelationship of the Three Types of Assessment Information

Although three different types of assessment information are needed for the development of program plans for young children with disabilities, the three categories are linked. Piaget (1952) and Vygotsky (1978) stated that it is children's experiences and interactions with their world that influence their development. It is therefore necessary to know those influences and to use them to the best advantage. A child with a hearing impairment does not respond to vocal speech or sounds in the environment in the same manner as a child without a hearing impairment. A child with severe cerebral palsy may not be

TABLE 4.9   Examples of Child, Family, and Environmental Information

BRAD: 40 months old with Down Syndrome and a moderate hearing impairment.

Child Information:

Brad can match objects of different colors, shapes, and sizes; he has begun to be able to categorize by two different characteristics (e.g., shape and color); he can sequence stories and events that have three or four discrete phases; he enjoys being in a group and with other children but sometimes hits or has tantrums, especially in open-ended, free-play situations.

Family Information:

Brad's family wishes that he become more independent and take care of himself more including feeding and dressing himself; that Brad become toilet trained; that Brad interact more with his peers without hitting or biting.

Environmental Information:

Brad spends eight hours a day in a child care program with fifteen other children, where there are two teachers; the room is very active and usually very noisy; while the noise is usually connected to active learning on the part of the children, it also can appear chaotic; children arrive in Brad's room between 7:30 and 10:00 am; they leave between 2:30 and 5:30; this makes for frequent transitions; there are three meal times during the period Brad is in the room, morning snack, lunch, and afternoon snack; there is a 90 minute nap/rest period from 12:00 noon to 1:30 p.m.

able to experiment with block towers, rolling balls, or matchbox cars on ramps. Her understanding of gravity will have to be developed through different, alternative interactions.

Finally, Vygotsky's contention that "learning is a profoundly social process . . ." (John-Steiner & Souberman, 1978, p. 131) is the basis for the argument that the family and the child's extended social system have an influence on development. The cultural and familial expectations work to influence the skills and behaviors that are important for the child's development. It is therefore necessary for early childhood educators to have available all three types of information in order to establish appropriate goals and objectives and to know what type of curricula and daily activities will promote the acquisition of the identified goals and objectives (see Table 4.7).

Methods for Collecting the Three Types of Information

Because the type of information being collected is individualized, collection procedures must be flexible and adaptable. Assessment procedures specific to the child and the setting enable teachers and other professionals to use a variety of methods to capture the three types of information (Grace &

Shores, 1991; Meisels, Jablon, Marsden, Dichtelmiller, & Dorfman, 1994; Puckett & Black, 1994). Some of these data collection procedures are described next.

PROCEDURES FOR COLLECTING CHILD SKILLS AND BEHAVIOR INFORMATION

The developmental and child preference information necessary for this category can be collected in numerous ways. Methods include observation, anecdotal records, work samples, behavior samples, communication samples, developmental checklists, activity preference records, and sociograms. Following are discussions of each of these methods.

Observations

The most widely used assessment method in early childhood is observation. By recording activities for brief periods of time (five to fifteen minutes) in different situations, different settings, and with different individuals, an observer sees a picture of a child's skills and behavior begin to emerge. Observations usually include the child's name, age, date, time, place, and activity, and the names of other individuals present. Careful analysis of observations yields information about the child's developmental skills and behavior patterns.

In the observation described in Table 4.10, Brad is building a block tower. Although the teacher who has recorded Brad's actions has not drawn any conclusions, it can be determined from the observation record that Brad can seriate blocks and has an understanding of what a pyramid looks like. Preliminary information is available about Brad's interaction style with his peers and about how he may cope with social situations when he is not asked to join a group. With repeated observations, conclusions about Brad's use of quiet areas and solitary activities as a coping method can be made. The determination can also be made as to whether Brad consistently uses his skills of construction to create something that he then uses to try to initiate interactions with others. It is important to note that only through repeated observations in a variety of situations, with a variety of individuals, can a conclusion be made about a child's skills or preferences. One observation of a skill or behavior does not mean that the child consistently responds in that manner or has mastered the skill. Multiple recorded observations, over time, can make patterns of a child's behavior apparent and can help early childhood educators determine what should be included in a child's skill repertoire. With this information, strengths and needs can be determined and goals and objectives identified.

TABLE 4.10   Example of an Observation Record

Name: Brad W.   Date: 05/25/95   Age: 3 yrs., 7 mo.
Time: 10:15–10:30 a.m.
Activity: Center Time (block corner)
Others Present: James, Keisha, Tammi, Mark

Brad walks to the block area and moves to the corner away from the other children. He gathers 10–12 unit blocks from the shelf and places them on the floor. He looks at James as J. creates a tower with his blocks. B. looks back to his blocks and begins to place them one on top of the other. He continues to periodically look at J. and the other children as he builds. When he has placed all the blocks in a tower, he twists them so that the tower turns. He is careful not to topple the tower. He slowly takes down the top block and proceeds to dismantle the tower. He moves closer to the group and places five unit blocks end to end. He then places four blocks end-to-end on top of his foundation. He continues with this pattern until there is one unit block on top. B. calls to Tammi, "Look, a pyramid." He points to his structure and smiles at Tammi. Tammi looks and smiles and then returns to her play with James and Keisha. B. waits until Tammi turns away and then knocks down his structure. He returns the unit blocks to their designated places on the block shelf and leaves the block corner with one glance at Tammi and the block structures the children are making. He goes to the reading center, selects a book, and sits in the bean bag chair.

Anecdotal Records

Anecdotal records are much like recorded observations of a child's skills and behaviors; however, they usually focus on one important or significant skill that is difficult to document or that occurs infrequently. This type of record may be used to stress a child's highest level of functioning, although it may not be his or her typical level of functioning.

An example might be when the director of a child care center brings a visitor to a classroom. If Brad greets the visitor by listening to the director's introduction and then responds by saying, "Hello, Mr. Duncan. It is good to meet you," the observer can write an anecdotal record of his interactions with adult strangers. The record might comment on his eye contact, posture, gestures, and the tone of his voice. Through this type of recording, we would have an example of how Brad responds in a situation that is atypical of his preschool and home life. (See Table 4.11 for an example of an anecdotal record).

Brad's interaction with strangers when he is introduced to them in a group situation is much more formal than his interactions with peers in the block corner. It is apparent that Brad uses sentences that are more complex than those he uses in the less formal play situation. The record provides ad-

TABLE 4.11   Example of an Anecdotal Record

Name: Brad W.   Age: 3 yrs. 8 mo.   Date: 06/17/95
Time: 2:15 p.m.
Place: 3 yr. old room
Others Present: Mr. D., Tammi, Rhonda, Tim K., & Ms. V.

Ms. V. brought Mr. D. to our room to visit. She introduced him to three of the children who were gathered at the door looking at the gerbil cage. She said, "Children, I would like you to meet Mr. D. He is visiting our school this afternoon." Brad looked at Ms. V. and then at Mr. D. He extended his hand and said, "Hello Mr. D. It is good to meet you." He looked Mr. D. in the eyes but did not smile. His voice was strong but without pleasure, as if this was a very formal occasion. Mr. D. responded that it was a pleasure to meet B. and asked him what he was doing? B. turned to the gerbil cage and said, "Watching Scat tear up the newspaper we put in the cage. He does that with his teeth and hands." B. then turned from Mr. D. and went to the easel.

ditional information about how he may cope with stressful situations. Mr. Duncan's direct question to Brad required a response. After responding, however, Brad immediately left the area and went to a solitary activity. This may be further evidence that Brad removes himself from stressful situations and finds solitary activities to accomplish.

Samples

Numerous types of samples can be collected from children. The most common is the *work sample*. This is an example of a child's work during an activity. Art work, dictated stories and letters, and photographs of block structures are all types of work samples that are the product of a child's efforts. An important aspect of the work sample is a brief note indicating the process the child used to create the sample. The date the work was produced and the child's name should also be included.

If a child with cerebral palsy, who cannot use her hands to grasp a string, uses her mouth to string paint, the resulting picture and a brief description of how she painted the picture would constitute a work sample. The picture itself would indicate how she could move her head, specifying range and direction. The note could describe how she was able to place the string in her mouth, how long she worked at painting, whether she rested and returned to the picture, and any social interaction that occurred with adults or peers while she was painting.

Behavior and *communication samples* are similar to work samples but focus on a child's behavior or communication. A communication sample records

TABLE 4.12   Example of a Communication Sample

Name: Brad W.   Age: 3 yrs. 9 mo.   Date: 07/28/95
Time: 11:00 - 12:00
Place: 3-yr.-old room
Activity: Free-play and clean up.

   The following words or phrases were spontaneously used by Brad: car, go, up, no, stop, under, mess, run, hit, outa-sight, Summer, momma, moon, trash, yuck, simple, more, hurt, sometimes, when, and, now.
   Brad was very verbal while in the block area. He talked little during clean up. He repeated many phrases that peers and adults used during clean-up.

the verbal and nonverbal communication a child uses during a given time period. This allows the early childhood educator to focus on the child's ability to communicate, strategies for communication, vocabulary, and responses to others' communication. If the teacher or other personnel are concerned about a specific area, such as vocabulary or spontaneous language, that aspect can be recorded. Table 4.12 is an example of a communication sample that focuses on Brad's spontaneous vocabulary use.

   In other situations, a communication sample might be an exact transcription of a recording of the child's vocalizations. In those cases, a narrative record also is kept to document the child's nonverbal behavior.

   A behavior sample focuses on the child's behavior and records interactions with others. Instead of recording all of the actions of the child, the behavior record concentrates on positive or negative interpersonal behaviors. A behavior record documents such activities as the child's offers to share toys with others and under what circumstances that behavior has occurred.

TABLE 4.13   Brad's Free-Play Activity Preferences

Free-Play Activity Preferences

Child: Brad W.   Age: 3 yrs. 9 mo.
Dates: Aug. 14–18, 1995

Water Table	Blocks	Dramatic Play	Manipulatives	Art	Books/Tapes
IIII IIII	IIII IIII IIII IIII IIII	II	I	IIII	II

Developmental checklists are sometimes used to determine what skills a child has acquired. The teacher, parent, or other professionals observe the child over time to see which skills, typical for a specific age, the child has or has not yet developed. The use of these checklists varies according to the type of information the program and family want to gather. The lists can be used to determine whether the child has ever exhibited the skills, whether the child frequently uses the skills, or even whether the child uses them in multiple settings.

In the case of Tarrel, a developmental domain of concern to his teacher might be communication. She can consult a checklist of typical communication skills of 4-, 5- and six-year-olds. Each time Tarrel exhibits one of the skills, his teacher can check off the skill to indicate it is present. For more detailed information, the teacher can place a check next to the skill each time she observes Tarrel exhibiting it.

Activity preference records are records of the activities and tasks a child chooses. They can be kept as frequency charts or time records. These records show a parent or teacher how the child spends his or her time during the day. Table 4.13 records the number of times Brad has chosen to play in each of six free-play centers over the course of one week. This information provides a profile of the activities Brad enjoys and where he chooses to spend time.

Sociograms are a method of graphically indicating how a child approaches and interacts with other children during a given period of time, and also who approaches and interacts with the child. Sociograms often provide a clear picture of the frequency of interactions with other children and the number of overtures a child makes toward other children during that time period. They are, however, notoriously unstable as predictors of future social interactions (Bailey & Wolery, 1989). If sociograms are used to determine the social interaction patterns of a child, it is important to collect numerous examples over a period of weeks to conclude that a specific social interaction pattern exists. Figure 4.1 depicts Brad's social interactions during one hour and fifteen minutes of free-play.

As can be seen, Brad approached a number of children during the free-play period. Very few children approached or interacted with him. Combining this information with additional sociograms and other forms of assessment data can begin to provide a profile of Brad's interactions, social skills, and preferences for activities.

Each of the methods described can assist early childhood educators in collecting information about young children's developmental skills, behaviors, and preferences. Using a variety of these methods in multiple settings, over time, a picture of the child will emerge that can be used to establish specific goals and objectives and help early childhood educators plan daily activities to enhance and develop children's skills, behaviors, and knowledge.

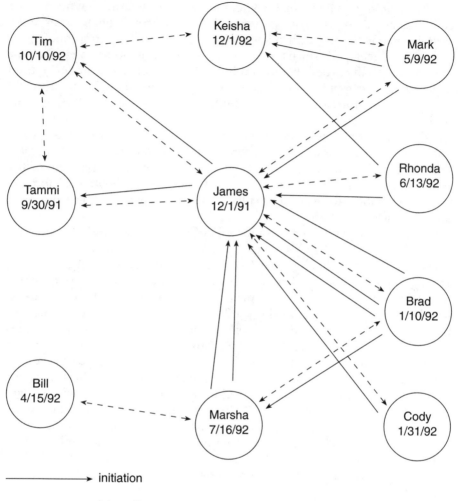

FIGURE 4.1   Sociogram for Ms. Walker's Classroom during Free-Play, 9/13/95, 10:00–11:15 a.m.

PROCEDURES FOR COLLECTING FAMILY PRIORITIES, CONCERNS, AND PREFERENCES INFORMATION

Just as numerous methods exist for collecting information about a child's developmental skills and behaviors, there are multiple ways to collect information about a family's priorities, concerns, and preferences for their child and for themselves. Two primary methods of collecting such information are written surveys and face-to-face conversations.

Bailey and Blasco (1990) found that a small majority of families (54 percent) prefer talking with educators and other professionals over writing responses about their concerns and priorities for their children. Research has indicated that interviews or discussions are most effective and better received by families when they are informal in nature (Summers et al., 1990). These interactions can take place in the family home, at neighborhood gathering spots, or at schools as long as the family member(s) are comfortable with the setting and feel that they are playing an important part in the development of their child's program (Summers et al., 1990; Turnbull & Turnbull, 1990).

To assist teachers and other personnel as they talk with family members, Winton (1988) has constructed a "structured family interview" that allows for informal interaction while also addressing specific issues (see Table

TABLE 4.14 The Structured Family Interview Process

Winton's Structured Family Interview

Phase One: Contact the family prior to the face-to-face interview to determine what topics they wish to discuss, establish when and how long the session will be and assure confidentiality of the information shared during the session.

Phase Two: At the beginning of the interview, review the purpose and confirm the amount of time allotted. Again, emphasize confidentiality.

Phase Three: Share any information that you have about the issues and ask for any information that the family member(s) might have. Synthesize all the information available.

Phase Four: Summarize the information and ask the family what they would like to do next. Be sure to establish what their priorities are for their child. Establish a plan to address these priorities.

Phase Five: Thank the family member(s) for their time and ask for feedback about the session.

Adapted from Winton, P., (1988). The family-focused interview: An assessment measure and goal-setting mechanism. In D. Bailey & R. Simmeonsson. *Family assessment in early intervention* (pp. 185– 205). Columbus, OH: Merrill Publishing.

4.14). Winton's interview structure begins with a contact with the family prior to the informal discussion to determine what topics will be addressed during the interview; provide the teacher with a general understanding of the family's priorities; and establish where, when, and for how long the discussion will take place. It is important that during this contact the teacher treat family members as equals and begin to establish the trust needed to work together.

The second phase of the interview is the beginning of the informal discussion. At this point, the teacher confirms the amount of time available for the interview and the topics to be discussed. The family has an opportunity to change the agenda and to communicate any events that may have occurred between the initial interaction and the interview. Confidentiality is emphasized at this time. These steps again emphasize that the family's concerns and priorities are important and allow for further trust to be established.

The third phase of the structured interview process is the sharing phase. Family members and the teacher discuss the topics on the agenda and share information that they have about those issues. This is the time to collect as much information as possible about the family's concerns and preferences for their child. Similarities and differences between the teacher and family are highlighted during this portion of the interview.

In the fourth part of the interview, the teacher summarizes what has been discussed and both parties explore plans to address the issues that have been raised. After discussing all possibilities, the family and teacher jointly decide upon a plan to address any identified priorities.

During the final phase of the interview, the teacher thanks the family members for their time, reiterates the plans for the future, and asks for other feedback. If necessary, arrangements are made for another meeting.

If some family members are not willing to meet with teachers or other professionals, information can be collected from them through the use of surveys or questionnaires. Surveys exist that allow family members to indicate the information or services they need (Bailey, 1987), the skills they feel are important for their child to develop (Vincent, 1983), and their preferences for programming for their child and family members (Turnbull & Turnbull, 1986). See Table 4.15 for examples of questions that appear on family surveys.

It should be noted that observing parents and other family members is a third method of gathering information about their concerns, priorities, and preferences for their child. However, observation of family members without their consent and understanding about why they are being observed is ethically questionable behavior (McGonigel, Kaufman, & Johnson, 1991; Winton, 1988). If a family member is concerned about her interactions with her daugh-

TABLE 4.15   Examples of Family Survey Questions

I need information about child growth and development (Andrew, 1990).

I have questions about respite care (Chesterfield, 1989).

I need more support from my family (Finn & Vadasy, 1988).

I need day care so I can get a job (Seligman & Darling, 1989).

I am interested in explaining my child's disability to others (Bricker & Cripe, 1992).

ter and she asks for assistance, a teacher might suggest an observation session in which the teacher shares her notes and suggestions with the parent at the conclusion of the session. To participate in such an activity without the knowledge or consent of the parent is not recommended and would be a barrier to establishing trust between the family and the early childhood program (Turnbull & Turnbull, 1990).

PROCEDURES FOR COLLECTING INFORMATION ABOUT THE CHILD'S ENVIRONMENTAL SETTING AND DEMANDS

Collecting information from the family about the settings in which a child spends time and the accompanying demands on the child can occur through three primary methods: a questionnaire, an informal interview, or observation. Surveys such as the Daily Routine Record (Vincent, 1983) ask parents to identify the settings in which their child spends time and the activities in which he or she participates in those settings. The form can be completed by the parents or can be used as an interview tool. (See Table 4.16 for a portion of this instrument).

If a family member does not want to complete a survey or be interviewed about the settings in which the child spends time, observations of the settings can be made. After a family member has indicated where the child spends time, a teacher or other staff person can observe those settings or interview people responsible for the child in those settings. For example, if a child spends a great deal of time at her grandmother's house, the teacher might observe at grandmother's (with permission) or interview the grandmother about the routine that occurs and what she expects from the child. In this manner, the teacher or other professional becomes aware of the demands made on the child and the skills to be developed for success in that setting.

TABLE 4.16   Example of Form to Record the Daily Routine

Time	Parent Activities	Child Activities	Days/ Weeks	Time for Interacting 1 = good time for child 2 = good time for other person 3 = not a good time for the child 4 = not a good time for other person	Amount of Assistance 1 = full assistance 2 = frequent 3 = minimal 4 = no assistance
10:00 A.M.					
10:30 A.M.					
11:00 A.M.					
11:30 A.M.					

Daily Routine Record (Vincent, 1983).

USING THE THREE TYPES OF INFORMATION TO DEVELOP CHILDREN'S GOALS AND OBJECTIVES

When the three types of information have been collected, they must be analyzed to establish goals and objectives. Teachers typically collect information and make decisions about programs on a regular and continuous basis. The process is disciplined and professional and is almost always under the control of the classroom teacher or a team of professionals.

The process of identifying goals and objectives for a young child with a disability is more formal, structured, and regulated by law. A team of the child's parent(s), early childhood educators, special educators, related service personnel (e.g., a speech-language pathologist or occupational therapist), and an administrator, must consider the child, family, and environmental information in order to develop an Individual Family Service Plan (IFSP), for a child aged birth to 36 months, or an Individual Education Program (IEP) for a child over 36 months of age. These plans are formal contracts that indicate the goals and objectives that teachers and other personnel will help the child to achieve. The plans also indicate which services will be provided to the child and the family. (See Chapter 5.)

The first responsibility of the team that creates the child's IEP or IFSP is to identify the goals and objectives for the child and staff. Based upon the collected information, the team comes to a consensus about which skills are important. Objectives are written to enable the teacher, parents, and any other staff members to work toward their attainment. The team must discuss all of the information and determine which skills the family considers important, which skills the child needs in the settings in which he or she spends time, and which are developmentally appropriate.

Brad's case provides a good example of how this process might work. Although he has Down syndrome and a moderate hearing loss, the information collected about his developmental skills shows some strengths in cognitive, written language, and social skills. It also suggests that Brad has difficulty in less structured, open-ended situations, such as center time or free-play. Family preferences are for Brad to be more independent and to interact with children his own age through acceptable means. The environmental information indicates that Brad spends a full day in child care and must make a number of transitions in an active and sometimes chaotic environment.

Given this brief profile and the three types of information, the team responsible for developing Brad's goals and objectives might select the following:

Goal 1: Brad will play with two classmates for an activity period without hitting or biting.

Goal 2: Brad will choose an activity after each of the three meals at his child care center and go directly to those activities.

Goal 3: Brad will feed himself complete meals at home and at child care.

These three goals take into account information from the child, family, and environmental sources and incorporate developmentally appropriate expectations, family preferences, and setting demands. Although no team of family members and professionals will generate exactly the same goals or do so in the same manner as another team, the availability of the three types of information to inform the decision-making process ensures that the program plans generated will be most likely to address the child's developmental needs, the family's preferences, and the skills necessary for success.

SUMMARY

A major component of all exemplary early childhood education programs is the formative assessment process. By collecting data about children's developmental skills, cultural and family backgrounds, learning styles, and activity preferences, teachers and other professionals are able to determine appropriate goals and plan routines and activities that address the needs of the children. Through the use of child-specific and setting-specific assessment strategies, program staff collect information that allows them to make informed decisions about short-term and long-term curriculum approaches.

The same strategies are important for programs that serve young children with disabilities alongside those without disabilities. By collecting information about their developmental skills and behaviors, determining the concerns and priorities of their families, and measuring the demands of the settings in which they spend time, teachers and families can jointly develop goals and objectives for the children. This multiple method, continuous process assessment meets the requirements of the legislation that regulates services to young children with disabilities and ensures that sound, developmentally appropriate strategies are being used to determine functional goals and objectives. The same information can then be used to help determine a curriculum program that will facilitate the children's acquisition of skills and behaviors as defined by their IEP or IFSP outcomes, goals, and objectives.

The developmentally appropriate, functional approach outlined in this chapter is consistent with the many regulations that guide and control services for young children with known or suspected disabilities. In addition, it ensures that the children's families are involved in the assessment process, that the goals and objectives identified are useful and functional, and that the process is similar to the assessment process for young children without disabilities.

In Chapter 5, formative assessment information, as discussed here, is used to develop specific program plans for young children with disabilities. Chapters 6 and 7 illustrate the use of this information as it pertains to daily routines, classroom arrangement, classroom management, and unit and theme plans.

ACTIVITIES AND RESOURCES

Activities

1. Interview a family, using one of the Concerns, Priorities, and Resources questionnaires. Have students identify and prioritize the family's three most important concerns.
2. Combine students into groups of three. Have one student conduct a quick norm-referenced, standardized screening of a child. (Have them use the Denver II or some other instrument.) Another student should observe the same child for about a fifteen-minute period during a typical classroom interaction. The third student should interview the teacher, a parent, and a caregiver of the child. The three students can compare the information they collected and discuss any similarities or differences.
3. Using each of three case studies presented in Chapter 1, review the three types of assessment information and identify the most important skills and behaviors for each child to develop. Also, identify the strengths and preferences of each child.

Class Discussion Questions

1. Assessment is the process of collecting information to make decisions. What types of decisions are made when teaching young children and why are different types of assessment procedures necessary for each type of assessment?
2. What is the difference between assessment for eligibility and assessment for program decision making? Why are there differences?
3. Why are norm-referenced, standardized assessment instruments less appropriate for making programming decisions for young children with disabilities than they are for nondisabled children?
4. Compare the types of information collected by a standardized assessment instrument and a ten-minute child observation. How can each of these sets of information be used?
5. What are the three types of assessment information necessary for the development of program plans for young children with disabilities? Why is each type important? How might a program be affected if one of these types of information was missing?
6. How do we ensure that assessment procedures are culturally and ethnically unbiased?
7. When determining a child's functional skills, why are work samples alone not sufficient for determining levels of functioning?
8. If a family is very different from yours (e.g., culturally, ethnically, socioeconomically), how might you go about collecting information about their concerns and priorities for their young child with a disability?
9. If it is impossible for you to observe the environments in which a child spends time, what other methods might you use to collect that information?
10. If the child, family, and environmental assessment collected by an assessment team is contradictory, how does the team decide which information is the most important?

Readings

The readings listed below provide expanded discussions of the ideas and strategies discussed in this chapter.

Fenichel, E. (Ed.) (1994). Developmental Assessment. *Zero to Three, 14*(6), 50 p.

Grace, C. & Shores, E. (1991). *The portfolio and its use*. Little Rock, AR: Southern Association on Children Under Six.

Linder, T. (1992). *Transdisciplinary play-based assessment* (rev. ed.). Baltimore, MD: Paul H. Brookes Publishing Company.

McGonigel, M., Kaufman, R. & Johnson, B. (1991). *Guidelines and recommended practices for the individual family service plan*. Bethesda, MD: Association for the Care of Children's Health.

Neisworth, J., & Bagnato, S. (1992). The case against intelligence testing in early intervention. *Topics in Early Childhood Special Education, 12*(1), 1–20.

Puckett, M., & Black, J. (1994). *Authentic assessment of the young child: Celebrating development and learning*. New York: Merrill.

Instruments That Assist Families in Identifying Concerns, Priorities, and Resources

The following instruments are a sample of those available to assist families in the identification of their concerns and priorities for their young children with disabilities.

Bailey, D. & Simeonsson, R. (1990). *Family needs survey* (revised). Chapel Hill, NC: Frank Porter Graham Child Development Center.

Child Development Resources. (1991). *How can we help?* Lightfoot, VA: Child Development Resources.

Cripe, J. & Bricker, D. (1993). *Family interest survey*. Baltimore, MD: Paul H. Brookes.

Finn, D. & Vadasy, P. (1988). *Prioritizing family needs scale*. Birmingham, AL: University of Alabama at Birmingham.

Seligman, M., & Darling, B. (1989). Parent needs survey. In M. Seligman & B. Darling. *Ordinary families, special children: A systems approach to childhood disability*. New York, NY: Guilford Press.

Vincent, L., Davis, J., Brown, P., Teicher, J., & Weynand, P. (1983). *Daily routine recording form*. Madison, WI: Madison, WI: Madison Metropolitan School District.

REFERENCES

Andrew, S. (1990). Survey of family needs. Charlottesville, VA: Author.

Bagnato, S., & Neisworth, J. (1990). *System to plan early childhood services: Administration manual*. Circle Press, MN: American Guidance Services.

Bailey, D. (1987). Collaborative goal-setting with families: Resolving differences in values and priorities for services. *Topics in Early Childhood Special Education, 7*(2), 59–71.

Bailey, D., & Blasco, P. (1990). Parents' perspectives on a written survey of family needs. *Journal of Early Intervention, 14,* 196–203.

Bailey, D., & Wolery, M. (1989). *Assessing infants and preschoolers with handicaps.* Columbus, OH: Merrill.

Bailey, D., & Wolery, M. (1990). *Teaching infants and preschoolers with disabilities.* (2nd ed.). New York: Merrill.

Bayley, N. (1993). *Bayley scales of infant development (2nd. Ed.).* San Antonio, TX: Psychological Corporation.

Bredekamp, S. (1987). *Developmentally appropriate practice in early childhood programs serving children from birth through age 8* (Expanded edition). Washington, DC: National Association for the Education of Young Children.

Bricker, D., & Cripe, J. (1992). *An activity-based approach to early intervention.* Baltimore, MD: Paul H. Brookes.

Chesterfield County Public Schools (1989). *Family needs checklist.* Richmond, VA: Author.

Congressional Record. (August 23, 1977). *Public Law 94-142: Education of the Handicapped Act.* Washington, DC: U.S. Government Printing Office.

Congressional Record. (October 7, 1991). *Public Law 102-119: Individuals with Disabilities Education Act.* Washington, DC: U.S. Government Printing Office.

Congressional Record. (October 8, 1996). *Public Law 99-457: Title I, Part H—Handicapped Infants and Toddlers.* Washington, DC: U.S. Government Printing Office.

Finn, D. & Vadasy, P. (1988). *Prioritizing family needs scale.* Birmingham, AL: Author

Frankenburg, W., Dodds, J., & Fandal, A. (1976). *Denver developmental screening test.* Denver, CO: LADOCA Project and Publishing Foundation.

Grace, C., & Shores, E. (1991). *The portfolio and its use: Developmentally appropriate assessment of young children.* Little Rock, AR: Southern Association on Children Under Six.

Hills, T. (1993). Assessment in context: Teachers and children at work. *Young Children, 48*(5), 20–28.

John-Steiner, V., & Souberman, E. (1978). Afterword. In M. Cole, V. John-Steiner, S. Scribner, & E. Souberman (Eds.), *L.S. Vygotsky—Mind in Society* (pp. 122–133). Cambridge, MA: Harvard University Press.

Lynch, E. & Hanson, M. (1992). *Developing cross-cultural competence: A guide for working with young children and their families.* Baltimore, MD: Paul H. Brooks Publishing Co.

McGonigel, M., Kaufman, R. & Johnston, B. (Eds.) (1991). *Guidelines and recommended practices for the individualized family service plan* (2nd ed.). Bethesda, MD: Association for the Care of Children's Health.

Meisels, S. (1985). A functional analysis of the evolution of public policy for handicapped young children. *Educational Evaluation and Policy Analysis, 7,* 115–126.

Meisels, S., Jablon, J., Marsden, D., Dichtelmiller, M., & Dorfman, A. (1994). *The Work Sampling System: An Overview* (3rd ed.). Ann Arbor, MI: Rebus Planning Associates.

Meisels, S., & Provence, S. (1989). *Screening and assessment: Guidelines for identifying young disabled and developmentally vulnerable children and their families.* Washington, DC: National Center for Clinical Infant Programs.

National Association for the Education of Young Children. (1988). Position statement on standardized testing of young children 3 through 8 years of age. *Young Children, 43*(3), 42–47.

National Association of Elementary School Principals. (1990). *Early childhood education: Standards for quality programs for young children in the elementary school*. Alexandria, VA: NAESP.

National Association of State Boards of Education. (1991). *Right from the start: The report of the NASBE task force on early childhood education*. Alexandria, VA: NASBE.

Newborg, J., Stock, J., & Wnek, L. (1984). *Battelle developmental inventory*. Chicago, IL: Riverside.

Piaget, J. (1952). *The origins of intelligence in children*. New York: Norton.

Puckett, M., & Black, J. (1994). *Authentic assessment of the young child: Celebrating development and learning*. New York: Merrill.

Seligman, M. & Darling, R. (1989). *Parent needs survey*. New York, NY: Guilford.

Southern Association on Children Under Six (1990). Developmentally appropriate assessment: A position paper. Little Rock, AR: SACUS.

Summers, J., Dell'Oliver, C., Turnbull, A., Benson, H., Santelli, E., Campbell, M., & Siegel-Causey, E. (1990). Examining the individualized family service plan process: What are family and practitioner preferences? *Topics in Early Childhood Special Education, 10*, 78–99.

Turnbull, A., & Turnbull, H. (1986). *Families, professionals, and exceptionality: A special partnership*. Columbus, OH: Merrill.

Turnbull, A., & Turnbull, H. (1990). *Families, professionals, and exceptionality: A special partnership*. (2nd ed.). New York: Merrill.

Vincent, L. (1983). Parent inventory of child development in nonschool environments. Madison, WI: Madison Metropolitan School District. ERIC # ED 265931.

Vygotsky, L. (1978). *Mind in society*. Cambridge, MA: Harvard University Press.

Weschler, D. (1989). *Weschler preschool and primary scale of intelligence-revised*. San Antonio, TX: Psychological Corporation.

Winton, P. (1988). Effective communication between parents and professionals? In D. Bailey & R. Simmeonsson, *Family assessment in early intervention*. Columbus, OH: Merrill.

Wortham, S. (1994). *Early childhood curriculum: Developmental bases for learning and teaching*. New York, NY: Merrill.

5

USING INDIVIDUALIZED PLANS AS A BASIS FOR DESIGNING DEVELOPMENTALLY APPROPRIATE LEARNING EXPERIENCES FOR YOUNG CHILDREN WITH SPECIAL NEEDS

OBJECTIVES

After studying this chapter, readers should be able to perform the following:

- Describe the purpose of, the components of, and the similarities and differences between the IFSP and the IEP.

- Discuss how the developmentally appropriate practices (DAP) guidelines provide the foundation in programs in which individualized goals and objectives are addressed.

- Describe how goals and objectives can be embedded into an early childhood routine.

- Discuss strategies for monitoring the progress made on the individual plans of young children with special needs and their families.

The purpose of this chapter is to provide an overview of the Individualized Family Service Plan (IFSP) and the Individualized Education Plan (IEP), planning documents designed to guide the services for young children with disabilities and their families.

INDIVIDUALIZED PLANS

The key to success in developmentally appropriate programs is recognizing the relationship between age-appropriate and individually appropriate practices. This section focuses on the individual needs, interests, and desires of the child and family through the use of Individualized Family Service Plans (IFSPs) and Individualized Education Plans (IEPs).

As described in Chapter 3, Part H of the *Individuals with Disabilities Education Act* (IDEA) requires IFSPs for children from birth to age 3; Part B of IDEA requires IEPs for children age 3 through 21. IEPs and IFSPs are formal planning documents that must be developed in order for children to receive early intervention, special education, and/or related services. The purposes, components, and processes involved in developing these plans are highlighted in this chapter.

Individualized Family Service Plan (IFSP)

IFSPs are written planning documents outlining services for infants and toddlers (ages birth to 3), who are eligible for early intervention services, and their families. The IFSP is somewhat different from the IEP in that it relies heavily on a family-driven orientation to service delivery. IFSPs are based on the multidisciplinary assessment of the child and the identification of the concerns, priorities, and resources of the child's family. The IFSP is written by, or its writing is monitored by, the family, with assistance from members of a qualified team of professionals from across disciplines. Parents or guardians serve as integral members of the team. The manner in which families are involved, however, depends on their individual preferences. The IFSP should provide a plan for services that enhance the development of the child and the capacity of the family to meet the special needs of the child.

According to regulations for Part H of IDEA, the specific components that must be contained in the IFSP are as follows:

1. A statement of the infant's or toddler's present level of development in five domains: physical, cognitive, communication, social or emotional, and adaptive development
2. Family information, including a statement of the family's resources, priorities, and concerns related to enhancing the development of the child
3. Outcomes to be achieved for the child and family, as well as the criteria, procedures, and timelines used to monitor progress
4. Specific services the child and family will receive
5. The name of the service coordinator responsible for the IFSP
6. A statement of the natural environments in which services are to be delivered
7. A plan to support the transition of the child at age 3 to preschool services or other services

More important than the IFSP product itself is the actual IFSP process. The development and implementation of the IFSP is an ongoing supportive activity. The end result should be a set of identified outcomes on the IFSP that address the changes that families have identified for themselves and their children As McGonigel, Kaufman, and Johnson (1991) stated, "a family need or concern exists only if the family perceives that the need or concern exists" (p. 32).

Bennett, Lingerfelt, and Nelson (1990) provide the following suggestions to professionals regarding the IFSP process:

1. Family-identified concerns, needs, and desires should receive the most weight in the IFSP process. Many families need help in prioritizing their objectives and identifying specific projects on which they want to work. For a child with extensive needs, the family may feel overwhelmed and unsure of where to begin. Professionals can provide information to help them sort out their concerns and needs and ultimately make informed decisions regarding their priorities. If the family indicates that they want their child to learn to

sit independently and to walk, they may need information from professionals about what they can do to assist the child in achieving these milestones.
The skill of sitting independently precedes the skill of walking; therefore, sitting independently is a priority skill to work on first. In this example, the
professional helped the family to realize which of their desired outcomes
would be realistic to work toward and shared strategies for achieving the
outcomes.

2. Families should identify and use their existing strengths and resources. They should be encouraged by professionals to use their own abilities to solve problems and obtain needed resources. Strengths and resources
often vary across families. Family strengths might include dedication to hard
work, commitment to one another, or a positive approach to challenging situations. One example of family members' commitment to one another is an
older sibling who provides childcare for her younger sibling with a disability, as well as for a neighbor's child who is nondisabled. Using the older sibling as a resource creates an opportunity for the child with a disability to
interact with a nondisabled child.

3. Families often need to develop strong informal social networks to promote the well-being of the family unit. Professionals must work with families
to identify and maintain the sources of informal social support readily available to them. Networks could include neighbors, church members, or those
in the extended family. For parents who work outside the home, co-workers
may provide a source of support. Many families of children with disabilities
find it helpful to link with other such families.

4. Families' repertoires of skills and competencies often have to be expanded. Professionals can create opportunities for the family to develop valuable new skills and capabilities. For example, after a family develops transition
skills for moving from one program to the next (e.g., hospital to home, home
to infant program, infant program to preschool services), they can use these
skills as their child makes subsequent transitions (e.g., preschool to kindergarten, primary to middle school, school to work).

The following is an example of an IFSP outcome written to address the
needs of the family. In this example, the family's number one priority was for
their child to have the opportunity to play with and develop friendships with
her normally developing same-age peers. However, because there were no
children Anna's age within several miles of their house, the parents, Susan
and Jeff, felt that a child care program would provide Anna with the opportunity to develop social and communication skills, which they considered a
priority. They decided on the following outcome: "Susan (Anna's mother)
will select a childcare program in which to enroll Anna so that she can play
with friends her own age."

After the outcomes have been determined, several activities or steps can be generated to achieve success for each outcome. In this example, Susan could visit the various child care options in the area or talk to other parents about the settings. The best way to go about achieving a desired outcome can vary tremendously across families. Some families many have a very clear idea of what they want for themselves and their children, as well as how to go about accessing the necessary resources. Others may need more assistance in identifying outcomes, strategies, and resources. The teacher or service coordinator must tailor the support to fit the amount of assistance a family needs or desires.

Individualized Education Plan (IEP)

The IEP is an annual document developed for children with disabilities from ages 3 through 21 who are eligible for special education services. The IEP is a direct requirement of IDEA, which mandates that all students with disabilities receive a free and appropriate public education. In essence, this requirement acknowledges that children with disabilities need a unique, specially designed instructional program.

The IEP is developed and signed by a team that must include the child's parent(s) or guardian(s), the child's teacher, an agency representative, and other representatives deemed appropriate by the parents or school district (e.g., related service personnel or advocate). The IEP contains the following information:

1. A statement of the child's present level of educational performance in each of the domains: adaptive, cognitive, communication, physical, and social or emotional
2. The child's annual goals and short-term objectives
3. The special education and related services to be provided
4. The extent to which the child will participate in the regular education program
5. The way in which the child's progress will be determined;
6. The date of initiation and projected duration of services
7. An optional transition plan (if the IEP team finds it appropriate)

The IEP can serve a variety of purposes. The primary purpose is to provide a written plan of the special education program designed to meet the needs of the child. Thus the IEP can provide direction for the teacher in meeting the needs of a child with a disability within a group of nondisabled children. There should be an integrated relationship among the child's needs, the IEP goals and objectives, and the instruction provided in the educational environment. A second purpose of the IEP is to serve as the basis for evaluation.

The annual goals become the standards against which to judge student progress and instructional effectiveness. A third purpose is to function as a vehicle for communication among team members in program planning and implementation.

Comparison of IFSP and IEP

The IFSP and the IEP have several similarities. For example, they both require a statement of the child's level of performance. However, the domains included in the documents are different. The domains in the IFSP are cognitive, communication, social/emotional, and adaptive skill development. In the IEP, the domains include academic achievement, social adaptation, prevocational and vocational skills, psychomotor skills, and self-help skills.

The IFSP and IEP have other differences as well. The IEP does not require a statement of the family's resources, priorities, and concerns, nor does it require a service coordinator and a transition plan. However, the regulations state that nothing prevents the IEP from focusing on transition in the same manner as does the IFSP. Another difference is that the IEP contains a statement on the extent of a preschool-aged child's regular classroom participation, while the IFSP requires a statement of the natural intervention environment. Table 5.1 compares the components of the IFSP and the IEP.

The major underlying difference between the two documents is that the IFSP is based on a family-centered orientation in which the family is the focus of services, while the IEP is based more on a service delivery in which the needs of the child are the focus of services. Some states have felt that the family-centered orientation is so important that they have made efforts to extend the use of the IFSP to preschool special education. Another difference is that the IEP must be completed before programming can officially begin; therefore, the IEP may seem more like a product than a continuous process.

DEVELOPING IEP/IFSP GOALS/OUTCOMES AND OBJECTIVES

The overall purpose of the IFSP and IEP is to develop individualized outcomes or goals with accompanying objectives and learning strategies so that each child's full potential may be realized. The IFSP outcomes and IEP goals should be developed to reflect the skills required for the child to participate in the activities and routines in the natural environment (e.g., home, classroom, and community) (Noonan & McCormick, 1993). Objectives represent learning expectations and are based on the child's and family's interests, abilities, and priorities.

TABLE 5.1 Comparison of the Required Components of the IFSP and the IEP

Individualized Family Service Plan (IFSP)	Individualized Education Plan (IEP)
1. A statement of the child's present levels of functioning in cognitive, communication, social/emotional and adaptive skill development.	1. A statement of the child's present levels of educational performance, including academic achievement, social adaptation, prevocational and vocational skills, psychomotor skills, and self-help skills.
2. A statement of the family's resources, priorities, and concerns related to enhancing the child's development.	2. A statement of annual goals which describes the educational performance to be achieved in all areas in which the child needs specially designed programs.
3. A statement of the expected intervention objectives (for the infant or toddler and the family) with schedules including the timelines used to determine progress.	3. A statement of short-term instructional objectives with criteria, evaluation procedures, and schedules including the criteria, evaluation procedures, and assessment measures for determining (at least once a year) if objectives are being met.
4. A description of specific early intervention services necessary to meet the unique needs of the child and family (i.e., frequency, intensity, and the method of delivering services).	4. A statement of specific educational services needed by the child including all special education services and any special instructional media and materials needed.
5. The projected dates for initiation of and expected duration of services.	5. The projected date for the initiation of services and anticipated duration of services.
6. The name of the service coordinator from the profession most immediately relevant to the child's or family's needs who will be responsible for carrying out the plan and coordinating with other agencies and persons.	6. A list of the individuals who are responsible for implementing the IEP.
7. Procedures to support the transition of the child to services provided under Part B of IDEA.	7. A justification of the type of educational placement that the child will have.
8. A statement of natural environments that occur where early intervention services will be provided.	8. A description of the extent of participation in regular education classrooms.

In the past, mistakes were made when IEP goals and IFSP outcomes with corresponding objectives were derived from developmental assessments (Noonan & McCormick, 1995). The end result was nonfunctional, impractical IEP goals such as "Rachel will demonstrate increased balance by standing on one foot for ten seconds," or "John Andrew will stack ten one-inch blocks." Developmental assessments were never intended to be used to determine the skills to target on the IEP. Instead, an approach should be utilized in which the skills identified are those needed for children to "participate actively in natural settings" (Noonan & McCormick, 1993, p. 1). The following are steps to be followed in the process of developing IEP goals and IFSP outcomes:

1. Begin by identifying skills that are partially acquired or that are demonstrated in some contexts but not others.
2. Identify skills that will permit the child to participate in routine daily activities within the natural environment and, therefore, increase the opportunities for interaction with peers.
3. Determine skills that would be instrumental in accomplishing the greatest number of other skills or functional tasks.
4. Identify skills that the child is highly motivated to learn and/or that the family wants him to learn.
5. Select skills that will increase participation in future environments.

After IEP goals and IFSP outcomes are identified, they must be broken down into smaller components or objectives. Objectives are subskills or steps that are critical to achieving the long-range goal or outcome. Objectives have three components: (1) the definition or description of the targeted skill or behavior, (2) the specification of the conditions under which the behavior will occur, and (3) the criterion or standard for judging the adequacy of the behavior when it is performed.

An example most people can relate to is the goal of losing weight, with the corresponding objectives leading to the goal. If a person's long-range goal is to loose fifteen pounds over several months, the first objective might be to lose five pounds during the first two weeks, five more pounds over the next four weeks, and five more pounds over the next four weeks. Each objective of losing five pounds is a step toward the overall goal of losing fifteen pounds. Various strategies may be used to achieve each of the objectives, and some strategies may be modified depending on how successful they were in accomplishing the objectives.

Many experienced teachers have difficulty formulating long-range goals/outcomes and short-term objectives. Notari-Syverson and Shuster (1995) suggest guidelines to follow in developing IEP or IFSP goals and objectives. These guidelines include five indicators of high-quality goals and objectives: functionality, generality, ease of integration within the instructional context, measurability, and the hierarchical relationship between long-range goals and short-term objectives. The indicators are broken down into components, which are listed in Table 5.2 and discussed in the following section.

Notari-Syverson and Shuster (1995) stress the importance of the functionality of skills. They describe two components of functionality. The first is that the skill should increase a child's ability to interact with people and objects within his or her daily environment. If a skill is included on the IEP or IFSP, it should be one that the child needs to perform in all or most of the

TABLE 5.2   Indicators of High-Quality IEP/IFSP Goals and Objectives for Infants and Young Children

FUNCTIONALITY
1. Will the skill increase the child's ability to interact with people and objects within the daily environment?
2. Will the skill have to be performed by someone else if the child cannot do it?

GENERALITY
3. Does the skill represent a general concept or class of responses?
4. Can the skill be adapted or modified for a variety of disabling conditions?
5. Can the skill be generalized across a variety of settings, materials, and/or people?

INSTRUCTIONAL CONTEXT
6. Can the skill be taught in a way that reflects the manner in which the skill will be used in daily environments?
7. Can the skill be elicited easily by the teacher/parent within classroom/home activities?

MEASURABILITY
8. Can the skill be seen and/or heard?
9. Can the skill be directly counted (e.g., by frequency, duration, measures of distance such as how far a child is able to ride a tricycle, throw a ball, or propel a wheelchair)?
10. Does the skill contain or lend itself to determination of performance criteria?

HIERARCHICAL RELATION BETWEEN LONG-RANGE GOAL
AND SHORT-TERM OBJECTIVE
11. Is the short-term objective a developmental subskill or step thought to be critical to the achievement of the long-range goal?

From: Notari-Syverson & Shuster (1995). Putting real-life skills into IEP/IFSPs for infants and young children. *Teaching Exceptional Children, 27*(2), 29–32.

environments (e.g., classroom, home, and community) in which he or she interacts. An example of a skill that increases a child's ability to interact with objects in his or her environments is placing an object into a container. At home, the child can put toys in the toy chest, items of clothing or silverware in a drawer, or lunch in his or her lunch box. At school, the child can place his or her coat and book bag in the correct cubby or place trash in a trash can. In the community, the child can place money in an offering plate at church or groceries in a grocery cart.

The second component of functionality has been described by the question, "If a child does not have this skill, will someone else have to perform the skill for the child?" Many skills or behaviors are critical for the completion of daily routines such as brushing teeth, combing hair, drinking from a cup, and eating with a spoon or fork. Eating, for example, is an event that occurs several times a day and is a behavior in which everyone engages. Children need to develop skills and independence in feeding themselves, thus increasing the opportunities to engage in mealtime activities.

Generality is the second characteristic of high-quality goals and objectives as described by Notari-Syverson and Shuster (1995). Generality means that skills should represent a general concept or class of responses. Further, they should emphasize a generic process rather than a particular instance. An example of this is the skill of fitting an object into an exact space. Numerous opportunities arise for a child to use this type of skill: putting mail in a mail slot, coins in a vending machine, crayons in a crayon box, or dishes in a dishwasher. Another aspect of skill generality to consider is whether or not a skill can be adapted or modified for various types of disabilities (e.g., visual impairment, hearing impairment, or motor impairment) so that the child's impairment interferes as little as possible with the performance of a particular skill. For example, the skill of using a simple toy in an appropriate manner can be adapted easily, regardless of the disability. For a child with a motor impairment, toys can be lightweight and easy to move (e.g., Nerf balls, Wiffle Balls, toys on wheels, or roly-poly toys). For a child with a visual impairment, toys should be large and bright and should make noise (e.g., musical instruments or balls containing bells).

Another consideration in skill selection is whether or not the skill can be generalized across a variety of settings, materials, and/or people. Targeted skills should be those that the child can perform with interesting materials and in meaningful situations. An example of this type of skill is manipulating two small objects simultaneously. There are numerous opportunities when this type of skill is needed and can be practiced. At home, the child can use the skill to thread his or her shoelaces or to place Cheerios into a Ziploc bag. At school, the skill could be used to sharpen a pencil using a pencil sharpener. In the community, taking coins out of a small wallet or coin purse requires the use of the same skill.

The ease of integration within the instructional context is another quality indicator to consider when determining skills to target. Questions to ask in considering the instructional context are "Can the skill be taught in a way that reflects the manner in which it will be used in the daily environments?" or "Can the skill occur in a naturalistic manner?" A good example is the use of one object to obtain another object, such as using a fork to obtain food, using a broom to sweep, or using a stool to reach a book on a shelf. It is also important to focus on skills that can be elicited by the teacher or parent within classroom or home activities and that can be initiated easily by the child as part of the daily routine. For example, "stacking objects on top of one another" is a skill that meets this criterion. The skill can be used to stack books, cups and plates, pieces of wood, cans of food, or items of clothing. An inappropriate skill is "stacking one-inch blocks." This skill is so narrowly focused that it is not required in a naturalistic manner across daily environments.

The measurability of a skill is a quality indicator requiring that each skill be seen and/or heard. Various observers must be able to identify the same behavior. An example of a measurable skill is "to indicate wants and needs"; it refers to objects, persons, and/or events. Examples of nonmeasurable skills are "to experience a sense of self-importance" or "to recognize colors"; it is difficult to define these behaviors as they are stated. Does "recognize colors" mean to point to colors, name colors, or match colors. It is also important to remember that the skill should be directly measurable. For example, the frequency of a behavior can be counted (e.g., indicating wants or needs during snack time), the length of a behavior can be timed (e.g., playing independently), or the distance involved in executing a skill can be measured (e.g., riding a tricycle).

The skill should represent a well-defined behavior or activity. For example, "grasps a raisin-sized object" is a measurable skill; however, "has mobility in all fingers" is a nonmeasurable skill. Skills should contain performance criteria or lend themselves to the determination of performance criteria, which is the standard by which the skill will be evaluated. Therefore, the extent and/or degree of accuracy of a skill should be stated in order for the skill to be evaluated. For example, the skill "follow one-step directions with contextual cues" meets this criterion; however, "increase receptive language skills" does not.

Finally, Notari-Syverson & Shuster (1995) recommend that there should be a hierarchical relation between long-range goals and short-term objectives. Short-term objectives are developmental subskills or steps that are critical to the achievement of the long-range goal. The following is an example of an appropriate goal and corresponding objective.

The long-range goal is "Place and release objects balanced on top of another object." An appropriate short-term objective might be "Release an object with each hand." A child must be able to release objects before he can perform the more difficult task of placing and balancing objects on top of one another.

Some mistakes are frequently made when goals and objectives are developed. Sometimes the short-term objective is a restatement of the same skill as the long-range-goal, with the addition of an instructional prompt. For example, the long-range goal is "Independently activates mechanical toy," and the short-term objective is "Activates mechanical toy with physical prompt." Another common mistake occurs when the short-term objective is not conceptually or functionally related to the long-range-goal. For example, the long-range goal is "Poke with index finger," and the short-term objective is "Release object readily."

By following these guidelines, teachers and other professionals serving young children with disabilities can become proficient in developing appropriate goals and objectives that are meaningful for children and their families. After the goals and objectives have been developed for individual children, careful planning must occur so that all of the children's individual goals and objectives can be addressed within a developmentally appropriate program.

DEVELOPMENTALLY APPROPRIATE PRACTICE PRINCIPLES AS THE FOUNDATION IN PROGRAMS THAT ADDRESS INDIVIDUALIZED GOALS AND OBJECTIVES

Although IEPs or IFSPs serve as the guide for an instructional program, daily routine and curriculum provide the basis for the intervention delivered to young children with disabilities and their families. Recommended practices have been the subject of much discussion in recent years and have evolved from the theories of normal child development and special education, and from research conducted with children who are disabled and nondisabled (Bruder, in press). As discussed in Chapter 3, most leaders in the field of early childhood special education and general early childhood education agree that the developmentally appropriate practice (DAP) guidelines (Bredekamp, 1987) represent appropriate practices for all young children, including those with disabilities. They typically stress, however, that although curriculum models emphasizing DAP are indeed appropriate and necessary, they are usually insufficient for young children with disabilities unless individualized adaptations and teaching techniques are applied (Carta, 1994; Carta, Schwartz, Atwater, & McConnell, 1991; Wolery & Bredekamp, 1994).

The role of the teacher is essentially the same in classrooms that include young children with special needs and those that do not; however, an increased amount of planning and adapting may be necessary to ensure that individual outcomes are achieved. The parameters of a developmentally appropriate environment often require modification or expansion, depending on a particular child's needs. Teachers must ensure that needed adaptations are made so that children with disabilities are able to meet and exceed their desired outcomes. Classrooms are relevant and engaging only when they reflect the needs and interests of all children.

The routine, activities, and physical environment may require modification if young children with disabilities are to be successful. For example, for a child with cerebral palsy who uses a wheelchair to ambulate, modifications may be required in the arrangement of the room to allow enough space for the wheelchair. In addition, the types of materials selected will have to be easy for the child to hold and manipulate. Often a single adaptation can be made, such as adding a piece of Velcro to a baseball glove or using a paintbrush with an extra large handle. For some activities, extra time or assistance may be required. This is particularly true in physical activities that require motor skills the child has not developed. It is important to remember that children with disabilities must not be excluded from activities if development is to be fostered in all areas. Strategies must be utilized to enhance the child's ability to participate in the same developmentally appropriate activities as their nondisabled peers.

Another assumption of a developmentally appropriate environment is that "planned activities emphasize interaction with materials, peers, and adults" (Bredekamp, 1987). Some children are low responders because of physical, cognitive, or speech/language delays or disabilities. Prompting, modeling, motivating, or modifying must be developed to encourage interaction. In the case of a child who is nonverbal, an alternative communication system such as sign language may be required for interactions with peers and adults. For a child with a physical disability to interact with his or her environment, modifications may be required, such as the use of an adapted switch that activates an electronic communication board.

In a developmentally appropriate environment, an assumption is that "planned activities are driven by the children's interests and experiences" (Bredekamp, 1987). The interests and experiences of young children with disabilities may be somewhat different from those of their nondisabled peers. Therefore, teachers must be creative and build on the past experiences of each child.

EMBEDDING SKILLS INTO A TYPICAL EARLY CHILDHOOD ROUTINE AND CURRICULUM

An approach recommended by many professionals and becoming widely used in early intervention and education is an embedding or matrix approach (Noonan & McCormick, 1995). Bricker and Cripe refer to this approach as "Activity Based Instruction," which is a process characterized by supporting and engaging children's interests within the context of the following:

1. Routine, planned, or child-initiated activities
2. Embedded intervention goals (IFSP or IEP goals)
3. Logical antecedents and consequences
4. Generalizable and functional skills (Bricker & Cripe, 1992, p. 253).

This type of approach utilizes the many naturally occurring events and opportunities that exist in a young child's day to address individual goals and outcomes. The activities can occur within the natural routine (e.g., meal time, toileting, or center time), can be planned by the teacher or primary caregiver, or can be child initiated. By capitalizing on children's interests, preferences, and actions, emphasis is placed on children's initiations rather than on the teacher's choices.

Skill embedding requires that teachers review the schedule and identify the activities in which the IEP objectives can be embedded. Skills are embedded by crossing developmental domains in the same activity. For example, during a group art activity in which children paint a mural, objectives from several developmental domains, such as fine motor, cognitive, social, and communication skills, may be targeted. It is possible to work on the fine motor skill of using tools appropriately (e.g., a paintbrush or a sponge), the cognitive skill of discriminating colors, the social skill of taking turns with peers, and the communication skill of indicating wants and needs in a group situation.

In an activity-based approach, an emphasis is placed on antecedents (what precedes the behaviors) and consequences (what follows the behavior). Teachers must be careful observers of children's behavior and be aware of ways to arrange the environment to facilitate children's initiations, maximize adult responsiveness to child-initiated interactions, or arrange other aspects of the environment to reinforce child-initiated interactions. Finally, activity-based intervention encourages the acquisition of generalized and functional skills. This means that skills should be critical for engagement in daily activities and should contribute to the child's ability to affect the environment.

One way to ensure that each child's individualized goals and objectives are being embedded within daily activities and routines is to use the Individualized Curricula Sequencing Model (Guess & Horner, 1978; Mulligan & Guess, 1984). In this approach, skills to be taught to the child are listed in a matrix across the daily activities within the environment. Table 5.3 contains the steps involved in completing an activity-by-skill matrix. A matrix approach can be very helpful in the planning process because it utilizes the many naturally occurring and planned events and opportunities that exist in a young child's life as "intervention opportunities" (Noonan & McCormick, 1995). Table 5.4 provides a sample activity by skill matrix.

In using an approach in which individual goals and objectives are embedded across ongoing activities, teachers often must adapt the activities. There are typically two broad categories of activities in general early childhood programs: daily routines and curriculum (McCormick & Feeney, 1995). Both types of activities often need to be adapted or extended, based on the individual plans, to facilitate the attainment of desired outcomes for young children with disabilities. These processes are discussed in detail in the following chapter.

TABLE 5.3 Steps for Completing an Activity-by-Skill Matrix

1. List the events (activities, etc.) in which the child will participate during the day down the left-hand column of the matrix. The events should be listed in the order in which they occur daily.

2. List the location of each event below each listing in the left-hand column of the matrix. The listing should include the entire day. The purpose is to provide instruction in all relevant locations.

3. In the left-hand column of the matrix, list the time each activity will start and its expected duration each day.

4. Also in the left-hand column of the matrix, list the name of the adult who is responsible for implementing the instruction. If peers also are used, they should be listed here as well.

5. Across the top of the matrix list all of the skills that have been identified for instruction. Each column should include one behavior.

6. In the cells of the matrix, list the materials and specialized instructional strategies that will be used. If a skill is not addressed at a given event/time, the cell should be left blank.

7. Check the matrix to ensure that skills will be taught across adults, materials, and settings to facilitate generalization.

Adapted from "Application of the Individualized Curriculum Sequencing Model to Learners with Severe Sensory Impairments" by E. Helmsletter and D. Guess, 1987, in *Innovative Program Design for Individuals with Dual Sensory Impairments*, L. Goetz, D. Guess, and K. Stremel-Campbell (Eds.), Baltimore: Paul H. Brookes.

TABLE 5.4   Sample Activity-by-Skill Matrix Form

Child: Walt

Activity	Time/Person	Verbal Request	Naming Colors	Controlled Release	Keep Glasses on	Problem Solving	Wash Hands	Compliance
Arrival/Breakfast	8:45–9:15	X		X		X	X	
Transition/Circle (Carlton)	9:15–9:35	X	X		X			
Transition/Directed Play	9:35–10:00	X	X	X				
Transition/Small Group (Carlton)	10:00–10:25	X	X	X	X	X		X
Transition/Centers	10:25–10:55	X	X	X		X		
Transition/Outside	10:55–11:20	X						X
Toileting Self-Help	11:20–11:35	X					X	
Lunch	11:35–12:05	X		X		X	X	
Small Group	12:05–12:25	X	X	X	X	X		X
Transition/Group (Carlton)	12:25–12:45	X	X	X	X			
Transition/Circle (Carlton)	12:45–1:00	X						
Transition/Dismissal								

X = Opportunity to embed objective into activity.
Jennifer L. Kilgo, Ed.D., Debbie Woodward, M.Ed. Virginia Commonwealth University, 1995

MONITORING PROGRESS

According to IDEA, the IFSP must be formally reviewed at least every six months and the IEP must be reviewed at least annually. In practice, however, educators must monitor the progress of young children with disabilities continuously in order to make proper adjustments in the plans. After IEPs or IFSPs have been developed for each child, a schedule is developed for daily and weekly monitoring of the acquisition of objectives. The IEP and IFSP were designed to be dynamic rather than static documents; they can be modified on an ongoing basis as the children change and progress occurs.

Monitoring must occur in order to ascertain whether children are changing and desired progress is taking place. Wolery and Wilbers (1994) define monitoring as "the process of determining whether one or more children are developing and learning as expected, and if not, determining what should be changed to improve the likelihood that they will progress as desired" (p. 80). In other words, monitoring serves the dual purposes of determining whether goals and outcomes identified on the IEPs or IFSPs have been achieved and whether adjustments or adaptations are needed in the daily routine or curriculum in order for individual children to be successful. Ongoing observation of children's skills and behaviors provides teachers and other team members with an accurate appraisal of whether outcomes have been achieved and whether modifications are needed in future planning. In planning for monitoring, Wolery and Wilbers (1994) suggest that decisions should be made regarding who will monitor progress (e.g., teacher, parents, related service professionals, or baby-sitter), what methods will be used (e.g., observations, anecdotal reporting, videotaping, or portfolio), how often the information will be collected (e.g., daily, weekly, or biweekly), and the situations or contexts in which the monitoring will occur (e.g., classroom, playground, home, baby-sitter's home, or other community settings).

The IFSP and IEP should serve as a guide for the teacher or service coordinator and other team members, including family members, who implement the plans and monitor the progress of particular goals and outcomes. A team process in gathering and using data is strongly suggested in order to capture the overall progress of each child. A variety and combination of methods, including direct observation, anecdotal records, checklists, teacher and family judgment, product collection, and video- and audiotaping, are appropriate for monitoring the progress of young children.

The context in which progress monitoring should occur is the natural environment (e.g., classroom, playground, and lunchroom). Monitoring should be directly linked to programming; therefore teachers usually must collect information while they are carrying out their daily responsibilities of teaching.

The frequency of monitoring varies according to the goals and objectives of the children. Table 5.5 provides a format that can be used to plan the

TABLE 5.5 Format for Monitoring Goals and Objectives

Student's Name: ___Anna___   Month: ___September___

Goals and Objectives

	Communication		Cognitive		Gross Motor		Fine Motor		Self-Care		Social-Emotional	
	multi-step direction	4–5 word phrases	sort objects	name ident.	riding toys	ball skills	writing strokes	object into squares	fastening	toileting	transitioning	turn-taking
8:00–8:25 Arrival									O		O	
Bathroom	O									O		
8:25–8:40 Social Time		V		V								V
8:40–9:00 Breakfast		O		O								O
9:00–9:15 Circle	V	V		V								V
9:15–10:15 Centers		T	V	T			P	V				V
Art	P	P		P			P					
Manipulatives			O					O				

TABLE 5.5 *Continued*

Student's Name: _____ Anna _____   Month: _____ September _____

Goals and Objectives

	Communication	Cognitive	Gross Motor		Fine Motor		Self-Care		Social-Emotional			
	multi-step direction	4–5 word phrases	scrt objects	name ident.	riding toys	ball skills	writing strokes	object into squares	fastening	toileting	transitioning	turn-taking
10:15–10:30 Clean Up	O		O					O				
10:30–10:40 Bathroom	O									O		
10:40–11:10 Movement					O	O						
11:10–11:30 Story		T		T								
11:30 Snack	O	O		O								O
11:45 Cleanup/ Bathroom	O									O		
12:00 Departure									O			

O = observation   P = products   V = video   T = tape recording methods for monitoring progress toward objectives. The progress children make toward the attainment of individual goals and objectives determines the modifications that should be made.

ADDRESSING INDIVIDUAL NEEDS: BRAD'S GOALS AND OBJECTIVES

Review the case study of Brad, who is described in Chapter 1. Brad's skills and his parents' priorities for the most important skills to target resulted in the development of the IEP contained in Figure 5.1.

After the IEP goals and corresponding objectives have been developed, they must be embedded into ongoing activities across the day. Table 5.6 shows the way in which Brad's objectives have been embedded in the activities of his daily routine. Progress must be monitored throughout the day for each of these objectives. A sample form for monitoring the individual objectives across the daily routine is contained in Table 5.7.

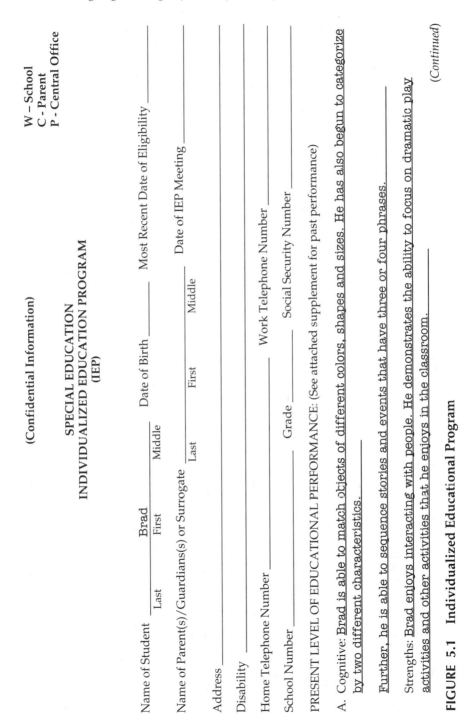

(Confidential Information)

W – School
C - Parent
P - Central Office

SPECIAL EDUCATION
INDIVIDUALIZED EDUCATION PROGRAM
(IEP)

Name of Student _____ Brad _____ Date of Birth _____ Most Recent Date of Eligibility _____
Last   First   Middle

Name of Parent(s)/Guardians(s) or Surrogate _____ Date of IEP Meeting _____
Last   First   Middle

Address _____

Disability _____

Home Telephone Number _____ Work Telephone Number _____

School Number _____ Grade _____ Social Security Number _____

PRESENT LEVEL OF EDUCATIONAL PERFORMANCE: (See attached supplement for past performance)

A. Cognitive: Brad is able to match objects of different colors, shapes and sizes. He has also begun to categorize by two different characteristics.

Further, he is able to sequence stories and events that have three or four phrases.

Strengths: Brad enjoys interacting with people. He demonstrates the ability to focus on dramatic play activities and other activities that he enjoys in the classroom.

(Continued)

FIGURE 5.1 Individualized Educational Program

(Confidential)

Name of Student _____ Brad _____   Date of Birth _____

PRESENT LEVEL OF EDUCATIONAL PERFORMANCE (*continued*):

B. Communication Skills: Brad uses some simple signs to express his desire to eat or drink. He typically points to things that he wants or pushes an adult toward what he wants to communicate. He has a vocabulary of approximately fifty words that he typically does not use.

C. Behavior: Brad has difficulty when transitioning from free-play to group settings. He will tantrum or hit at times when transitions occur.

D. Social: Brad enjoys being in groups with other children. At times he has difficulty interacting appropriately with peers and may hit others when he gets excited.

E. Motor: Brad is able to walk independently but has trouble walking long distances (he tires easily) and on uneven surfaces. His overall low muscle tone also affects his ability to manipulate small objects with his hands.

F. Self-care: Brad is able to use a fork/spoon for a short period of time to feed himself. He is not yet toilet trained and prefers having his parents put on his clothes and coat because dressing tasks are difficult for him.

FIGURE 5.1   Individualized Educational Program (*continued*)

Name of Student ___Brad___   Date of Birth ___

LEAST RESTRICTIVE ENVIRONMENT JUSTIFICATION FORM

Check the following items YES or NO. A written explanation for negative responses for items 1 through 9 must be provided.

	YES	NO
1. The school the student would normally attend, if not handicapped, is the recommended placement or is the placement.	X	
2. The child is educated in the regular class with the use of supplementary aids and services.	X	
3. The quality and intensity of services which the handicapped student requires will be provided by IEP.	X	
4. The placement is appropriate taking into account the potential harmful effects to the handicapped student.	X	
5. The child is educated with age-appropriate peers.	X	
6. The students are being educated with peers with the same handicapping condition.		X
7. The amount of travel time and distance to and from school is appropriate.	X	
8. The student will receive 5½ hours instructional time per day.		X
9. The child is educated with non-handicapped peers.	X	
10. The placement in a more restrictive environment is based on the individualized needs of the student.	NA	
11. Given the consideration to items 1–9, the following placement is appropriate:		
a. Direct instruction and/or consultative services within the regular class.	X	
b. Regular class with instruction in the resource room.		
c. Self-contained class with full-time academic instruction in regular public school facility; non-academic instruction with peers.		
d. Self-contained class with full-time academic and non-academic instruction in regular public school facility.		
e. Separate day school.		
f. Public and/or private residential facility.		
g. Private day school for the handicapped.		
h. Homebound.		
i. Hospital.		
j. Homebound instruction for pre-school age handicapped children.		

FIGURE 5.1   Individualized Educational Program (*continued*)

Name of Student: _____ Brad _____ Date of Birth _____ Page _____

Area of Instruction: _____ Communication _____

Annual Goal: _____ Brad will be able to communicate his thoughts, wants and needs to peers and adults.

SHORT TERM OBJECTIVES	PROJECT INITIATED	DATES COMPLETED	PROGRESS NOTES
Objective # __1__ : Brad will consistently use one word when making requests for objects / activities during the daily routine. (See strategies #3 and #5) Evaluation Criterion: 3 one word requests in a 30 minute observation (could be over 1 or more activities) Frequency: 2, 30 minute observations per month Procedure: Language sample/teacher observation/speech-language pathologist (SLP) observation			
Objective # __2__ : Brad will make one word comments about activities to peers and adults. (See strategy #3). Evaluation Criterion: 1 one word comment in a 30 minute observation Frequency: 2, 30 minute observations per month Procedure: Language sample/teacher observation & SLP			
Objective # __3__ : Brad will ask a peer to play with him by using a one word request ("Play"). Evaluation Criterion: 1 play request during free-play time per observation Frequency: 2, 30 minute observations per month Procedure: Language sample/teacher observation & SLP			

Evaluation Schedule: Annual goals will be evaluated during the annual review.
Short term objectives will be monitored each six week marking period.
No mark—objective not initiated. P—progressing on the objective.

FIGURE 5.1 Individualized Educational Program (*continued*)

Name of Student: _____Brad_____ Date of Birth _____ Page _____

Area of Instruction: _____Communication_____

Annual Goal: _____Brad will respond appropriately to other's communications with him._____

SHORT TERM OBJECTIVES	PROJECT INITIATED	DATES COMPLETED	PROGRESS NOTES

Objective # __1__ :
Brad will consistently follow a 1 step direction during the daily routine.
 	
Evaluation
  Criterion: Following 3 one step directions during an observation
  Frequency: 2, 30 minute observations per month
  Procedure: Language sample/teacher observation & SLP			

Objective # __2__ :
Brad will respond to a peer's request to play with him by saying "yes/no" or shaking his head yes/no.
 	
Evaluation
  Criterion: Responding approximately one time during observation
  Frequency: 2, 30 minute observations per month
  Procedure: Language sample/teacher observation & SLP			

Objective # __3__ :
Brad will consistently express protest by saying the word "No."
 	
Evaluation
  Criterion: Saying "No" in protest one time during observation
  Frequency: Two, 30 minute observations per month
  Procedure: Language sample/teacher observation & SLP			

Evaluation Schedule: Annual goals will be evaluated during the annual review. Short term objectives will be monitored each six week marking period. No mark—objective not initiated. P—progressing on the objective.

FIGURE 5.1 Individualized Educational Program (*continued*)

Name of Student: _____ Brad _____   Date of Birth _____   Page _____

Area of Instruction: _____ Motor _____

Annual Goal: _____ Brad will increase his endurance when using his small and large muscle groups. _____

SHORT TERM OBJECTIVES	PROJECT INITIATED	DATES COMPLETED	PROGRESS NOTES
Objective # __1__ : Brad will play with classroom manipulatives (i.e., large Legos) beginning for 2 minutes and increasing to 5 minutes (see strategy #2). Evaluation Criterion: Playing for 4 minutes during observations Frequency: Two observations per month (15 minutes each) Procedure: Teacher observation/occupational therapist (OT) observation			
Objective # __2__ : Brad will walk to and from the playground sitting down no more than one time each way (see strategy #8). Evaluation Criterion: Sitting down no more than one time during observation Frequency: Two 15 minute observations per month Procedure: Teacher/physical therapist (PT) observation			

Evaluation Schedule: Annual goals will be evaluated during the annual review. Short term objectives will be monitored each six week marking period. No mark—objective not initiated. P—progressing on the objective.

FIGURE 5.1 Individualized Educational Program (*continued*)

Name of Student: ___Brad___ Date of Birth: _____ Page _____

Area of Instruction: ___Social/Behavior___

Annual Goal: ___Brad will relate to others in socially appropriate ways.___

SHORT TERM OBJECTIVES	PROJECT INITIATED	DATES COMPLETED	PROGRESS NOTES
Objective # __1__ : Brad will make a smooth transistion (no hitting or tantrumming) from freeplay to group settings (see strategy #1) Evaluation Criterion: No instances of hitting during observation of transitions Frequency: Five observations of transitions per month Procedure: Teacher observation/data collection			
Objective # __2__ : Brad will express his excitement during play or other activities in socially appropriate ways (i.e. clapping hands together, saying "yeah"). Evaluation Criterion: No instances of hitting during observation Frequency: Two, 30 minute observations per month Procedure: Teacher observation/data collection			
Objective # __3__ : Brad will share a toy with a peer during play when asked by peer. Evaluation Criterion: 50% of opportunities to share during observation Frequency: Two, 30 minute observations per month Procedure: Teacher observation collection			

Evaluation Schedule: Annual goals will be evaluated during the annual review. Short term objectives will be monitored each six week marking period. No mark—objective not initiated. P—progressing on the objective.

FIGURE 5.1 Individualized Educational Program (*continued*)

Name of Student: ____Brad____ Date of Birth ____ Page ____

Area of Instruction: ____Self-help____

Annual Goal: ____Brad consistently will pull his pants up and down and remove his own diaper when toileting.____

SHORT TERM OBJECTIVES	PROJECT INITIATED	DATES COMPLETED	PROGRESS NOTES
Objective # __1__ : Brad will consistently pull his pants up and down and remove his own diaper when toileting. Evaluation Criterion: Pulling pants up and down during observation Frequency: Five observations of toileting routine per month Procedure: Teacher observation/data collection			
Objective # __2__ : Brad will sit on the toilet for 2 minutes beginning one time per day moving to 3 times per day within 6 months time. Evaluation Criterion: Sitting on toilet for 2–3 minutes Frequency: Five observations of toileting routine per month Procedure: Teacher observation/data collection			

Evaluation Schedule: Annual goals will be evaluated during the annual review.
Short term objectives will be monitored each six week marking period.
No mark—objective not initiated. P—progressing on the objective.

FIGURE 5.1 Individualized Educational Program (*continued*)

Name of Student: ___Brad___   Date of Birth _____   Page _____

Area of Instruction: ___Self-help___

Annual Goal: ___Brad will become more independent when eating.___

SHORT TERM OBJECTIVES	PROJECT INITIATED	DATES COMPLETED	PROGRESS NOTES
Objective # __1__ : Brad will use a utensil with the appropriate foods during lunch. Evaluation Criterion: Using utensil 100% with appropriate foods Frequency: Three lunch time observations of 30 minutes each Procedure: Teacher observation/data collection			
Objective # __2__ : Brad will serve himself a portion of food during lunch with a large spoon. Evaluation Criterion: Serving self one time during lunch Frequency: Three lunch time observations of 30 minutes each Procedure: Teacher observation/data collection			
Objective # __3__ : Brad will have no more than one spill of his cup during lunch time. Evaluation Criterion: No more than one spill during lunch time Frequency: Three lunch time observations for 30 minutes each Procedure: Teacher observation/data collection			

Evaluation Schedule: Annual goals will be evaluated during the annual review.
Short term objectives will be monitored each six week marking period.
No mark—objective not initiated. P—progressing on the objective.

FIGURE 5.1   Individualized Educational Program (*continued*)

Name of Student: _____ Brad _____ Date of Birth _____ Page _____

Area of Instruction: _____ Self-care _____

Annual Goal: _____ Brad will become more independent when dressing. _____

SHORT TERM OBJECTIVES	PROJECT INITIATED	DATES COMPLETED	PROGRESS NOTES
Objective # __1__ : Brad will put on his coat/jacket by himself. Evaluation Criterion: Putting on coat one time during observation Frequency: Three observations per coat wearing months, within daily routine Procedure: Teacher observation/data collection			
Objective # __2__ : Brad will button large buttons on his clothing independently. Evaluation Criterion: Buttoning large button one time during observation Frequency: Three observations per month of this activity within routine Procedure: Teacher observation/data collection			
Objective # __3__ : Brad will zip large zippers on his clothing independently. Evaluation Criterion: Zipping large zipper one time during observation Frequency: Three observations per month of this activity within routine Procedure: Teacher observation/data collection			

Evaluation Schedule: Annual goals will be evaluated during the annual review.
Short term objectives will be monitored each six week marking period.
No mark—objective not initiated. P—progressing on the objective.

FIGURE 5.1 Individualized Educational Program (*continued*)

Signature of Participants	Relationship to Student	Date
_____	_____	_____
_____	_____	_____
_____	_____	_____
_____	_____	_____

I give permission for my child, _____, to be enrolled in the special education program described in this Individualized Education Program. I understand the contents of this document, and I have been informed of my due process rights. I understand that I have the right to review my child's records and to request a change in the IEP at any time. I also understand that I have the right to refuse this placement and to have my child continue in his/her present placement pending further action.

Month Day Year	Signature of Parent(s) / Guardian(s) or Surrogate

I do not give permission for my child, _____, to be enrolled in the special education program described in the Individualized Education Program. I understand that I have the right to review his/her records, and to request another placement. I understand that the action described above will not take place without my permission or until due process procedures have been exhausted. I understand that if my decision is appealed, I will be notified of my due process rights in this procedure.

Month Day Year	Signature of Parent(s) / Guardian(s) or Surrogate

Parent Contact Log:

Date	Name of Person Contacted	Type of Contact	Comments

(Confidential)

FIGURE 5.1   Individualized Educational Program (*continued*)

Name of Student: ___Brad___   Date of Birth _____

LEAST RESTRICTIVE ENVIRONMENT (Type and Intensity of Services)

Special Education and Related Services	Frequency and Duration (per week)	Date to Begin	Anticipated Completion Date	Environment Location/Provider
Early Childhood Special Ed.	4 hr/wk	_____	_____	Child Care Classroom Center/ECSE
Collaborative— Team Mtg.	1 hr/wk	_____	_____	Child Care Classroom Center/ECSE
OT	1 hr/wk/30 min. each	_____	_____	Child Care Center Classroom/OT
PT	1 hr/wk/30 min. each	_____	_____	Child Care Center Classroom/PT
Speech-Language Therapy	2 hr/wk/30 min. each	_____	_____	Child Care Center Classroom/SLP

Extent of Participation with Non-handicapped Students

ACTIVITIES   **AMOUNT OF TIME PER WEEK**

Academic   ___In a fully inclusive setting at Child Care Center.___   ___100%___   and

Non-Academic   ___All interventions will be integrated into Brad's daily activities.___

Transportation   ___N/A___

Vocational Educational Program:

a. _____ applicable at this level   b. __X__ not applicable at this level
          (see goals and objectives attached)

Name of course in which student will be enrolled _____

This class is:

a. _____ regular vocational offering
b. _____ special vocational offering for handicapped students only.

FIGURE 5.1   Individualized Educational Program (*continued*)

SUGGESTED STRATEGIES FOR THE CLASSROOM

1—When transitioning from one activity to the other have a set song or signal to let all the children know that a transition will occur. Also, give a five minute warning prior to transition for all children. Another suggested strategy to try with Brad to make transitions more smooth is to have a peer encourage Brad or hold Brad's hand when coming to the group.

2—Keep two or three of the manipulatives in the manipulative area consistent instead of changing them all every month–six weeks. This will help Brad to continue to feel successful in this area if there are two or three manipulatives that he can master and then move on to others.

3—Discuss the possibility of adding a bit of structure for Brad (or the whole class) during the free-play time (e.g., changing areas every 20 minutes, having a set number of people to play in a center at one time). Within these structured settings Brad will be able to establish a script he can consistently use in the area. The added structure and established certainty of the situation may also help to reduce some of Brad's challenging behaviors.

4—Have children choose where they will play during free choice by either naming the area or pointing to a picture.

5—Expect verbal language from Brad when he points or pushes an adult toward what he wants. Since verbal language is the goal (but is not frequently used) try pairing a gesture or sign with a one word phrase when making a request.

6—Have Brad use a cup with a lid (not a spout, but one with an inverted hole so the lip of the cup remains the same because working on lip closure is important) and then move to a cup without a lid.

7—It sounds like social relationships are important to Brad and fostering those in the classroom may help to decrease some challenging behaviors. Try seating him next to peers and having an adult behind him sometimes to assist when necessary. Also, structuring some activities or simple games that require two or more children may help. Trying to guide Brad when someone else needs help and encouraging him to help the other child will foster a sense of responsibility.

8—Have a peer walk with Brad to and from the playground either walking beside him or holding his hand to help encourage him and build up his endurance/balance.

9—Discuss the use of pairing signs and words with the parents as a means of facilitating spoken language. If they agree to it as a strategy begin using it in the classroom. If they would like to do it at home a repertoire of signs/words could be established and used in both environments.

FIGURE 5.1 **Individualized Educational Program** (*continued*)

TABLE 5.6   Sample Activity-by-Skill Matrix for Brad's Objectives

Student's Name: ___Brad___   Month: ___September___

Objectives: Activity Time:	Dress Self	Feed Self	Toileting	Verbally Communic.	Play Approp.	Change Activities	Problem Solving
8:30–9:00 Arrival/Breakfast	X	X	X	X		X	X
9:00–9:30 Social Group				X		X	
9:30–10:30 Centers				X	X	X	X
10:30–10:45 Snack		X		X		X	
10:45–11:20 Outside	X				X	X	X
11:20–11:30 Toileting/Handwashing			X			X	
11:30–12:10 Lunch		X		X		X	
12:10–1:30 Rest						X	
1:30–3:00 Centers/FreePlay				X	X	X	X
3:00–3:30 Closing Circle/Prepare for Home/Toileting	X		X	X		X	X

X = Opportunity to embed objective into activity.

TABLE 5.7   Planning Matrix with Brad's Objectives and Corresponding Data Collection

Student's Name: Brad   Month: September

Objectives: Activity Time	Dress Self	Feed Self	Toileting	Verbally Communic.	Play Approp.	Change Activities	Problem Solving
8:30–9:00 Arrival/Breakfast	O	O	O	V		O	O
9:00–9:30 Social Group				V		O	
9:30–10:30 Centers				V	V	O	P
10:30–10:45 Snack		O		V		O	
10:45–11:20 Outside	O				O	O	O
11:20–11:30 Toileting/Handwashing			O			O	
11:30–12:10 Lunch		O		V		O	
12:10–1:30 Rest						O	
1:30–3:00 Centers/Free Play				V	V	O	O
3:00–3:30 Closing Circle/Prepare for Home/Toileting	O		O	V		O	O

O = Direct observation   P = Product   V = Video tape   A = Audio tape

SUMMARY

The intent of this chapter was to show how IEPs and IFSPs serve as planning guides for young children with disabilities within developmentally appropriate programs. The components of the IFSP and IEP were described, and comparisons were made of the two documents. Guidelines were offered for developing appropriate goals and outcomes, embedding children's individual goals and outcomes into natural routines and activities, and monitoring progress toward the attainment of the goals and outcomes. Finally, a sample IEP was included, as well as sample formats for embedding goals and objectives and monitoring progress.

ACTIVITIES AND RESOURCES

Case Study Activities

After reviewing the case study of Brad in Chapter 1, please answer the following application questions:

1. Is the IEP in compliance with IDEA? (Are all required components included? Were timelines met? Were all appropriate people included in the development of the document?)
2. Are the goals and objectives developmentally appropriate based on what you know about Brad from the case? Are the goals and objectives functional?
3. How does the IEP reflect family-centered practices?
4. What changes would you make in the content of the document? Why?
5. Would you make any improvements to the organization (layout and format) of the IEP? What changes? Why?
6. Select one of the Brad's long-range IEP goals and corresponding short-term objectives. Determine how Brad's progress toward these objectives will be monitored.
7. Describe a developmentally appropriate activity that allows for at least two of Brad's goals to be addressed.
8. For each of Brad's goals, indicate the daily routines or activities in which they can be addressed.

Activities

1. Interview the parent of a young child with a disability who has an IFSP or IEP. Ask the parent to explain how he or she was involved in the development of the plan and ways in which professionals can help to make it easier for families to actively participate in the IEP/IFSP process.
2. Develop three objectives to correspond to the following goal: "Grasp a raisin-sized object." Identify how progress can be monitored for one of the objectives.
3. Design three activities that provide an opportunity to embed one of the objectives developed in activity #2.

Class Discussion Questions

1. Compare and contrast the IFSP and the IEP. Explain the benefits of having the IEP process become more similar to the IFSP process.
2. Describe what constitutes a high-quality IFSP or IEP goal and objective for young children with disabilities.
3. Provide a rationale for developmentally appropriate practices' providing the foundation in programs in which individualized goals and objectives are addressed.
4. Describe the approach teachers must use to embed children's goals and objectives into an early childhood routine.
5. Explain the various ways in which objectives can be monitored in ongoing early childhood routines.
6. What is the advantage of using multiple sources of data to determine children's progress?

Resources

Activity-based intervention. Bricker, D., Veltman, P. & Munkres, A. (1995). Baltimore, MD: Brookes Publishing Company.
   This 14-minute video presents strategies to foster learning within natural contexts. The strategies include tips on promoting functional skill development; facilitating routine, planned, and child-initiated activities; and fostering learning through natural consequences and reinforcers.

REFERENCES

Bennett, T., Lingerfelt, B.V., & Nelson, D.E. (1990). *Developing individualized family support plans.* Cambridge, MA: Brookline.

Bredekamp, S. (Ed.). (1987). *Developmentally appropriate practice in early childhood programs serving children from birth to age 8 (exp. ed.).* Washington, DC: NAEYC.

Bricker, D., & Cripe, J. (1992). *An activity-based approach to early intervention.* Baltimore: Paul H. Brooks.

Bruder, M.B. (in press). Early childhood intervention. In J. Wood & A Lazzari (Eds.), *Exceeding boundaries: Understanding exceptional lives.* Ft. Worth, TX: Harcourt-Brace Publishing.

Carta, J.J. (1994). Developmentally appropriate practices: Shifting the emphasis to individual appropriateness. *Journal of Early Intervention, 18*(4), 342–343.

Carta, J., Schwartz, I., Atwater, J., & McConnell, S. (1991). Developmentally appropriate practice: Appraising its usefulness for young children with disabilities. *Topics in Early Childhood Special Education, 11*(1), 1–20.

Guess, D., & Horner, R.D. (1978). The severely and profoundly handicapped. In E.L. Meyer (Ed.), *Exceptional children and youth—An introduction* (pp. 218–268). Denver, CO: Love Publishing.

Helmsletter, E., & Guess, D. (1987). Application of the individualized curriculum sequencing model to learners with severe sensory impairments. In L. Goetz, D.,

Guess, D., Stremel-Campbell, K. (Eds.), *Innovative program design for individuals with dual sensory impairments*. Baltimore: Paul H. Brookes.

McCormick, L., & Feeney, S. (1995). Modifying and expanding activities for children with disabilities. *Young Children, 50*(4), 10–17.

McCormick, L., & Feeney, S. (1995). *Teaching Exceptional Children*.

McGonigel, M., Kaufmann, R., & Johnson, B. (Eds.). (1991). *Guidelines and recommended practices for the individualized family service plans* (2nd ed.). Bethesda, MD: Association for the Care of Children's Health.

Mulligan, M., & Guess, D. (1984). Using an individualized curriculum sequence model. In L. McCormick & R.L. Shiefelbusch (Eds.), *Early language intervention* (pp. 300–323). Columbus, OH: Merrill Publishing Co.

Noonan, M.J., & McCormick, L. (1993). *Early intervention in natural environments: Methods and procedures*. Pacific Grove, CA: Brookes-Cole Publishing Co.

Noonan, M.J., & McCormick, L. (1995). "Mission impossible"? Developing meaningful IEPs for children in inclusive preschool settings. *The Frontline, 2*(1), Baltimore: Brooks-Cole Publishing Co., 1–3.

Notari-Syverson, A., & Schuster, S. (1995). Putting real-life skills into IEP/IFSPs for infants and young children. *Teaching Exceptional Children , 27*(2), 29–32.

Wolery, M., & Bredekamp, S. (1994). Developmentally appropriate practices and young children with disabilities: Contextual issues in the discussion. *Journal of Early Intervention, 26*(4), 45–48.

Wolery, M., & Wilbers, J. (Eds.). (1994). *Including children with special needs in early childhood programs*. Washington, DC: NAEYC.

6

USING PRINCIPLES OF DEVELOPMENTALLY APPROPRIATE PRACTICE TO MAKE DECISIONS ABOUT THE LEARNING ENVIRONMENT

OBJECTIVES

After studying this chapter, readers should be able to perform the following:

- Explain how developmentally appropriate practices can serve as the basis for planning learning environments for all young children.
- Discuss the teacher's role in a developmentally appropriate learning environment.
- Determine appropriate intervention strategies and practices to meet the individual needs of children with disabilities within developmentally appropriate learning environments.
- Design physical environments that address the needs of all young children and be able to make the necessary environmental modifications for children with disabilities.
- Develop a daily schedule that addresses all curriculum areas and maximizes instructional time.

The purpose of this chapter is to describe how the developmentally appropriate practice (DAP) guidelines (Bredekamp, 1987) can provide the foundation for making decisions about optimal early education environments for all young children. The focus is on two critical classroom components: the physical environment and the social/programmatic environment. Space, furniture, equipment, and materials are elements of the physical environment. The scheduling of time and resources, the roles and responsibilities of the teacher, and the types of intervention strategies and practices that can be used are social/programmatic variables (McEvoy, Fox, & Rosenberg, 1991).

THE TEACHER'S ROLES AND RESPONSIBILITIES IN MAKING DECISIONS ABOUT THE LEARNING ENVIRONMENT

As defined by Hanson and Lynch (1995), a curriculum is "an organized set of activities and experiences designed to achieve particular mental or learning objectives" (p. 185). Vincent (1988) described the curriculum as a "road map" or tool that helps teachers know where they are going and how to get there. Curriculum and recommended practices for young children with disabilities have been the subject of much discussion in recent years and have evolved from theories of child development, early childhood education, special education, related services, and research conducted with children experiencing typical and atypical development. As discussed in Chapter 2, most leaders in the fields of early childhood special education and general early childhood education agree that the DAP guidelines (Bredekamp, 1987) should be addressed in the early education of all young children, including those with disabilities. They are quick to point out, however, that while curriculum models emphasizing DAP are indeed appropriate and necessary, they are usually insufficient unless individualized adaptations are made and instructional techniques are adopted to meet the needs of young children with disabilities (Carta, 1994; Carta, Schwartz, Atwater, & McConnell, 1991; Wolery & Bredekamp, 1994; Wolery, Strain, & Bailey, 1992). Recommended practice in early childhood special education requires that teachers build on the DAP guidelines and move beyond them when necessary for young children with disabilities.

As presented in Chapter 2, a developmentally appropriate curriculum is one that is appropriate to the age span of the children in the program, as well as appropriate to their individual needs, abilities, learning styles, and interests. Table 6.1 contains a list of the basic assumptions of a developmentally appropriate classroom. These assumptions and their application to young children with disabilities have significant implications for the roles and responsibilities of teachers in planning for the social and programmatic aspects of the environment.

First, it is important to consider carefully these assumptions and their applicability to young children with disabilities. One assumption of a developmentally appropriate classroom, for example, is that planned activities are driven by the children's interests and experiences. This assumption is based on the belief that successful learning depends on the provision of meaningful

TABLE 6.1   Assumptions of a Developmentally Appropriate Learning Environment

- Planned activities are driven by the children's interests and experiences.
- Planned activities address all areas of the children's development.
- Planned activities emphasize interaction with peers, adults, and the physical environment.
- Planned activities are concrete, real, and relevant to children's lives.
- A finite set of activities are planned and adapted to address the wide range of abilities of the children.
- Planned activities incorporate meaningful educational goals.
- There is a balance of individual, small group, and large group activities.
- Adults act as facilitators who can adapt, change, and expand activities to meet the individual needs and learning styles of the children.
- Planned activities foster self-control and independence in all children.

These assumptions have been adapted from Bredekamp, S. (1987). *Developmentally appropriate practice in early childhood from birth to age 8 (exp. ed.).* Washington, DC: NAEYC and Bredekamp, S., & Rosegrant, T. (1992). *Reaching potentials: Appropriate curriculum and assessment for young children.* Washington, DC: NAEYC. Copyright 1987 by NAEYC. All rights reserved.

curriculum that helps children make sense of what they are learning. The experiences that are meaningful to a young child with a disability may be somewhat different from those of his nondisabled peers. Children who are blind may have had very different experiences, particularly in terms of the information they have received visually, than their nondisabled peers or even their disabled peers who do not have visual limitations. Teachers must be creative when it comes to learning more about children's individual experiences and interests. Often the teacher may have to probe to learn more about the interests of children who are shy, withdrawn, nonverbal, or have physical, sensory or cognitive limitations.

Another assumption of a developmentally appropriate classroom is that adults adapt, change, and expand activities to address the wide range of needs in the classroom. This is often true to a greater degree when they are working with young children with disabilities. The physical environment, daily schedule or routine, and activities may require modification in order for young children with disabilities to be successful (Carta et al., 1991). Developmentally appropriate classrooms reflect the importance of interactions with peers, adults, and the physical environment. For a child who has a disability that results in his making infrequent initiations or responses, strategies such as prompting or modeling can be used to encourage interactions. For a child who is nonverbal, for example, an alternative communication system (e.g., sign language, communication board, or gesturing) may be required to facilitate interactions with peers and adults. Teachers must ensure that all children participate with peers as well as with adults on an ongoing basis.

Initially it is important for teachers to consider the roles they will assume in a developmentally appropriate classroom. When children with special needs are included, the roles of the teacher are basically the same; however, the amount of planning and adapting may be increased to address the learning styles of the young children with disabilities and to ensure that their individual objectives are met. Some of the typical teacher roles within developmentally appropriate classrooms include the following:

1. Planning: Teachers plan appropriate learning activities designed to address the overall needs of the children. Planning must be completed before the children arrive each day.

2. Environmental arrangement: Teachers prepare and arrange materials and activities in learning centers and make appropriate adaptations for young children with disabilities.

3. Engagement: Teachers engage in activities with children and serve as assistants to children who need enhanced or extended learning experiences.

4. Facilitation: Teachers facilitate children's self-directed learning by modeling, coaching, questioning, and/or providing additional material and information.

5. Interaction: Teachers interact with children while they are working independently or in small or large groups. Teachers must be aware of ways to arrange the environment to increase social interactions, facilitate child initiations and maximize adult responsiveness within social and nonsocial environments.

6. Support: Teachers recognize, encourage, and support children's individualized development and learning across all areas of the curriculum.

7. Monitoring progress: Teachers observe and evaluate children's learning. In using an approach in which individual goals and objectives are embedded across ongoing activities, teachers must be careful observers of behavior. They should be aware of when it is necessary to adapt or extend practices to accommodate and individualize them for young children with disabilities.

8. Communication/Collaboration: Teachers must communicate and collaborate with families and other professionals to support learning, particularly when addressing the IEP/IFSP goals and objectives of young children with disabilities.

INSTRUCTIONAL STRATEGIES AND MODIFICATIONS

As described previously, a variety of activities and routines take place each day in most preschool or primary learning environments. The activities may include work in learning centers, dramatic play, music activities, art activities, science discovery, exploration of various materials, and a variety of others. The routines are regularly occurring events that often involve caring for basic needs such as snack, lunch, grooming, toileting, napping, and dressing (Wolery, 1996). McCormick and Feeney (1995) report that all activities have three basic elements in common. The first element to consider is the desired outcome. McCormick and Feeney suggest asking the following question: "Is the desired outcome at the appropriate level of difficulty for the child?" If not, modifications should be made.

The second element is the special arrangements that may be necessary to help children attain the desired outcome. If modifications are needed, the questions to be addressed, as emphasized by McCormick and Feeney, include the following: (1) Does the child need more or less time for the activity? (2) Does the child need an additional or different type or amount of space? (3) Does the child need additional or different materials? (4) Does the child need additional or different directions or instructions? (5) Does the child need special instructional assistance? and (6) Does the child need special positioning or equipment?

The third element is the assessment or monitoring of progress. Mc-Cormick and Feeney refer to the moment-to-moment decision making that is often required of teachers. This is particularly important in addressing the needs of young children with disabilities because ongoing, frequent adjustments are often necessary.

The following example demonstrates how these three elements can be applied. For a child with cerebral palsy who is participating in snack time with the goal of eating his food and drinking his juice independently, the outcome of the activity is the same as it is for other children in the class. Not only does the snack time provide opportunities to practice eating finger foods and drinking from a cup, but the child must also use conversational skills with peers, develop motor skills during snack preparation, and indicate wants and needs. To address the goal of eating his food and drinking his juice independently, however, this child needs more time to eat, more space for his adaptive chair, a sticky mat to stabilize the food, a cup with a wide base to avoid spillage, and physical assistance with more difficult food items. Careful observation will indicate to the teacher when the assistance can be faded or gradually reduced.

A wide range of instructional strategies and practices can be used to address the goals and objectives of young children with disabilities in a developmentally appropriate environment. The key to utilizing these procedures in naturalistic teaching situations lies in tailoring the classroom environment to the unique needs, abilities, and learning style of each child.

PHYSICAL ENVIRONMENT CONSIDERATIONS

We all recognize that learning environments for young children must be safe, clean, attractive, and comfortable. However, they should also be engaging, flexible, stimulating, challenging, and enjoyable. The challenge to teachers is to provide for both the age-appropriate and individually appropriate needs of children and to do so in a way that allows for a great deal of child-centered learning. The following are guidelines that must be addressed when planning the learning environment.

1. *Address the Whole Child.* When designing a developmentally appropriate environment, the educator must consider the interrelated nature of each child's social, emotional, physical, and intellectual development. It is particularly important that each of the developmental areas be given equal emphasis within the environment. When one area of development is emphasized at the expense of other areas, the overall needs of children often are not being addressed adequately. Teachers must realize that children rarely focus

on one skill at a time; thus an environment for young children should be planned in a way that allows for the integration of the major developmental areas. Many areas of the classroom and activities within those areas can be designed to support the development of two or more domains. For example, a group water play activity in which containers of various sizes and weights are used can facilitate the development of social, physical, and intellectual skills. The social growth comes through sharing and taking various roles, and physical growth is enhanced through activities such as using sponges, which facilitate eye-hand coordination. Intellectual skills might include counting, conservation of liquid, or the concepts of sinking and floating.

2. *Foster Independence.* One of the primary objectives of the environmental arrangement should be to foster independence. There is a tendency to do more for children with disabilities than is often necessary or beneficial. This concept has been described as *learned helplessness*. In other words, children learn to be helpless or dependent when they are not encouraged to do as much for themselves as possible. One way to foster independence is through subtle guidance. Visual cues can be added to the environment to encourage independence. For example, pictures can be used in an activity to indicate what is to be done, in what order, and what to do when the activity is completed. Another example is to set up the materials for an activity in the order in which they are to be used (e.g., top to bottom, left to right). Other ways in which students can be guided are through the use of such techniques as color coding, letter coding, or providing outlines of shapes. Appropriate strategies can provide children with opportunities to complete activities independently but with some structure to guide them. Thus all children can experience the sense of accomplishment that can come from the successful completion of tasks.

3. *Provide Access to Learning.* Learning environments must be accessible to children with disabilities. Accommodations such as ramps, widened doors, bathroom modifications, and water fountain adaptations may be necessary so that all children can participate fully in learning activities.

For some children, specific adaptations will be required to help maximize their participation. For a child with cerebral palsy, access to learning may require an adapted chair for table activities, a wheelchair to get from one activity to the next, and a floor seat for free-play activities. In addition, modifications may be required in the room arrangement to allow enough space for the child's wheelchair and other equipment (e.g., communication board). The types of materials selected should be easy for the child to hold and manipulate. Often adaptations can be as simple as adding Velcro to a baseball glove or using a paintbrush with an extra large handle.

In certain activities, an increased amount of time or assistance may be necessary for some children. This is particularly true in physical activities that require motor skills the child does not possess. Strategies must be developed that enhance each child's ability to participate in the same developmentally appropriate activities as his nondisabled peers; otherwise, we are contributing to learned helplessness.

An optimal goal for children with disabilities is for them to participate in the same activities as their nondisabled peers, and in a similar manner. Teachers should select space, furniture, equipment and materials that allow children to participate with as few adaptations as possible. When an adaptation is made, it must be naturalistic, and the goal should be to fade the adaptation as soon as feasible. For example, a spoon or fork with a built-up handle may help a child with a physical disability feed himself; however, this type of adaptive utensil is not available in all environments (e.g., restaurant, friend's house, or church picnic). Therefore, the adaptations should be as minimal as possible, with the eventual goal of reducing the need for the adaptation. If a child-sized chair can be modified for a child with a physical disability to use at school, this is preferable to a special piece of equipment. The idea is to allow children with disabilities to participate in the environment in a fashion similar to that of their nondisabled peers.

4. Create a Sense of Community. Teachers play a central role in creating a sense of community and in fostering the positive peer relationships that are critical to successful inclusion. Nondisabled peers often serve as excellent models for children with disabilities. Rather than children with disabilities being singled out for one-on-one instruction, they should be included as equal members of the group whenever possible. Group relationships can be enhanced when teachers model acceptance and responsiveness to individual differences.

5. Foster Social Skill Development. Interpersonal skills also can be addressed within the design of the physical environment. Providing adequate space and materials for groups of children facilitates child-child interaction. There should be opportunities for one-on-one, small-group, and large-group activities during the day, and the composition of the groups should change constantly. Although many areas such as blocks, dramatic or imaginative play, gross motor activities, and sand and water play naturally allow for social interactions, a teacher can take advantage of other opportunities to develop social skills or encourage social interactions. Teachers can carefully select toys and materials such as kitchen equipment in the housekeeping area and gross motor equipment such as balls, slides, and tunnels that allow for more than one child to participate. They can plan cooperative activities that require partners or groups of children to work together, for example, mural painting or buddy projects in art, using props such as puppets in the book area, or working with a table map or floor puzzle in the discovery area. In addition, children can work together to complete classroom chores such as cleanup, passing out materials, or taking notes to the office.

6. Reflect Classroom Uniqueness. The physical environment should be driven by the different interests and needs of the teacher and children. Various elements evolve over the year to reflect the growth in skills and the changes in the tastes and interests of the children and teachers who work in the classroom. Classrooms should demonstrate respect for cultural diversity and always reflect the children's experiential backgrounds. One kindergarten might like the color red, trucks, and gardening, and another may prefer the color blue, pets, and dress-up time. The differences make the classroom unique and help the room become a familiar and secure place for children.

7. *Address Various Learning Styles.* A critical factor to consider in arranging the physical environment is the various learning styles of children within a given classroom. Some children have natural ways of learning and preferences about how they learn best. Some learn optimally through incidental observations of others in their environment, while others require more direct instruction. For example, one child may make the transition to a new activity area at the appropriate time by watching others. Another child may require a number of prompts or cues to make a transition at the proper time. Similarly, some children require a more highly prepared learning situation to learn new skills or meet individual objectives. The various learning styles of children must be addressed so that they have an optimal learning environment.

The discussion that follows is focused primarily on the guidelines to be followed in arranging the physical environment of the classroom. However, many of the guidelines and strategies can be applied to other environments such as the home or community.

Guidelines for Arranging the Physical Environment

The physical environment of early education programs can be described as the setting in which learning takes place. It includes the physical layout, the organization of various activity areas, furniture and equipment, and learning materials. In essence, the physical environment sets the stage for learning and dictates the types of behaviors and activities that occur within the environment. The arrangement of the physical environment can either facilitate or interfere with learning. The teacher must consider all of the children as the room is being arranged so that modifications can make it accessible and conducive to learning for children with disabilities.

Types of Classroom Space

The types and organization of physical space should be consistent with the program goals. Therefore, they vary from program to program. In general, the following types of physical space are found in most early childhood classrooms:

1. Active play space. Floor space is needed for gross motor activities, dramatic play, and games. Open areas are recommended for these types of activities so that children have sufficient room to move around.

2. Table space. Uncluttered table space is needed for activities such as manipulatives, writing, and art work.

3. Quiet space. Areas are needed for quiet activities such as reading books, listening to tapes, and engaging in a variety of quieter activities. Corners with overstuffed pillows, lofts, or rocking chairs are all good quiet spaces.

4. Group space. Ample space is needed for whole-group and informal and formal small-group activities. Although table space is usually available for small-group work when it is not being used for manipulatives, often large-group space has to be dedicated for circle and other opening and closing activities.

5. Wet space. Space is needed near a water source for use in cooking, science, and art activities. A water play area or water table is also recommended. At various times during the year, the water table can be filled with materials such as sand, rice, and Styrofoam packing materials to provide new challenges for children.

6. Personal space. Each child in the class needs space for storing personal belongings such as book bag, coat, lunch box, snacks, supplies, finished work, and correspondence between home and school. The teacher has an obligation to see that children's work and belongings are protected.

7. Teacher space. A space is needed to be used solely for adult materials such as attendance records, lesson plans, confidential information such as Individual Education Plans (IEPs), and authentic assessment portfolios.

8. Storage space. Ample storage space is needed in any early learning environment for materials, equipment, and books. Storage is also needed for consumables such as paper, paint, marbles, and other supplies that have to be kept out of the sight of children.

9. Parent space. Space is needed for private meetings and interactions with parents and other family members. Some programs may find it helpful to have a parent information center, bulletin board, or library materials area.

A sample floor plan for a center-based preschool classroom is shown in Figure 6.1. The layout provides examples of various types of space described in the previous section. Figure 6.1 should be seen as an ideal room arrangement; it should not be held up as a model to be emulated. It is designed to show some of the possibilities that may exist when a teacher takes the time to analyze a room carefully and strives to make decisions that will add to the quality of the teaching-learning experience.

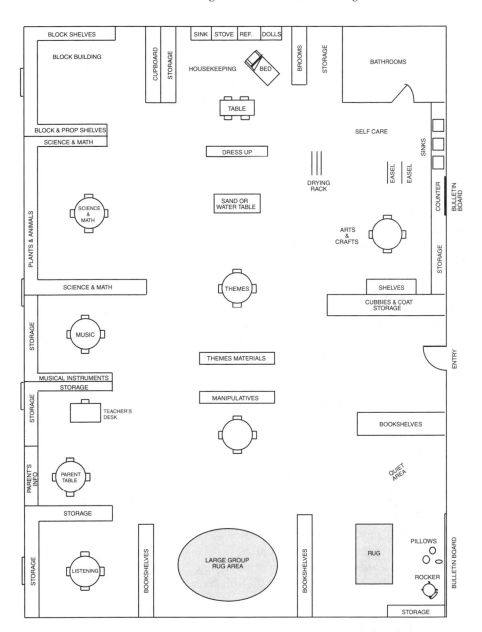

FIGURE 6.1   Sample Floorplan for a Center-Based Preschool Classroom

Amount of Space

Most states have established their own requirements regarding the amount of space needed in public school classrooms. For preschool classrooms, regulations are generally established by the licensure boards within each state. The recommendation of the National Academy of Early Childhood Programs (1991) is that there be at least thirty-five usable square feet per child in a preschool classroom (e.g., ten children = 350 square feet) and seventy-five square feet of outdoor space per child.

The needs of children with disabilities must be considered carefully when determining the allocation of space in a classroom. Some areas may have to be increased in size for children who require extra equipment. For example, a child with a physical disability who uses a wheelchair may require that the floor space for blocks be increased so that he or she can participate. Children with visual impairments may require adaptations to ensure their safety and access to all activities. Tactile cues, such as duct tape, can be added to indicate where areas of the room begin and end, and sharp edges and hazardous items must be removed from the classroom. As a general rule, it is best to minimize the space adaptations so that only the necessary changes are made. This means that children with disabilities must learn to negotiate the barriers of the natural environment and keeps undue attention from being directed toward disabled children (Noonan & McCormick, 1993).

Outdoor Space

The guidelines published by the National Academy of Early Childhood Programs (1991) state that outdoor areas should include a variety of surfaces such as soil, grass, and blacktop, and equipment for riding, climbing, swinging, sliding, water play and other types of activities. The guidelines also address the importance of enclosing the outdoor areas with fences or other barriers. As with indoor space, modifications may be necessary to ensure that young children with disabilities have access to all equipment. Playground equipment can be adapted by the addition of rails to the slide or a ramp leading up to the sandbox or the play house. For children with visual impairments, tactile cues such as boundaries can be added to indicate where the swings are located so that children can avoid getting hit. Adaptations vary according to the individual needs of the children.

INDIRECT GUIDANCE WITHIN THE ENVIRONMENT

Indirect guidance enables the teacher to facilitate both classroom movement and children's activities without excess oral direction. The ways in which children can be guided indirectly include, but are not limited to, the following:

1. The arrangement of the environment should be organized in a consistent and predictable manner so that children know what to expect and what is expected of them. Children often experience a sense of security when the organization of the environment helps them to know where they can find materials and participate in certain activities (Crosser, 1992). Boundaries can be used to define given areas of the classroom so that children can see where instructional areas begin and end. For example, the shelving and rugs that define the block area can serve as visual indicators of the area for block play. In addition, activity area signs, symbols, or pictures can be prominently displayed to indicate the activities that should occur in different areas.

2. The location of the classroom fixtures should be considered when the teacher arranges space in the physical environment. The teacher must utilize or work around fixed features of the classroom such as the sink, doorways, bathroom, and windows. Cubbies or lockers should be located by the entrance to the classroom and at the children's level. This provides a visual cue for children to remove their coats and hang them in the lockers. Activity areas should be located in close proximity to the fixtures needed to carry out the activities. For example, art, cooking, and snack tables should be on uncarpeted areas near the sink. Teachers must be aware of potential safety problems and recognize that the three areas must be separated so that children do not interfere with each other. Garbage cans should be located at strategic places in the classroom to encourage independent cleanup. Accessibility of materials and activities allows children to participate with minimal adult assistance. (Caution: electrical appliances and water do not belong together.)

3. The teacher should create clear pathways and traffic patterns that are logical, avoid interference, and minimize distractions. Furniture should be arranged to encourage natural traffic paths so that children and adults do not have to go through one activity area to get to another. Paths should be clearly seen from the child's point of view and may have to be widened to make them accessible to all children. Well-planned traffic patterns can lead to independence and minimize interference.

4. The room design should discourage running by avoiding long, narrow "runways." When running is controlled, the safety of all children, but especially those who are smaller, medically fragile, or physically disabled will not be jeopardized.

5. The environment should have uncluttered walls, floors, and work spaces. With clutter eliminated, children, particularly those with attention problems, have more room to explore the environment, direct their attention to relevant materials, and engage in meaningful learning activities.

6. Equipment, materials, and toys should be arranged attractively and logically from a child's point of view. Materials and toys should be labeled, visible, accessible, and stored in the area in which they are to be used. For example, the bin for crayons can have the word *crayons* and a picture of crayons

clearly displayed. Silhouettes or outlines can be used to indicate where blocks, woodworking, cooking, and dramatic play items belong. Placing materials in the appropriate context provides a visual cue for their use. Costumes in the housekeeping or dramatic play area; paper, markers, and paper clips in the writing area; or puzzles with attribute shapes in the manipulative center let the children know where and how the items should be used. Items that are not for students' use should be stored out of their reach. The logical organization and labeling of toys, materials, and equipment assists adults in locating misplaced items.

7. The noise level should be considered in the arrangement of space. Social and active areas such as blocks and dramatic play or housekeeping areas should be located near one another when possible. Similarly, individual work areas and quiet areas for manipulatives and language arts should be next to each other to encourage attending behavior. Sound-absorbing materials such as carpet, pillows, and curtains can be used to cut down on excessive noise.

8. Private spaces can be created for individual or group activities in an area by the addition of elements such as rugs, cushions, or comfortable chairs. Children can work alone in these private spaces, or ongoing project work can take place. Areas that provide solitude facilitate sustained work on engaging activities.

9. Placing the names and/or pictures of the children on their special space (e.g., lockers, cubbies, or tubs) helps them to identify their own personal space. They can use this space to keep belongings such as coats, books, lunch, special equipment, or extra clothes.

10. Reasonable limits should be placed on the number of children in one space to prevent behavior problems and encourage appropriate interaction. Teachers should consider the number and type of materials and the amount of space needed for the activity when determining limits. Overcrowding has a tendency to create behavior problems for young children because they become frustrated when they cannot utilize materials they find interesting and exciting.

11. The environment should provide for a sense of success and competence. For example, art galleries can be created to exhibit work at the children's eye level, demonstrating the importance of their work. Activities that are age appropriate and individually appropriate, materials that are easily accessible, and teachers who continually validate the child's worth all lead to success and competence.

TROUBLESHOOTING

All classroom arrangements have problems at various times during the year. When children wear heavy clothing and boots during the winter, they may need more space in front of the lockers. The addition of a guinea pig may require another table in the science section. A child who learns to ambulate with a walker needs a place to store the walker when it is not being used. These are opportunities to fine-tune the environment to make it work better for everyone. Observations, anecdotal records, and children's behaviors and verbalizations can all provide insight into needed changes. However, as pointed out previously, children often find security in a predictable classroom. Therefore, changes should usually be kept to a minimum. Teachers who change their room arrangement every few days or weeks force children to learn new ways of operating, which takes away time that would otherwise be available for learning.

THE SOCIAL AND PROGRAMMATIC ENVIRONMENT IN EARLY CHILDHOOD PROGRAMS

The social and programmatic environment of the early childhood classroom includes the scheduling of time and resources, the grouping of children, the roles and responsibilities of the teacher and other adults, and a variety of appropriate intervention strategies and practices (McEvoy et al., 1991). Factors to consider when designing this environment are discussed in the sections that follow.

CONSIDERATIONS IN THE SCHEDULING OF TIME AND RESOURCES

A variety of activities and routines take place each day in most preschool, kindergarten, and primary classrooms. Examples include dramatic play, music activities, art activities, science discovery, exploration of various materials, and those that vary according to the season and the children's interest. *Scheduling* refers to the organization of time and resources to meet the needs of the children within the early childhood program. The schedule is a framework for the flow of activities based on interests and ability levels. A predictable classroom schedule can have a number of benefits for children with disabilities, such as anticipating scheduled transitions and increasing time on task (Ostrosky, Skellenger, Odom, McConnell, & Peterson, 1994).

The following factors must be considered in establishing the daily routine in a classroom environment. Some of the factors are applicable to all young children, and some are unique to young children with disabilities.

1. What are the program's goals? This is the most important question.

2. What is the time period in which the children attend the program? Is it a half-day or full-day program? How many hours do the children attend per day?

3. What are the arrival and dismissal patterns of the children? Do they all arrive at once, or do they come in at staggered times? How is time allotted for communication with family members or caregivers?

4. How many children are in the class? What are the individual strengths and needs of the children?

5. How many adults (e.g., teachers, paraprofessionals, parents, and volunteers) are assigned to the class, and when are they available? When are the related service personnel in the classroom (e.g., occupational therapists, physical therapists, and speech-language pathologists)?

6. How is time allotted for communication among the adults (e.g., parents, teachers, and related service personnel)?

7. What are the fixed activity periods for the children outside the classroom (e.g., music, art, physical education, lunchroom, and playground)?

8. At what times of day are the children at their best or most alert? When do they rest or have quiet time?

9. How will the type and length of activities be balanced during the day? What is the appropriate length for various activities?

10. What types of activity choices can be offered during the same time block?

11. How is time for transitions between activities planned?

12. How is time for cleanup allotted?

By considering these factors carefully, teachers can plan so that daily activities and routines are established to ensure that program goals are achieved and that all involved (e.g., children, teachers, related service personnel, and families) know what to expect. The adults in the environment should know where each activity of the day will occur, who will be responsible for the activity, the children participating in the activity, and the objective to be addressed.

Guidelines for Scheduling

Time Segments

It is recommended that the schedule be divided into approximate time segments that reflect the needs and abilities of the children. Commonly accepted practice is that the younger the children, the shorter their attention span, and the shorter the activities. A general guide is the "three-minute rule," which suggests that for each year of a child's life, three minutes should be added to the length of an activity. Therefore, fifteen minutes is the recommended length of a formal group activity for a five-year-old. However, individual appropriateness means that some children are capable of much longer sessions and some need shorter sessions. A careful balance must be achieved so that children have enough time to engage in activities without being rushed, yet not so much that they become bored or engage in inappropriate behavior. Time periods often have to be extended or shortened, depending on the interest levels of the children. The quality of the activity and the interest of the children should serve as a guide for the length of the activity.

After a schedule is developed, it is imperative that it be viewed as a dynamic guide rather than a rigid one. Teachers should follow the schedule but adjust the amount of time allocated for an activity as the children's needs indicate. For example, a child with a physical disability may need extra time ambulating from the classroom to other areas of the school building such as the gym, lunchroom, or playground. A child with a feeding problem may require a longer time for snack or lunch. In such cases, modifications are required in the schedule to accommodate the individual needs of children.

Schedules vary from classroom to classroom depending on a number of factors, the most important one being the individual needs of the children. A careful balance must be achieved to allow for necessary one-to-one opportunities, small-group activities, and large-group activities. Similarly, quiet and active times, and structured and unstructured times must be balanced to meet the individual needs of the children. Table 6.2 shows sample daily schedules. After a schedule is developed, young children often must be taught to follow it. Table 6.3 suggests strategies that may be used to help children learn to follow the schedule, thus increasing their independence.

TABLE 6.2   Sample Daily Schedule

A. Full-Day Preschool Program

8:30 - 9:00	Arrival and Free Play
9:00 - 9:20	Group/Theme Presentation
9:20 - 10:30	Centers (e.g., Art, Blocks, Music, Dramatic Play, Manipulatives, Computer)
10:30 - 10:45	Clean-up, Transition to Group
10:45 - 11:00	Group: Follow-up to Theme—Language Oriented
11:00 - 11:30	Outside/Movement
11:30 - 11:45	Wind Down Group/Story
11:45 - 12:00	Transition to Lunch
12:00 - 12:30	Lunch/Grooming
12:30 - 2:00	Rest/Nap
2:00 - 2:15	Grooming
2:15 - 2:45	Centers/Free Play
2:45 - 3:00	Music Group
3:00 - 3:15	Dismissal

TABLE 6.2   *(Continued)*

B. Full-Day Preschool Program

8:15 - 8:30	Arrival/Health Check/Grooming
8:30 - 8:50	Morning Circle and Planning Time
8:50 - 9:45	Work Time/Centers
9:45 - 10:00	Clean Up
10:00 - 10:20	Small Group/Individual Work
10:20 - 10:50	Gross Motor/Outside Time
10:50 - 11:00	Preparation for Lunch/Grooming
11:00 - 11:45	Lunch
11:45 - 12:45	Nap/Rest Time
12:45 - 1:00	Grooming
1:00 - 1:30	Centers
1:30 - 2:00	Snack
2:00 - 2:20	Afternoon Circle
2:20 - 2:30	Dismissal

C. Half-Day Preschool Program

8:30 - 9:00	Arrival and Free Play
9:00 - 9:20	Group: Routines and Theme Presentation
9:20 - 10:30	Centers (e.g., Art, Blocks, Music, Dramatic Play, Manipulatives)
10:30 - 10:45	Clean-up
10:45 - 11:00	Story Group
11:00 - 11:30	Outside/Movement
11:30 - 11:45	Wind Down Group/Story
11:45 - 12:00	Transition to Lunch
12:00 - 12:30	Lunch/Grooming
12:30 - 12:45	Dismissal

D. Half-Day Preschool Program

8:15 - 8:30	Arrival/Health Check/Grooming
8:30 - 8:50	Morning Circle/Planning Time
8:50 - 9:45	Work Time/Centers
9:45 - 10:00	Clean-up Time
10:00 - 10:30	Recall and Snack Time
10:30 - 10:50	Small Group/Individual Work Time
10:50 - 11:20	Gross Motor/Outside Time
11:20 - 11:40	Circle Time
11:40 - 11:45	Dismissal

Full-Day (B) and Half-Day (D) Sample Preschool Schedules are adapted from Hohmann, M., Banet, B., & Weikart, D. (1979). *Young Children in Action*. Ypsilanti, MI: High/Scope Press (p. 61).

TABLE 6.3   Suggestions for Teaching Children to Follow the Schedule

1. Teachers can refer to the periods by name throughout the day (e.g., group time, outside time, snack, lunch, centers, journal work) and can indicate the purpose or what is expected during each segment. For example, "It's time for journal work. I know you can't wait to write about our field trip to the pumpkin patch." "I'm putting my coat on now because it's outside time and we all need to be ready."
2. It is helpful if teachers follow the order of the routine as closely as possible to allow the children to anticipate what will happen next. The consistency of the routine can help to foster independence because children know what to expect. Predictability in the routine may also help the children to develop a stronger sense of security.
3. Photographs can be taken of activities during each time period of the day. During group or circle time, children can look at the photographs and talk about what is happening in them. This can help children connect the name of the time period to each activity. Later on, some children may be able to sequence the photographs in the order of the daily routine.
4. After the children have talked about the photographs of the daily routine, some of them may be interested in helping construct a schedule. For children with cognitive delays or disabilities, the pictures can be referred to when following the schedule. Pairing the name of the activity with the picture can lead to children following the written schedule rather than the pictures.
5. At circle time, songs can be developed with the children about the daily routine. As they sing about each time period, the children can act out some of the things they do during that period to help them remember the purpose and order of the activities.
6. At the end of each period, teachers can review what has happened and talk with the children about what is coming next: "Now that we've finished with center time and we've cleaned up, we need to get ready to go to the library." Gentle reminders help to let children know what is expected rather than telling them directly what to do. It is important to tell children in advance if there is to be a change in the routine, so they can incorporate it into their thinking about the day's events.
7. Time can be allowed at the end of the day for closure and recall of the classroom experiences. The order and time allowed during each period should be discussed and adjusted when needed. When problems arise, such as children not having enough time to get from one activity to the next, children with disabilities can often be assisted by their nondisabled peers.

Curriculum Areas

All areas of the curriculum should be addressed throughout the daily schedule. Routines and activities should distribute the amount of emphasis placed on the skill areas. Time should be scheduled at the end of the day for closure and discussion of the day's activities and experiences.

Arrival and Departure Times

Programming should begin as soon as children arrive at school and should continue until the end of the day. Arrival and departure periods are especially important teaching opportunities because they can provide linkages between home and school. A staff member should be assigned to greet children and family members or caregivers when they arrive and depart.

Transition Periods

Transitions are periods of time in which children are moving from one activity to the next. When children are required to wait for long periods between activities, with no direction from the teacher, valuable time is wasted and behavior problems are likely to occur. Children must be taught what is expected of them during transitions, particularly the difference between changing activities within the room and leaving the room to go to lunch. Goals such as moving independently from one activity to the next, selecting an activity, gathering the needed materials, or choosing a partner can be addressed as part of transition time. These transitions should be short and smooth, thus allowing more time for children to engage in other activities (e.g., group activities and learning centers). Table 6.4 provides suggestions for facilitating smooth transitions.

TABLE 6.4   Strategies for Facilitating Smooth Transitions between Activities

1. The schedule can be planned so that active times alternate with quieter, more sedentary periods. For example, going from outside time to small group time is an easier and more natural transition than going from small-group time to planning time, because it gives children a different type of focus and a chance to release some energy.
2. Teachers should alert children a few minutes before an activity or time period is over. This will allow children to finish an activity, anticipate what is next, and accomplish what is expected of them. The teacher might say, for example, "Work time is almost over. Then it will be clean-up time."
3. Signals can be established to mark the end of the periods. For example, a bell could be rung, a song could be sung, or a timer could go off. One of the more competent children in the class could be the time keeper in certain activities or remind another child that it is time to change activities.
4. Meeting places can be designated for transition times. For example, as they finish cleaning up and before they go to snack, children can meet in the circle. Between small-group time and outside time, children can meet by the door.
5. Once children have gathered, they can be helped as they make up special ways to move to the next activity (e.g., walking with their hands way up high, touching something blue, moving as quietly as a mouse).
6. Children who finish an activity early should be allowed to begin another activity. This may prevent boredom, behavior problems, or interference with other children's completion of work.

Adapted from Hohmann, M., Banet, B., & Weikart, D. (1979). *Young Children in Action.* Ypsilanti, MI: High/Scope Press. (p. 98).

Cleanup

Cleanup activities are important across the daily routine. Participating in cleanup activities can foster self-discipline and self-satisfaction in young children. Table 6.5 provides examples of creative ideas to help children learn to clean up. This list is not exhaustive but is intended to help spark other creative strategies that will lead to successful cleanup during the day.

Lunch and Snack Time

Lunch and snack time are opportunities for social, emotional, physical and intellectual development. Adequate time must be provided for children to engage in conversations about food, colors, the weather, and any other topic of interest. Additional time may be needed to accommodate young children with disabilities who have oral-motor or feeding difficulties and/or communication delays.

TABLE 6.5   Suggestions for Helping Children during Clean-up

1. Children can be encouraged to clean up when they finish an activity and are ready to begin another. This "clean-as-you-go" policy will cut down substantially on the amount of clean-up at the end of the day.
2. Since children may not know automatically what constitutes cleaning up, teachers may need to show them how to clean-up or help individual children define their own specific clean-up tasks. For example, "What are you cleaning up first, Alan, the cars and the trucks or the blocks?" A specific comment helps children see where to begin more than a general statement like "Come on, Alan, it's clean-up time." A direct suggestion or choice may help children to get started. This can be particularly helpful on messy days when it is difficult to know where to begin.
3. Teachers may need to work along with children as they put things away and use the opportunity to talk with them about what they are doing and observing. They may need to design ways that children with disabilities can participate in clean-up activities. A basket attached to a walker or wheelchair can provide a container to hold the objects that are being put away, thus freeing up the child's arms to operate the wheel chair or walker.
4. Clean-up activities can provide opportunities for problem solving or concept development. For example, "That's a good way to get the furniture to the shelf, John Andrew. Do you think it will all fit into your basket or will you need to make another trip?"
5. Once an entire area is clean, children can be encouraged to move to another area still in need of assistance or to a central gathering place. Moving to a central gathering place cuts down on random play that distracts and interferes with children still putting things away. It also gives children a place from which they can survey the room and spot other jobs that still need to be done.
6. Children should understand the reason for cleaning up. For example, "As soon as everything is cleared from the table, we'll be ready for snack time."

Balance

A variety of activities should be provided across the day. Teachers should try to achieve a balance of quiet/active, large muscle/small muscle, group/individual, and formal/informal learning. Active gross motor activities should be alternated with quiet small-group activities so that children will not become too excited or too passive during the day. Another suggestion is to move gradually from an outdoor or gross motor activity to rest or nap time. Having a calm, quiet activity such as story reading between an outdoor play period and rest or nap time can help children to calm down before resting.

Outdoor Time

A period of time each day should be provided for children to engage in outdoor physical activities. Rather than serving only as times for children to release energy, outdoor activities can provide opportunities for dramatic play, motor skill development, socialization, gardening, and a wealth of other learning activities. Children with disabilities should be provided the necessary adaptations or assistance so they can participate fully in outdoor play with their nondisabled peers.

Maximizing Instructional Time

Every effort should be made to increase the amount and effectiveness of instructional time in order to meet the needs of all children. Suggestions for increasing instructional time are listed in Table 6.6. These strategies are extremely important to consider in addressing the needs of children with disabilities, who need ample opportunity to practice learned skills.

TABLE 6.6   Scheduling Suggestions

1. All personnel (e.g., teachers, paraprofessionals, related services professionals) can be included on the daily schedule.
2. Areas in which children will be working for various time periods should be specified on the daily schedule and each child should be accounted for during each time segment.
3. Periods can be lengthened for bathroom, dressing, undressing, and eating to permit adequate time for teaching during these natural times.
4. Children can be rotated so that every child participates in various types of groups: 1:1, small group, large group. The adults working with children in these various groupings should also be rotated.
5. The schedule can help to ensure that skills are taught in a variety of situations when and where they are normally used rather than only during a set time period. For example, dressing/undressing skills should be taught during arrival and dismissal times, when going to the bathroom, in preparation to go to the playground and upon return, or when an accident occurs and clothing needs to be changed.
6. When family members or volunteers are in the classroom, they can be worked into the daily schedule. They can work on skills that are emerging or they can provide "supervised practice" opportunities for skills that children have just learned.

TROUBLESHOOTING SCHEDULING PROBLEMS

The adage "If it ain't broke, don't fix it" is certainly appropriate to consider in designing the classroom schedule. When evaluating the classroom schedule, the classroom teacher can ask the following questions:

1. Does the current schedule minimize organizational time and maximize instructional time?
2. Are the instructional activities on the schedule efficient? That is, will they help children learn what they need to learn? Is there time for children to make choices?
3. Is there a balance to the day (e.g., large versus small group, active versus quiet activities)?
4. Are the times at which planned activities begin and end being managed well? Is enough time allotted for each activity?
5. Is the routine predictable for the children, yet flexible enough to allow for teachable moments?
6. Is there time for all children to be engaged in activities?
7. Are procedures being used to minimize outside interruptions and in-class disruptions, and are these procedures working well?

If the answer to any of these questions is no, then this may be the logical place to begin modifying the daily schedule. If yes is the answer to all of the questions, apparently no modifications are required. Even when the schedule is working well, however, teachers must be continually aware of the changing needs of the children and must adjust the classroom schedule accordingly. Time spent early in the school year teaching the children the schedule will benefit everyone by making each day more productive.

GROUP SIZE

Group size and teacher-student ratio have been the subject of much discussion as the inclusion movement has gained momentum. The National Academy of Early Childhood Programs (1991) suggests the teacher-student ratios presented in Table 6.7. As the age of the children increases, the number of children in a classroom increases and the teacher-student ratio decreases. This is based on the assumption that as children grow older, they become more independent and need less adult assistance. Ratios must be flexible, however, to accommodate children with disabilities in inclusive settings. For example, children with physical, behavioral, or sensory impairments may require more staff time and, thus, a higher teacher-student ratio. Similarly, children who are not toilet trained or who do not eat independently may require additional staff

TABLE 6.7   Recommended Staff–Child Ratios within Group Size

Age of Children	Group Size									
	6	8	10	12	14	16	18	20	22	24
Infants (birth–12 mos.)	1:3	1:4								
Toddlers (12–24 mos.)	1:3	1:4	1:5	1:6						
2-year-olds (24–36 mos.)		1:4	1:5	1:6						
2½-year-olds (30–36 mos.)			1:5	1:6	1:7					
3-year-olds					1:7	1:8	1:9	1:10		
4-year-olds						1:8	1:9	1:10		
5-year-olds						1:8	1:9	1:10		
6-year-olds								1:10	1:11	1:12

Source: From *Accreditation Criteria and Procedures of the National Academy of Early Childhood Programs (rev. ed.)*, 1991, Washington, DC: The National Association for the Education of Young Children. Copyright 1991 by NAEYC. Reprinted by permission. All rights reserved.

time. Depending on the needs of the children, appropriate teacher-student ratios must be determined in each class. The greater the needs of the students, the greater the need for additional adults to support learning.

SUMMARY

In this chapter, we have taken a close look at two important aspects of the learning environment: the physical and the social and programmatic components. The emphasis is on how developmentally appropriate practices provide the foundation for young children's learning environments. Specific strategies are suggested for adapting the environment as needed to address the needs of young children with known or suspected disabilities. As specified throughout the book, the key to a successful learning environment is a well-trained, experienced teacher who is able to make decisions that reflect both age-appropriate and individually appropriate practice.

ACTIVITIES AND RESOURCES

Activities

1. Draw a diagram of the floor plan for a kindergarten classroom with eighteen children, with appropriate activity areas, equipment, and furniture. Show where modifications are necessary for a child in a wheel chair, a child who uses a walker, or a child with a visual impairment.

2. Select a routine activity such as art or snack time and describe how the activity can be modified to meet the needs of a child with a physical impairment, visual impairment, or hearing impairment.
3. Develop a daily schedule for fifteen preschoolers (three children with disabilities) who attend a center-based program for five hours per day. Describe strategies that allow for both consistency and flexibility.
4. Select one of Terrell's IEP objectives and plan an activity designed to address it. Describe how the activity arrangements will be adapted to meet Terrell's needs.
5. Observe in an infant and toddler, preschool, or primary classroom where young children with disabilities are served with their nondisabled peers. Select a child with a disability and focus on his daily activities and routines. Describe how the physical and the social and programmatic elements of the environment have been adapted to meet this child's objectives.

Class Discussion Questions

1. Discuss possible adaptations in the physical environment to address Brad's needs. Compare these to the adaptations for Tiffany.
2. Describe how the daily schedule should be designed to address all curriculum areas and maximize instructional time.
3. Explain how developmentally appropriate practices serve as the foundation for learning environments for all young children.
4. Discuss the role of the teacher in a developmentally appropriate learning environment in which young children with disabilities are served. How does this differ from the traditional role of the teacher?

Resources

Noonan, M.J., & McCormick, L. (1993). *Early intervention in natural environments*. Pacific Grove, CA: Brooks/Cole.
This is a practical book that offers guidelines for implementation of a naturalistic curriculum and describes numerous specialized methods of instruction.

Peters, J., and the staff of the Teaching Research Early Childhood Training Department of Western Oregon State College (1992). *Supporting children with disabilities in community programs*. Monmouth, OR: Teaching Research Publications.
This manual was developed to describe the authors' experiences and learning in their work with young children with disabilities and their families, community based programs. Excellent examples and strategies are provided.

Space to grow: Creating an environment that supports language acquisition. (1989). Portland: OR: Educational Productions, Inc.
This tape provides the viewer with specific, easy-to-implement strategies for developing an environment that motivates children to use language. Specific examples for such support are provided.

The creative curriculum for early childhood. St. Paul, MN: Redleaf Press.
This video demonstrates the importance of a well-planned environment. The scenes of children working and playing in seven learning centers capture the essence of teachers' using the environment to support their curriculum.

REFERENCES

Bredekamp, S. (Ed.). (1987). *Developmentally appropriate practice in early childhood programs serving children from birth to age 8* (exp. ed.). Washington, DC: NAEYC.

Bredekamp, S., & Rosegrant, T. (1992). *Reaching potentials: Appropriate curriculum and assessment for young children.* Washington, DC: NAEYC.

Carta, J.J. (1994). Developmentally appropriate practices: Shifting the emphasis to individual appropriateness. *Journal of Early Intervention, 18*(4), 342–343.

Carta, J., Schwartz, I., Atwater, J., & McConnell, S. (1991). Developmentally appropriate practice: Appraising its usefulness for young children with disabilities. *Topics in Early Childhood Special Education, 11*(1), 1–20.

Crosser, S. (1992). Managing the early childhood classroom. *Young Children, 47*(2), 23–29.

Hohmann, M., Banet, B., & Wiekart, D. P. (1979). *Young Children in Action: A Manual for Preschool Education.* Ypsilanti, MI: High/Scope Press.

Hanson, M., & Lynch, E. (1995). *Early intervention: Implementing child and family services for infants and toddlers who are at-risk or disabled.* (2nd ed.) Austin, TX: Pro-ed, p. 185.

McCormick, L., & Feeney, S. (1995). Modifying and expanding activities for children with disabilities. *Young Children, 50*(4), 10–17.

McEvey, M., Fox, J. J., & Rosenberg, M. S. (1991). Organizing preschool environments: Suggestions for enhancing the development/learning of preschool children with handicaps. *Topics in Early Childhood Special Education, 11*(2), 18–28.

National Academy of Early Childhood Programs. (1991). *Accreditation criteria and procedures.* Washington, D.C.: National Association for the Education of Young Children.

Noonan, M.J., & McCormick, L. (1993). *Early intervention in natural environments: Methods and procedures.* Pacific Grove, CA: Brookes-Cole Publishing Co.

Ostrosky, M., Skellenger A., Odom, S., McConnell, S., & Peterson, C. (1994). Teacher's schedules and actual time spent in activities in preschool special education classes. *Journal of Early Intervention, 18*, 25–33.

Vincent, L. (1988, March). *Curriculum development.* Inservice training for early childhood special education teachers, Los Angeles Unified School District.

Wolery, M. (1996). Using assessment information to plan intervention programs. In M. McLean, D. Bailey, & M. Wolery (Eds.). *Assessing infants and preschoolers with special needs.* (pp. 491–518). Englewood Cliffs, NJ: Merrill, An imprint of Prentice Hall.

Wolery, M., & Bredekamp, S. (1994). Developmentally appropriate practices and young children with disabilities: Contextual issues in the discussion. *Journal of Early Intervention, 26*(4), 45–48.

Wolery, M., Strain, P., & Bailey, D. (1992). Reaching potential of children with special needs. In S. Bredekamp & T. Rosegrant (Eds.). *Reaching potentials: Appropriate curriculum and assessment for young children (Vol. 1)* (pp. 92–111). Washington, DC: NAEYC.

7

USING PRINCIPLES OF DEVELOPMENTALLY APPROPRIATE PRACTICE TO MAKE DECISIONS ABOUT MATERIALS, LEARNING CENTERS, AND INTEGRATED THEMATIC UNITS

OBJECTIVES

As a result of studying this chapter, readers should be able to perform the following:

- Identify guidelines for selecting materials and equipment that reflect the developmental needs of young children.
- Design and plan learning centers for children with and without disabilities.
- Use an integrated theme approach to address the objectives of young children with disabilities.

The topics discussed in this chapter include the materials and equipment used with young children, the design and implementation of learning centers, and the use of integrated thematic units. The suggested strategies are derived from the principles of developmentally appropriate programming and are appropriate for all children. The approaches take into account the wide range of differences that occur in children of similar age and recognize that children with disabilities are often more similar to children without disabilities than they are different.

HOW CHILDREN LEARN AND HOW TO CREATE CURRICULA THAT HELP THEM LEARN

As discussed in Chapter 2, young children learn through the active exploration of their environment. It is through interactions with the materials, peers, and adults in their homes, schools, and communities that children create social, physical, and conceptual knowledge. Through the decisions they make about materials, equipment, child social arrangements, and adult interactions, teachers foster the acquisition or development of children's skills. If Tiffany is interested in bright, shiny objects, the teacher who places one-inch balls covered with Mylar into wide-mouthed containers is encouraging Tiffany to use her hands. Through the selection of simple materials that are engaging to Tiffany, the teacher has created a learning situation that fosters Tiffany's acquisition of a major objective.

Although children with disabilities often have a barrier between themselves and the settings in which they spend time, they, like all other children, learn through their interactions with peers, materials, and people. It becomes the responsibility of the teacher to choose materials that circumvent those barriers, design peer social situations that use the children's strengths, and foster the attainment of specified skills.

Materials and Equipment

One of the primary means by which early childhood programs facilitate children's development is through the use of materials and equipment that are part of the concrete environment with which children interact. Well chosen, developmentally appropriate materials and equipment are valuable for at least three reasons: (1) they motivate children, (2) they foster growth and expand skills, and (3) they enable teachers to structure the choices that children have in their environments (Bredekamp & Rosegrant, 1992; Sutton-Smith, 1992).

Materials that Motivate Children

In general, materials and equipment can possess specific characteristics that make them more attractive and motivating to young children. Bronson (1995) indicates that at least five considerations should govern the choice of materials for young children:

1. They should possess characteristics that appeal to the children's interests and experiences.
2. They should possess appropriate physical characteristics so that the children may interact with them.
3. They should be of a complexity that is understood by the children both cognitively and socially.
4. They should be appropriate for children in group situations.
5. They should be well constructed, durable, and safe (p. 8).

Developmentally appropriate materials for early childhood programs should appeal to the children's interests and experiences. If a classroom of first graders has made a recent trip to a pond or river and the members of the class showed an interest in the plants and animals during their visit, reeds, straw, milkweed, and other plant materials would be appropriate during an art activity.

Materials should be unique and interesting for children in a program and at the same time familiar to them. If a unit on gases is being conducted in a kindergarten classroom and the children are familiar with balloons that are filled by mouth, a unique but similar material would be balloons filled with helium. The helium balloons are similar to balloons in their past experiences but different enough to be motivating.

Appropriate materials for young children also should possess physical characteristics and uses that allow children to easily interact with them. For example, for 2- or 3-year-olds, Duplo building blocks are large enough for hands that do not have highly refined motor abilities. The physical characteristics of these blocks indicate to children that they are to be pieced together, and the size allows younger children to be successful in building with them.

Developmentally appropriate materials also have characteristics that make them complex enough for children, both socially and cognitively. Four-year-olds, in general, can adopt various social roles, identify multiple properties of objects, make simple predictions, and classify. Appropriate materials for 4-year-olds are those that capitalize on these abilities. Teachers should ensure that their classrooms have materials that allow children to experiment with various social roles and expand or enhance their cognitive skills of discrimination, classification, and prediction.

Developmentally appropriate materials in early childhood programs also should be well constructed, durable, and safe. Materials in group settings have significantly greater utilization than those in children's homes. The number of children and opportunities for contacts are greatly increased in early childhood programs; therefore, materials must be durable. Wooden doll houses, unit blocks, and tubular steel wheel toys are examples of well-constructed materials that are durable enough to be used over long periods of time with large groups of young children.

In addition to the previously mentioned characteristics, materials and equipment for young children also should be real, flexible, and representative or symbolic in nature. Because young children learn through their interactions with the real world, the materials and equipment they interact with should be real. Using actual objects and materials, such as a firefighter's coat and helmet, is more engaging to young children and advances developmental skills more than does using toy replicas. With the actual coat and helmet, the children are able to feel the texture of rubber or latex, experience the mass and weight of the large helmet, and experience what it is like to walk with large, knee-high boots. These interactions help children understand what it is like to be a firefighter (development of social roles), explore the properties of thick cloth (cognitive and language skills of labeling, observation, comparison, and physical knowledge), and practice personal adaptive skills (putting on hats, coats, and boots).

Materials and equipment also should be flexible. That is, as much as possible, they should be usable in more than one manner and should address multiple needs. Although there are reasons to have puzzles in an early childhood program, these types of materials provide for limited interactions. A puzzle is designed to be taken apart and put back together in a predesigned pattern. A very creative child might put the puzzle together outside of its frame, stack the pieces into a tower, or place the pieces standing on their ends in Play Doh. These uses of the puzzle are outside the design and intent of the material.

Materials that are more flexible, such as clay, blocks, and nonthematic dramatic play clothing allow children to adapt the materials to their needs. A simple felt hat can be a formal Easter bonnet, a bowl in which to put fruit, a police officer's helmet, or a construction worker's hard hat. Children can interact with Play Doh in the simplest manner of rolling, pulling, and flattening the dough, or they can sculpt and construct specific shapes and representational forms. Such flexibility in materials makes them engaging to a wide range of children with multiple needs and skill levels. These types of materials can help to advance the skills of a child who is cognitively gifted as well as those of a child with mental retardation.

Finally, good materials for early childhood programs can be representational and symbolic without being overly prescriptive. Materials such as unit blocks let children create representational structures but do not dictate the types of structures that will be produced. Unit blocks can be turned into walls, houses, roads, towers, spaceships, tables, or even a bed and pillows. The properties of unit blocks allow children to create representational structures without being told what to build or how to build it.

Materials that Foster Development

It is important for materials to be engaging, from an educational perspective, but they must also foster the children's development and skills. Materials that are real, flexible, and representational can be used to enhance children's development. In a developmentally appropriate early childhood setting, materials with these characteristics can be used to address the multiple needs and developmental levels of young children with and without disabilities. For example, bristle blocks, which are construction materials that stick to one another when pressed together, fit the definition of good materials for an early childhood program. They are "real" in the sense that they can be interacted with and manipulated by young children. They are flexible and can be used for many different purposes. They are representational because they can become cars, people, rocket ships, roads, and many other objects with which young children are familiar.

Because they are real, flexible, and representational, bristle blocks can also advance the development of various skills and several levels of the same skill. Very young children can dump the blocks from one container and place them in another. Children whose hand skills are limited can put them together and take them apart in an exploratory fashion. Children whose cognitive skills are greater can use them to create representational structures such as houses, ships, and roads. In this manner, bristle blocks can contribute to the development of fine motor, language, social, and cognitive skills of children from developmental levels as young as 9–12 months of age to prekindergarten and kindergarten age, provided that teachers understand the relationship between materials and development.

CHOOSING MATERIALS AND EQUIPMENT TO STRUCTURE CHILDREN'S ENVIRONMENTS

Well-chosen materials and equipment enable the teacher to structure children's environments. As discussed in Chapter 6, the environmental arrangement of a program's space influences children's interactions, their opportunities for social encounters, and their understanding of expected classroom behaviors. The materials and equipment included in programs' environmental arrangements convey similar messages. Materials and equipment structure children's environments in at least three ways: (1) the initial choice to include a material in the classroom, (2) the physical characteristics of the materials, and (3) the flexibility of the materials.

By choosing to include specific pieces of equipment and materials in a setting and excluding others, a teacher structures the parameters of learning in the environment. For example, by choosing to include a climbing structure, a slide, and a large crawling tube in one portion of a classroom, the teacher has indicated to the children that it is acceptable for them to engage in gross motor activities inside. The teacher who excludes these types of materials or places them in a separate room conveys the idea that large muscle activity is not expected or encouraged during inside, free-play periods.

Characteristics of materials add structure and convey specific messages regarding appropriate behavior. For example, puzzles, Montessori seriation cylinders, and shape sorters or form boards communicate to children that they should be working on a structured task, primarily in solitary play. Because these materials are self-correcting (that is, children know when they have not placed the materials together in the manner in which they were designed), they encourage children to work on a task that has a specific end product. Shape sorters encourage children to determine which shapes fit into which openings. The end product is successfully putting all of the shapes into the corresponding holes.

On the other hand, materials such as clay, Play Doh, paint, and collage supplies structure the environment in a very different manner. The characteristics of these materials indicate to children that they may explore and create. Because the materials do not have a specific end product or procedure by which to accomplish a task, they foster creativity and open-ended thinking.

The flexibility of materials structures the environment. Although well-chosen children's books are rich in the images, words, and ideas they bring to children, their intrinsic flexibility is limited. They can be read by teachers to the children, read by individual children, or shared by small groups of children. In each situation, the reading of these books conveys to children the idea that they are to observe, listen, possibly comment on the content, and ask questions. It generally excludes or discourages behaviors such as active gross motor activities.

Materials such as unit blocks are inherently flexible. Although they are uniform and predictable, they also can be combined into unlimited combinations. Props can be added to them to create unique situations. The message that children receive from unit blocks is that they should be active and creative.

Reviewing the program mission and philosophy as well as the general goals for children enables the staff to determine the criteria and messages they should consider when choosing materials and equipment.

MATERIALS AND EQUIPMENT FOR CHILDREN WITH DISABILITIES

The characteristics of materials and equipment are important for all children, but materials and equipment that will be used with children with disabilities must also possess the five characteristics of Bronson (1995), discussed previously in the chapter. They should be interesting and familiar to the children, physically accessible to them, and appropriate for their social and cognitive skill levels. It is especially important that materials be accessible. If a child has fine motor difficulties, manipulatives must be large enough to be used comfortably. Puzzles with large knobs, larger blocks (e.g., unit blocks), and thick writing and art utensils are all examples of materials that are more accessible to a child with fine motor needs. For a child with a visual impairment, materials that have an auditory component are more accessible. For example, books that can be read by pressing buttons that activate a speech component enable the child to participate in a language and literature center.

Two primary characteristics that increase the likelihood that these materials will be more accessible to young children with disabilities are enhanced sensory characteristics and enhanced physical characteristics. Materials with *enhanced sensory characteristics* possess characteristics that provide more than one sensory cue to the child. A visually attractive material may draw a child without a disability to a toy. For a child with a visual impairment, an enticing tactile surface and/or an auditory component makes the toy more accessible. Materials that have two or three obvious sensory characteristics are more likely to motivate children with disabilities.

Toys or other materials with *enhanced physical characteristics* can be used by children who have motor delays or disabilities, especially fine motor and hand use delays. Bristle blocks are physically enhanced because they stick to one another when gently placed together and hold their placement, unlike interlocking blocks or unit blocks.

Many commercially manufactured toys have undergone a transformation during the past thirty years, becoming more physically accessible. Toys that were once difficult to use and sometimes unsafe for all children have been redesigned to be safer and more accessible to children whose developmental skills are different from the norm. A case in point is Mattel's See 'N Say.® As originally designed in the sixties, this toy used a ¾-inch plastic ring that was pulled to activate a recording. To use the toy, a child needed the following physical capabilities:

1. Isolation of at least one finger to insert in the plastic ring
2. The ability to grasp the ring with the isolated finger
3. The strength to pull the ring and the attached string nine inches from the toy
4. The ability to balance and stabilize the toy with the hand not pulling the ring (the toy had no handle or grip)
5. A range of motion in the arm pulling the string to move the ring nine inches from the toy
6. The ability to release the ring completely at the moment the string was fully extended

For the average 3- or 4-year-old, this was a difficult task. For a child with a physical disability, motor planning problem, or cognitive delays, it was almost impossible to use this toy.

In the late eighties, "See 'N Say" was redesigned to make it more accessible for all children but especially for children with physical disabilities. A handle was added to the top to stabilize the toy. The plastic ring and string were removed and replaced with a large, easy-to-use push down lever. The necessary skills for using this toy now are as follows:

1. Stabilizing the toy with one hand, using the built-in handle
2. Pushing the lever with the other hand to activate the recording

The redesign of this toy has reduced the number of skills necessary to access the toy from six to two. The two skills are similar and are easier for children with disabilities to accomplish. Similar redesigns have occurred with such common toys as jack-in-the-boxes, Slinkies, and building blocks. Thirty years ago, many jack-in-the-boxes were opened by cranking a very small, tight lever in a circular motion. They required a neat pincer grasp, a stable shoulder and elbow, and refined wrist control. Redesigned jack-in-the boxes often have a mechanism that a child can move by passing an open or closed hand over a roller that opens the box.

Slinkies, the flexible metal snakes introduced in the sixties have been redesigned to provide greater visual input. The original Slinkies were made of a flat, colored steel. The current versions can be found in numerous fluorescent colors that help children locate the toy and follow the movement, even if they have decreased visual skills.

Many building blocks have been redesigned for easier access for younger children and children with physical disabilities. When first introduced, Leggos were a miniature version of unit blocks, but could be locked together. The basic Leggo block was four units by two units and measured approximately $1\frac{1}{4}$ inches by $\frac{5}{8}$ inch. To lock together two of these blocks, a neat pincer grasp, using the thumb and forefinger, was necessary. Although these materials had many of the benefits of unit blocks (e.g., uniform design, durability, consistent relationship among the pieces), for very young children or children with fine motor impairments they were difficult to use. The introduction of the Duplo series of blocks, which are larger versions of the Leggo blocks, allowed children greater access to the benefits of block building. The standard Duplo unit block is also four units by two units; however, it measures approximately $2\frac{1}{2}$ inches by $1\frac{1}{4}$ inches. The increased size means that a palmar grasp can be used to lock the blocks together.

Even though many materials for young children have been adapted to allow for greater access by children with various ability levels, teachers can also adapt materials and enhance their accessibility. The sensory characteristics of materials often can be enhanced easily. Commercial toys can be covered with textured cloth or paper to increase the tactile input available to children. Mylar wrapping paper, fluorescent colored paper, and foil paper can be attached to the exterior of toys and materials to increase their visual characteristics. The auditory component of materials can be enhanced by bells, chimes, or even digital computer chips as added sound for objects that do not have auditory characteristics.

Adding knobs or handles to make materials more physically accessible allows children with low muscle tone or fine motor impairments to use new and different objects. Adding Velcro strips enables children with significant motor disabilities to interact with and pick up materials when they are wearing an accompanying Velcro mitt.

Even when teachers enhance the sensory and physical properties of materials, they must place them carefully for children to benefit from them. Materials intended for independent use should be placed at an accessible level. For children with disabilities, this means that teachers must consider children's ability to reach, the range of motion of their arms, and any adaptive equipment (e.g., a walker or wheelchair) that may keep them at too great a distance from a traditional shelf.

When teachers evaluate materials for young children with disabilities, they should look for real, flexible materials with the potential to be used in a representational fashion. In addition, they should look for materials whose sensory and physical characteristics are enhanced to increase accessibility, or for materials that can be modified to enhance their sensory and physical properties. Materials and equipment that meet these standards will, with the proper arrangement and teacher support, enhance the developmental skills of all children.

LEARNING CENTERS

Learning centers are the physical areas of a classroom in which small groups of children gather or individual children work by themselves. Centers usually are designated by a type of activity or by skill content. For instance, one center designated by the type of activity is the sensory area. Sand, water, snow, beans, rice, or other sensory materials are placed there. A center designated by skill is the manipulative area. Puzzles, Peg-Boards, stacking rings, shape sorters and form boards, lock and latch boards, and other manipulatives are found in this center. Table 7.1 lists typical learning centers found in early childhood classrooms.

Learning centers, whether defined by skill or type of activity, focus on the development of multiple skills. Although an activity may be more likely to develop one or two targeted skills, often other skills are being developed simultaneously. For example, children working with unit blocks are primarily developing spatial awareness and fine motor abilities. In addition they may be enhancing social, cognitive, and communication skills. The mix of skills being developed is directly related to the number and types of props, the number of children, and the size of the block area.

TABLE 7.1   Typical Learning Centers in Early Childhood Classrooms

Learning Centers Defined by Skill	Learning Centers Defined by Type of Activity
Gross Motor	Art
Literacy and Listening	Blocks
Manipulatives (fine motor)	Cooking
Writing	Discovery
	Dramatic Play
	Music
	Sensory (e.g., sand and water)
	Woodworking

A sensory learning center that has primarily finger painting available may be fostering the development of prewriting skills and gross motor abilities such as shoulder stabilization and controlled use of the arms, wrists, and hands. The same area, however, can encourage the development of cognitive skills such as observation, classification, and discrimination when comparing colors, textures, lines, and images produced. The same sensory area can foster social skills when children work together on the same large sheet of paper, communication skills as they label their creations, and self-care skills as they clean up.

A gross motor learning center primarily fosters the development of motor skills such as climbing, jumping, balancing, pulling, and pushing. The center can also be designed to encourage the development of awareness of one's body in space, social interactions, and cognitive awareness of physical-world concepts such as weight, movement, and inertia.

Rationale for the Use of Learning Centers with Young Children with Disabilities

Learning centers are highly versatile and are valuable for children of all developmental levels. They assist teachers in addressing the multiplicity of children's needs without having to plan activities for each child. For example, a simple activity with Play Doh can address a wide variety of objectives through simple additions to the materials and the manner in which the teacher interacts with the children. A Play Doh activity with rolling pins and cookie cutters can foster objectives relating to hand strength, upper trunk and shoulder stabilization, and grasp and release skills. By using different colors of Play Doh and mixing sand or oatmeal into the dough, cognitive skills of observation, discrimination, and classification can be addressed and language skills such as labeling and using adjectives (e.g., smooth, gritty, chunky, rough) can be targeted.

Teachers' adaptations of their interactions with the children can address other skills. Language skills can be fostered through such teacher structures as giving simple instructions for putting on a smock before working with the dough, asking questions, or providing a very small amount of dough so that children will have to ask for more. Teachers can foster fine motor objectives by modeling the construction of "snakes" or balls of dough. Table 7.2 illustrates how three children with different fine motor needs can have their IEP objectives met at an art center, using one activity.

The ability of learning centers to address multiple developmental skill needs is only one reason for their efficiency at meeting the needs of young children with disabilities. Learning centers also enable young children with disabilities to work on the following skills:

TABLE 7.2 **An Art Center Activity Addressing IEP Objectives of Three Different Children in an Integrated 5-Year-Old Kindergarten Class**

Art Center Activity: Finger painting on butcher paper at a table with six chairs. Two containers of finger-paint are available for children to reach into, smooth on paper with their hands, and create any picture or design they desire.

Child and Objective	Adaptation
LaKeisha—follow two step directions	At the conclusion of her participation in the painting, a staff member can ask LaKeisha to "put her painting on the drying rack and wash her hands;" at clean-up time for the day, a staff member can ask LaKeisha to "wash the containers and put them on the art shelf."
Amber—use tools and utensils	A staff member can provide a spoon for Amber to use to scoop paint from the container to her paper; sponge tipped brushes or other tools can be provided for Amber to paint with or to make marks on her painting.
Tarrel—request assistance from peers and adults	A staff member should not have butcher paper available until a child sits at the table; he should wait until Tarrel asks for paper and provide prompts if necessary; a staff member should have only one container of paint that is passed from child to child; he should wait until Tarrel asks a peer for the paint; models of other children requesting the paint can be provided.

1. Making choices. The availability of four, six, or eight centers creates a built-in need to decide where to work. For children who are not able to make choices among eight, six, or even four centers, teachers can limit the choice to only two or even have children choose between two types of activities within one center.

2. Developing social skills. Because centers are designed so that small groups of children work side by side, they are ideal for focusing on social development. Centers for blocks or dramatic play allow children to work at the parallel, associative, or cooperative levels of play. Children can even participate in onlooker or isolated play in many centers.

3. Integrating skills. Because centers do not focus solely on one developmental skill, young children can integrate the skills they are developing with other, logically associated skills. For instance, in dramatic play, children who are working on taking turns when communicating with peers can also work on eye contact, social proximity, and voice level while learning to wait for another child to finish what he or she is saying and then responding.

4. Allowing functional use of skills. Because centers provide natural, logical, typical tasks for young children, the skills children develop are functional skills that allow them to be successful in groups of young children.

5. Natural repetition of skills. Centers provide multiple opportunities for children with disabilities to repeat skills until they master them. A child who is working on buttoning can put on and take off a smock in numerous locations (e.g., the paint easel, the art table, the dramatic play area, and the cooking center) and thereby practice that skill until it is achieved, mastered, and maintained.

6. Using motivating materials. Teachers can select materials that are intrinsically motivating to children and provide them in centers where the children must work on specific skills. A child who needs to work on release and grasp skills and is motivated by zoo animals may be drawn to a block center if figures of zoo animals are provided with the unit blocks.

Because the activities and materials placed in learning centers are flexible and constantly changing, teachers and other staff members can choose activities that are naturally motivating to the children. The information that teachers collect about the young children should indicate the childrens' preferences in activities and materials. The teachers use that information to plan activities that draw children to specific learning centers.

One of Brad's preferred activities is playing in the dramatic play center. He likes social groups, taking on roles, and interacting with small groups of children. By considering these preferences, the teacher can address Brad's objectives, including learning to button, fasten, and zip clothing, and using words to communicate his needs. The use of dramatic play clothing that has fasteners and the creation of scenarios that are highly social will motivate Brad to work on objectives that have been identified as important to his development.

If Tiffany's teachers and family feel that she should begin to use a communication board, her participation in a number of learning centers can allow for continued repetition and practice of that skill. For instance, in a gross motor area with a swing, Tiffany can use her communication board to ask to be swung. When the swing stops, she can use the board to ask for a push. As the teacher asks her questions, Tiffany can use the board to respond. In this way, she will have the opportunity to repeat a skill and work toward mastering it.

The activities, social interactions, and materials available in learning centers help to foster the development of functional skills for young children. Such skills as following directions, responding to social cues, greeting peers

TABLE 7.3 Benefits of Using Learning Centers with Young Children with Disabilities

1. Enables teachers to address multiple skills for multiple children simultaneously.
2. Allows children opportunities for repetition of skills in natural settings.
3. Allows teachers and other staff to provide materials and activities that incorporate preferences of children.
4. Allows children to make choices of activities, materials, and peers with whom to work.
5. Allows children to use social skills in natural settings.
6. Integrates children's skills in natural settings.
7. Allows children to work on necessary functional skills in a natural setting.

and adults, manipulating common early childhood materials, and participating in small groups allow children with disabilities to function in the settings in which all young children spend time. Table 7.3 reviews the benefits of using learning centers with young children with disabilities.

Types of Learning Centers

As mentioned earlier, learning centers can be divided into two categories: those that focus primarily on a specific type of skill and those that focus on a type of activity. Although the skills and behaviors enhanced in a center are dependent upon the activities, materials, and interactions that take place, each center has specific characteristics that enable a child to emphasize a set of primary skills or concepts.

The various attributes of centers fall into five categories: (1) level of structure, (2) level of open-endedness, (3) level of cognitive opportunities, (4) level of physical opportunities, and (5) level of social and communication opportunities. A teacher can develop a profile for any learning center by using these five attributes. For instance, in Figure 7.1, two centers have been rated on the five attributes mentioned above. A dramatic play center has many opportunities for social and communication interactions and for creativity, while a manipulative center is usually highly structured and has many opportunities to focus on the acquisition of cognitive skills. For a child whose program objectives focus on social and communication needs, the dramatic play center might be an area for which a teacher could design activities that would be inviting for him. For a child who needs to develop many cognitive skills and also needs to work on fine motor skills or visual and spatial skills, the manipulative

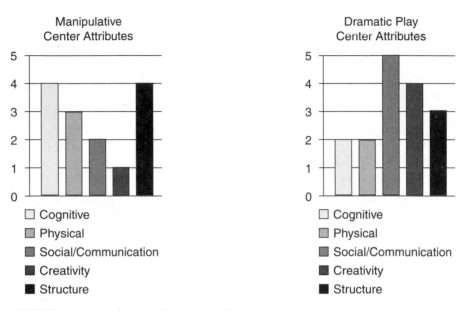

FIGURE 7.1   **Learning Center Attributes**

center can provide valuable learning activities. Teachers can use the assessment information they have about a child's learning style, activity preferences,
and motivators to plan activities that address specific needs.

Using the five center attributes to understand the skills and behaviors
that can be addressed by a given learning center, teachers can determine how
to balance the experiences of children who participate in those centers. For
example, the materials that make up a manipulative center are often highly
structured materials such as puzzles, shape sorters, and counting and classification figures (e.g., teddy bear counters). Such materials often help children
work on the development of their cognitive skills. However, social and communication skills are not easily addressed in a manipulative center. For a
child who is attracted to these types of materials and also needs assistance
with language development, the teacher can provide adaptations to the center, addressing social and communication skills. The teacher may choose to
intervene by discussing the activity with the child or by adding materials that
can be used simultaneously by two children (e.g., floor puzzles).

Different learning centers allow teachers to focus on different skills. Table
7.4 details the centers usually found in a program for young children and the
general skills that can be addressed in each one.

More important than the attributes of the learning center are the interactions that occur with the materials, children, and adults. A round, one-inch,

TABLE 7.4 Typical Early Childhood Classroom Learning Centers and the General Skills Fostered by Work in Those Centers

Center	Skills Fostered
Gross Motor Center	large muscle development locomotion spatial awareness persistence and endurance
Block Center	spatial relationships classification skills visual–motor coordination grasp and release object placement cooperation and sharing of resources
Dramatic Play Center	assuming social roles dressing skills symbolic representation problem solving abilities cooperation and sharing of resources communication skills
Manipulative Center	grasp and release spatial relationships classification visual–motor coordination object placement visual discrimination sorting and matching skills sequencing and seriation concepts
Art Center	self-esteem creativity cooperation and sharing of resources labeling and descriptive communication skills grasp and release spatial relationships visual–motor coordination object placement classification skills use of tools
Sensory Center	comparing and contrasting language skills cause and effect wrist pronation and supination visual–motor coordination social interactions following rules and guidelines development of concepts such as volume, weight, mass, float/sink, and gravity
Literacy and Listening Center	assuming social roles listening skills sequencing skills understanding of social roles

rubber ball in a gross motor area with three children becomes the vehicle for a simple game. The same ball in the dramatic play center may be a piece of "fruit," and when used in a water table in the sensory center, it becomes a mechanism for talking about sinking and floating. Teachers must be aware of the multiple ways that the ball is being used and be prepared to build on the children's choices and experiences. The versatility and flexibility of learning centers makes them an ideal mechanism for addressing the multiple needs of young children with disabilities and the wide spectrum of developmental needs of all young children.

INTEGRATED THEMATIC UNITS

What Are Integrated Thematic Units?

Integrated thematic units are a form of curriculum planning for early childhood education programs. They are based on the addressing of multiple areas of development simultaneously (Bredekamp & Rosegrant, 1995). Usually designed around a topical area such as transportation, community helpers, animals, or other real-life experience, integrated thematic units use planned activities to enhance and reinforce the development of children's skills. The thematic unit approach integrates curriculum for all young children in two important ways: developmental skills are integrated into the natural context in which those skills are used, and the approach integrates related developmental skills.

In early childhood settings that use an integrated thematic unit approach, activities designed to assist a child in the development of social skills are not isolated from activities designed to develop communication, cognitive, or motor skills. The approach recognizes that skills in one domain are often linked to skills in another. For young children, social and communication skills are intimately linked (Cripe, Slentz, & Bricker, 1993). Greeting peers or adults is both a communication skill in terms of language and a social skill in terms of determining when to greet, how to address, and deciding how formal to be with the person being greeted.

Likewise, cognitive and communication skills are linked (Bailey & Wolery, 1994). Identifying such common objects as toys, people, clothing, and foods is both a communication skill, in that words are used to label the object, and a cognitive act, in that the skills of observation, classification, discrimination, symbolic representation, and memory are used to determine what the object is. The integrated thematic unit approach lets early childhood educators address related skills such as these simultaneously.

This approach to programming is a flexible method for addressing children's IFSP or IEP objectives. Table 7.5 is a two-day portion of an integrated

TABLE 7.5   Example of Two Days from an Integrated Theme Unit with One Child's IEP Objectives Embedded in the Activities

Integrated Theme Unit

Daily Schedule for Copeland Preschool   Theme: TRUCKS

Time	Activity	Description
8:30	Arrival/Greeting	Drop off, greeting, choose activities.
8:30 – 9:15	Limited Free-Play	Simple activities in four or five interest areas are available for the children (e.g., puzzles, Leggos and bristle blocks, markers).
9:15 – 9:30	Morning Circle	All children join in for morning routines such as the "Good Morning" song, selection of daily helpers, and calendar and weather.
9:30 – 11:00	Free-Play	Eight different interest centers are available to the children (i.e. blocks, housekeeping, manipulatives, art, sand, books, writing center, and computer); the activities at these centers change every four to six weeks.
11:00 – 11:10	Song Circle	The children gather in a large group to sing the classes' repertoire of songs.
11:10 – 11:40	Outside Time	The children go to the playground where swings, a sand box, and riding toys are available. During inclement weather, the children go to a gym to use riding toys, mats, and climbing structures.
11:40 – 12:10	Lunch	The children eat in the classroom, family style.
12:10 – 1:40	Rest Time	All children take a nap or rest on their cots.
1:40 – 1:55	Story Group	All children gather to hear a picture book story.
1:55 – 3:25	Free-Play	The eight activity areas offered in the morning are again available.
3:25 – 3:40	Movement Group	All children participate in a music and movement activity lead by the teachers.
3:40 – 4:00	Dismissal	

(continued)

TABLE 7.5   *(Continued)*

Schedule for Monday	TOPIC: Introduction to Trucks	Brad's Targeted Objectives
8:30 - 9:15 Arrival, limited free-play, and breakfast	Pictures of different types of trucks around the room; truck books available in the library; matchbook style trucks available to play with at the manipulative table.	Use one word when making requests for objects/activities. Make one word comments about activities. Respond to peer's request to play. Express protest by saying the word "no." Play with manipulatives. Make smooth transition from free-play to group. Express excitement in play. Share a toy with a peer.
9:15 - 9:30 Morning Circle	Morning circle activities and an introduction to trucks. Pass around different types of toy trucks (e.g., pick-ups, garbage, tractor trailers). Go out to the play ground to look at a pick-up truck and a garbage truck; explore the cabs of each and observe what they carry. Return to the classroom and tell the group about the centers available for the day.	Follow one step directions during routines. Express protest by saying the word "no." Play with manipulatives. Express excitement in play. Share a toy with a peer.
9:30 - 11:00 A.M. Centers Blocks	Unit blocks and 6"–8" toy pick-up and trailer trucks. Small (<1") colored wooden blocks.	Use one word when requesting objects/activities. One word comments about activities. Ask a peer to play with him by using one word. Respond to peer's request to play. Express protest by saying the word "no." Play with manipulatives. Express excitement in play. Share a toy with a peer.

TABLE 7.5 *(Continued)*

Schedule for Monday	TOPIC: Introduction to Trucks	Brad's Targeted Objectives
Dramatic Play	Chairs arranged in the form of truck seats. A steering wheel attached to a block of wood, saw horse or some other stable base. A large box placed horizontally with the top portion cut open and a flap at the back to simulate a tailgate. Large traffic signs. Objects to be used as cargo.	Use one word when making requests for objects/activities. Make one word comments about activities. Ask a peer to play with him by using one word. Respond to peer's request to play. Express protest by saying the word "no." Express excitement in play. Share a toy with a peer.
Art	(a) Outlines and pre-cut square, rectangular, triangular and circular shapes; paste; 11" × 14" construction paper. Children can create any type of collage or picture they design; some may choose to represent trucks or other vehicles. (b) A second large box, large paint brushes, two or three colors of paint in wide based pans, shower curtain or other drop cloth. Allow the children to paint this "truck" to be used later in the week in the dramatic play area.	Use one word when making requests for objects/activities. Make one word comments about activities. Follow one step directions during routines.
Manipulatives	(a) Matchbox truck one-to-one correspondence. Make five "garages" from small boxes and place dots on the "roof", one dot on the first box, two dots on the second box, up to five dots. Take five matchbox size trucks and place corresponding dots on the roofs of the trucks. (b) Matchbox truck color match. Make five different color "garages" and provide a basket of five trucks that correspond with the colors of the garages.	Use one word when making requests for objects/activities. One word comments about activities. Play with manipulatives.

TABLE 7.5 *(Continued)*

Schedule for Monday	TOPIC: Introduction to Trucks	Brad's Targeted Objectives
Manipulatives *(cont.)*	(c) Truck lotto. Make a lotto game using truck stickers. Make lotto cards with four, six, nine, and sixteen places. (d) Truck puzzles.	
Easel	Butcher paper cut out in the shape of trucks; large print brushes; two primary colored paints.	Use one word when making requests for objects/activities. One word comments about activities.
Listening/Literacy Center	Books: Mike and Ruth Wolverton's *Trucks and Trucking*, Donald Crews' *Trucks*, Sara Wilson's *Garage Song*, Charlotte Pomerantz' *How Many Trucks Can a Tow Truck Tow?*, and Magee's *Trucks You Can Count On*.	Share a toy with a peer.
Sensory Table	Sand and small (~1"–2") trucks.	Use one word when making requests for objects/activities. Make one word comments about activities. Respond to peer's request to play. Express protest by saying the word "no." Play with manipulatives. Express excitement in play. Share a toy with a peer.
Discovery Table	Construct a simple 6" crane that is secured to a table top. Allow the children to place different objects in a basket and attempt to raise the basket with the crane. Objects might include foam pieces, stones, wooden beads. Allow children to classify the objects as "heavy" or "light."	Use one word when making requests for objects/activities. Make one word comments about activities. Respond to peer's request to play. Play with manipulatives. Express excitement in play. Share a toy with a peer.

TABLE 7.5 (*Continued*)

Schedule for Monday		TOPIC: Introduction to Trucks	Brad's Targeted Objectives
11:00 - 11:10	Music Circle	Teach the children the fingerplay *Wheels* from Louise Scott's *Rhymes for Learning Times.* Sing *Old MacDonald's Truck* from Jean Warren's *Piggyback Songs for Infants and Toddlers.*	Follow one step directions during routines. Make smooth transition from free-play to group. Express excitement in play.
11:10 - 11:40	Outside	Large plastic trucks in the sand box. Hollow wooden blocks and a mounted steering wheel. Tricycles and wagons.	Use one word when making requests for objects/activities. Make one word comments about activities. Ask a peer to play by using one word. Respond to peer's request to play. Express protest by saying the word "no." Walk to and from the playground. Express excitement in play. Share a toy with a peer.
11:40 - 12:10	Lunch	Wash hands, toileting, family style lunch, clean up. Have truck shaped placemats at each child's seat.	Make one word comments about activities. Follow one step directions during routines. Pull pants up and down. Sit on toilet.
12:10 - 1:40	Rest Time	Nap or rest on cots.	Follow one step directions during routines.
1:40 - 1:55	Story Group	Read Donald Crew's *Trucks.* Ask the children to tell the story; what is happening to the trucks, where they are going, what they are carrying, who is driving.	Make one word comments about activities. Follow one step directions during routines.
1:55 - 3:25	P.M. Centers	Repeat morning activities.	Make smooth transition from free-play to group. Express excitement in play. Share a toy with a peer.

TABLE 7.5 *(Continued)*

Schedule for Monday		TOPIC: Introduction to Trucks	Brad's Targeted Objectives
3:25 - 3:40	Movement Group	Collect sounds of different types of trucks (e.g., on the highway, backing up with a warning beeper, an air horn, a slow moving truck, a pick-up truck, an 18-wheel tractor trailer). With the children standing and with instructions to remain in their places, ask them to move like the sound that they hear. Ask them to try to identify the sounds or describe the sounds.	Make one word comments about activities. Follow one step directions during routines. Express excitement in play.
3:40 - 4:00	Outside/ Dismissal	Ask the children to gather their belongings and get in the wagons. One child can be the "driver" and pull a group of children.	Follow one step directions during routines. Walk to and from the playground. Express excitement in play.
Schedule for Tuesday			
8:30 - 9:15	Arrival, limited free-play and breakfast	Pictures of different types of trucks around the room; truck books available in the library; matchbook style trucks available to play with at the manipulative table.	Use one word when making requests for objects/activities. Make one word comments about activities. Ask a peer to play by using one word. Respond to peer's request to play. Express protest by saying the word "no." Play with manipulatives. Make smooth transition from free-play to group. Express excitement in play. Share a toy with a peer.
9:15 - 9:30	Morning Circle	Show children large replicas of traffic signs (e.g., stop, yield, go [green traffic light]). Talk about what the signs mean. Play a game of stop and go with the signs. Allow some children to choose the signs to indicate "stop" or "go."	Make one word comments about activities. Follow one step directions during routines. Express protest by saying the word "no." Share a toy with a peer.

TABLE 7.5 (*Continued*)

Schedule for Tuesday	TOPIC: Introduction to Trucks	Brad's Targeted Objectives
9:30 - 11:00 A.M. Centers Blocks	Continue to have unit blocks and 6″–8″ toy pick-up and trailer trucks available with small (<1″) colored wooden blocks. Add traffic signs.	Use one word when making requests for objects/activities. Make one word comments about activities. Ask a peer to play by using one word. Respond to peer's request to play. Express protest by saying the word "no." Play with manipulatives. Express excitement in play. Share a toy with a peer.
Dramatic Play	Continue with truck arrangement of chairs. Add the box that was painted on Monday. Add typical truck driver clothing (e.g., overalls, jumpsuits, caps).	Use one word when making requests for objects/activities. Make one word comments about activities. Ask a peer to play by using one word. Respond to peer's request to play. Express protest by saying the word "no." Express excitement in play. Share a toy with a peer.
Art	1) Wheel painting. Have available a variety of small (1″–2″) trucks with wheels that turn. Using shallow pans, make available different colors of paint into which the trucks can be dipped. Allow the children to paint on different textured papers (e.g., construction, manila, newsprint). 2) Have automobile dealer catalogs of trucks, some cut out and others not. On 11″ × 14″ construction paper, children can create a truck collage.	Use one word when making requests for objects/activities. Make one word comments about activities. Follow one step directions during routines. Play with manipulatives. Express excitement in play. Share a toy with a peer.

TABLE 7.5   *(Continued)*

Schedule for Tuesday	TOPIC: Introduction to Trucks	Brad's Targeted Objectives
Manipulatives	Repeat manipulative activities from Monday. Add a truck graph. Have a basket of three different colored trucks and a graph of three columns. Allow the children to categorize the trucks into the appropriate columns and count the number of trucks in each category.	Follow one step directions during routines. Respond to peer's request to play. Play with manipulatives. Share a toy with a peer.
Easel	Large manila paper in the shape of traffic signs. Large brushes with yellow, red, and green paint.	Use one word when making requests for objects/activities. Make one word comments about activities.
Listening/Literacy Center	Have large traffic signs available (e.g., stop, slow, go). Record a tape that tells the children which sign to find.	Make one word comments about activities. Ask a peer to play with him by using one word. Follow one step directions during routines. Respond to peer's request to play. Express protest by saying the word "no." Express excitement in play. Share a toy with a peer.
Sensory Table	Small trucks, traffic signs, and a shallow level of garden size stones (~2"–3"). The level of the stones should be shallow enough so that the children can make roads or pathways by pushing aside the stones.	Use one word when making requests for objects/activities. Make one word comments about activities. Respond to peer's request to play. Express protest by saying the word "no." Play with manipulatives. Share a toy with a peer.
Discovery Table	Use a large plastic dump truck (~15"–18") to carry a waterproof plastic container with one open side. Using a plastic bellows pump, allow the children to fill the container from a separate reservoir of water.	Make one word comments about activities. Follow one step directions during routines. Walk to and from the playground. Smooth transition from free-play to group. Express excitement in play. Share a toy with a peer.

TABLE 7.5 (*Continued*)

Schedule for Tuesday		TOPIC: Introduction to Trucks	Brad's Targeted Objectives
11:00 - 11:10	Music Circle	Teach the children *Watching Traffic* from Darlene Hamilton and Bonnie Flemming's *Resources for Creative Teaching in Early Childhood Education*. Repeat *Wheels* from Louise Scott's *Rhymes for Learning Times* and Old MacDonald's *Truck* from Jean Warren's *Piggyback Songs for Infants and Toddlers*.	Follow one step directions during routines.
11:10 - 11:40	Outside	Large plastic trucks in the sandbox. Large hollow wooden blocks and a mounted steering wheel. Tricycles with ropes, large boxes with cut out handles that have been reinforced by duct tape. Allow the children to "tow" the boxes.	Make one word comments about activities. Ask a peer to play by using one word. Respond to peer's request to play. Express protest by saying the word "no." Express excitement in play. Share a toy with a peer.
11:40 - 12:10	Lunch	Toileting, washing hands, family style lunch, clean up. Use truck collages as placemats.	Follow one step directions during routines. Pull pants up and down. Sit on toilet.
12:10 - 1:40	Rest Time	Nap or rest on cots.	Follow one step directions during routines.
1:40 - 1:55	Story Group	Read *Trucks You Can Count On* by Magee. Talk about what these trucks carry and where they take their cargo.	Make one word comments about activities. Follow one step directions during routines.
1:55 - 3:25	P.M. Centers	Repeat morning activities.	Make smooth transition from free-play to group. Share a toy with a peer.
3:25 - 3:40	Movement Group	Play two adjacent notes (e.g., C and D) on the piano or any other musical instrument to simulate the sound of an engine. Have the children move in place or in a designated circle or other pattern in time to the "engine."	Follow one step directions during routines. Express excitement in play.
3:40 - 4:00	Outside/ Dismissal	Fill up a wagon with children's backpacks and "drive" it to the door.	Follow one step directions during routines. Walk to and from the playground.

theme unit on trucks. In this example, all of Brad's IEP objectives (see Chapter 4) have been targeted. There are either routine times or planned activity times during which program staff can address Brad's skill development related to his objectives.

Some IEP objectives have multiple opportunities to address skill development. During the first day of this unit, there are at least ten different opportunities for Brad to work on using one-word clauses to comment about activities. Other objectives, such as toileting, can be addressed at fewer times during the day.

It should be emphasized that not all of the multiple opportunities must be used as times for teaching a certain skill. Overemphasis can diminish the child's interest in any activity. After planning the unit and determining the activities and routines during which children's specific skills can be addressed, priority activities can be identified as optimal times with the children. For example, it may be appropriate to emphasize Brad's skill in using one word to request an item when he arrives and at the beginning of morning and afternoon free-play. Although other opportunities to foster this skill exist, the staff may decide that these are the times when Brad is most motivated and rested and, therefore, the times with the highest probability of success.

When activities for integrated units are chosen carefully, they address children's individual objectives across multiple activities. One of Brad's primary objectives is to increase his fine motor skills. Because we know that Brad generally does not like to play with manipulatives, small toys that require the same type of fine motor skill as manipulatives have been included in his activities throughout the day. On Monday Brad has the opportunity to develop his fine motor skills in the morning circle by passing around the toy trucks, in the block center (trucks again), at the sensory table with trucks in sand, and at the discovery table by using a crane and small wooden beads. By using these materials throughout the room, Brad will be more likely to foster his fine motor development.

Selecting Integrated Theme Topics

At least five factors must be considered in the selection of integrated thematic units for a classroom containing children with and without disabilities. A primary consideration is that the theme should be broad enough to address the wide spectrum of skills and abilities found in a typical group of young children.

A second important consideration is the IEP or IFSP objectives for the children with disabilities. The thematic topic must be broad enough to enable teachers to generate activities that address the IEP or IFSP skills children need to acquire. Units such as transportation, community helpers, the restaurant, the farm, and other topics familiar to children are flexible enough to incorporate skills from communication, cognitive, social, adaptive, fine motor, and gross motor domains.

A third consideration is choosing a unit of high interest to the children. Topics should be generated from the experiences and interests of the children (Bredekamp & Rosegrant, 1992; Bredekamp & Rosegrant, 1995; Dodge & Colker, 1992; Isbell, 1995). One theme might focus on the topic of babies because one of the children has a new baby brother. Another might be trees because of the children's interest in falling leaves. With a focus on the children's interests and experiences, activities are intrinsically motivating to the children and their descriptive language is richer and more complex.

A fourth consideration when selecting topics is the availability of materials and resources. If the program staff do not have access to resources that allow them to create concrete, child-directed activities, it will be difficult to maintain the children's interest and motivation. Teachers can plan integrated units that address specific objectives, are highly motivating, and capitalize on interests and experiences. However, if there is no time for the teachers to collect the necessary materials, create the activities, and organize the learning environment, the unit will not be successful.

A final consideration is the staff's interests. The children's interests and the ability to address skill development are critical to the selection of a theme, but it is also important that staff be enthusiastic about the theme. Without the power of the teachers' interests, an integrated unit can lose many of the inherent benefits characteristic of this instructional approach.

Rationale for Using Integrated Themes with Young Children with Disabilities

Historically, teaching specific skills to young children with disabilities has been accomplished through massed trial instruction or drill and practice. Children have learned a skill by working one-on-one with an adult who cues their behavior and reinforces a correct response. This has proven to be an extremely effective method of instruction for specific skills, but it has not been effective in helping children to generalize those skills in other settings. In many cases, the opportunity to use the skill that has been taught in a massed trial instructional situation occurs rarely in the child's daily environment. An integrated thematic unit approach provides a natural context for learning the skills. Depending upon the needs of the children, subtle or significant cues can be used to support them as they learn new skills. Naturally occurring reinforcers can be used as consequences in the integrated thematic unit approach.

A typical example of this type of skill acquisition might be a young child who is learning to greet adults or children who enter a play area. Using a multiple or massed trial approach, an adult might work with the child in a separate room or in a space to the side of a classroom. The adult might repeatedly enter the area and cue the child to say "Hello" or some other such greeting until the child greets the adult with minimal or no prompting. The child may successfully learn the skill in this context but not transfer it to his or her daily activities with the other adults or children.

Using an integrated thematic unit approach, the child can learn this skill in multiple settings throughout the classroom. Wherever the child spends time during the preschool day—the dramatic play area, the art table, or the manipulatives table—a staff member can cue the child to greet children or adults who enter the area. The child has multiple opportunities to practice the skill in a real-life setting where the skill is actually used. The child will still receive reinforcement for displaying the skill successfully, possibly in the form of a hug or verbal acknowledgment.

A second important reason for using the integrated thematic unit approach with young children with disabilities is that it allows teachers, therapists, and other staff members to address related developmental skills simultaneously. Curricula can be developed such that they promote the acquisition of skills and behaviors that complement one another. Using the example of greeting others when they enter a room, a complementary skill might be making eye contact. These two social and communication skills are complementary in that they may be cued by the same behaviors or circumstances in the child's environment (a new person entering a room) and may be reinforced by similar or identical consequences (a verbal acknowledgment or a hug). The skills can be taught in multiple areas of the typical early childhood classroom, providing numerous opportunities for practice throughout the program day.

A third important reason to use an integrated thematic unit approach with young children with disabilities is that the curriculum planning process can use children's strengths as the basis for learning new skills. For instance, if we want to increase Tiffany's ability to maintain eye contact with adults, we can consider her strengths. Because she likes brightly colored objects and can track them, we might play a game in which she follows brightly colored toys to an adult's face. The toy is the cue or situation that initiates the skill, and the reinforcement might be smiles or hugs from the adult when eye contact is maintained.

A final reason to use the integrated thematic unit approach with young children with disabilities is that the curriculum is based upon children's interests, preferences, and experiences. This method of planning day-to-day activities ensures that children are interested in the curriculum and are motivated to participate in the activities. For young children with disabilities, providing adequate motivation is a key component to successful skill development (Bailey & Wolery, 1994; Bricker & Cripe, 1992; Cook, Tessier, & Klein, 1996; Linder, 1993). In the example of enhancing a child's ability to greet others, a teacher can plan activities that focus on the child's preference to play with blocks, which may increase motivation to practice the skill of greeting in the block area. The teacher can structure the block activity so that it is necessary for the child to greet others when they enter the block area. Using children's preferences and interests, as well as building on their strengths, ensures that young children are much more likely to participate actively in the activities designed to enhance their skill development.

SUMMARY

Through the use of appropriate materials, learning centers, and integrated themes, the multiple needs of young children with and without disabilities can be addressed in early childhood programs. Carefully chosen materials, well-conceptualized learning centers, and high-interest integrated themes motivate children with disabilities to become actively involved in their environments. They foster interactions with materials and peers and through those interactions enhance skills and abilities.

The use of developmentally appropriate materials, equipment, learning centers, and units address two of the largest problems of teaching young children with disabilities: motivation to develop skills and natural, functional settings in which to practice and master them. Creating learning environments following the guidelines cited in this chapter will provide engaging settings where children can participate in activities that allow them to develop skills identified on their individual program plans and, over the course of time, provide them with the opportunities to master those skills.

ACTIVITIES AND RESOURCES

Activities

1. Using a book such as one of the following, identify activities appropriate for Brad. Which of Brad's objectives can be addressed by the activities you chose?

    Hamilton, D. and Flemming, B. 1990. *Resources for creative teaching in early childhood.* 2d ed. New York: Harcourt, Brace, Jovanovich.
    Rainer, S. and Canady, R. 1991. *Story stretchers.* Mt. Ranier, MD: Gryphon House.

2. Visit a preschool, child care center, or early childhood classroom in your community. Identify materials and equipment in the program that can be used by children with physical, visual, and auditory impairments.
3. Choose a toy or piece of equipment typically found in an early childhood program. How can you make the toy or equipment accessible to young children with visual impairments? Auditory impairments?
4. Walk through a local toy store or look through an early childhood materials and equipment catalog. Identify ten toys that can be used with children with physical disabilities and ten that cannot.

Class Discussion Questions

1. Why are the types of materials chosen for an early childhood classroom important to the learning process? Why are they even more important to young children with disabilities?
2. How can early childhood materials be adapted or enhanced so that young children with disabilities can use them or obtain the greatest benefits from them?
3. How do learning centers foster functional skill development in young children with disabilities?
4. Identify the typical skills that can be fostered at the art center, block center, and dramatic play center.
5. What information should you have in order to decide what theme to choose for an integrated theme unit for your classroom? Specifically, what information do you need regarding the young children with disabilities in your classroom?

REFERENCES

Bailey, D., & Wolery, M. (1994). *Teaching infants and preschoolers with disabilities.* New York: Merrill.

Bredekamp, S., & Rosegrant, T. (Eds.). (1992). *Reaching potentials: Appropriate curriculum and assessment for young children, Volume 1.* Washington, DC: NAEYC.

Bredekamp, S., & Rosegrant, T. (Eds.). (1995). *Reaching potentials: Transforming early childhood curriculum and assessment, Volume 2.* Washington, DC: NAEYC.

Bricker, D., & Cripe, J. (1992). *An activity-based approach to early intervention.* Baltimore, MD: Paul H. Brookes Publishing Co.

Bronson, M. (1995). *The right stuff for children birth to eight: Selecting play materials to support development.* Washington, DC: NAEYC.

Cook, R., Tessier, A., & Klein, M.D. (1996). *Adapting early childhood curricula for children in inclusive settings* (4th ed.). Englewood Cliffs, NJ: Merrill.

Cripe, J., Slentz, K., & Bricker, D. (1993). *AEPS curriculum for birth to three years.* Baltimore, MD: Paul H. Brookes Publishing Co.

Dodge, D., & Colker, L. (1992). *The creative curriculum* (3rd Ed.). Washington, DC: Teaching Strategies, Inc.

Isbell, R. (1995). *The complete learning center book.* Beltsville, MD: Gryphon House.
Linder, T. (1993). *Transdisciplinary play-based intervention: Guidelines for developing meaningful curriculum for young children.* Baltimore, MD: Paul H. Brookes Publishing Co.
Sutton-Smith, B. (1992). *Toys as culture.* New York: Gardner.

8

USING DEVELOPMENTALLY APPROPRIATE PRACTICES TO MAKE DECISIONS ABOUT GUIDING THE BEHAVIOR OF YOUNG CHILDREN

DEBBIE C. WOODWARD

Class Rules

1. Please do not fight in the classroom.

2. Please do not punch anybody in the classroom or outside or anywhere.

3. Please flush the toilet when you finish in the bathroom.

4. Boys, please lift the toilet seat up when you use it.

5. Please be nice to your classmates and don't kick.

6. Please walk in the classroom.

7. Do not bring spitballs or throw them in the classroom.

OBJECTIVES

As a result of studying this chapter, readers should be able to perform the following:

- Provide a definition of developmentally appropriate behavior guidance and explain how the principles of age appropriateness and individual appropriateness apply to behavior guidance.
- Look at challenging behaviors from a child's perspective and ask "new questions" about how to help children develop positive behaviors and the opportunity to be valued.
- Describe strategies for teaching appropriate behaviors, preventing misbehaviors, and responding to misbehaviors.
- Discuss strategies for including families in behavior guidance planning, implementation, and evaluation.
- Use a six-step decision-making process to develop behavior guidance plans.

FOCUSING ON BEHAVIOR

Parents, teachers, school administrators, public leaders, and others interested in the welfare of children and communities are concerned about raising children who understand limits, have a strong sense of right and wrong, use appropriate self-discipline, resolve conflicts peacefully, and, in general, demonstrate positive social skills that contribute to the shared life of society. As society becomes increasingly complex and social problems more prevalent, childhood discipline and helping children develop positive social behaviors stand out as issues of dire importance. Children must learn a complicated set of social rules and the contexts in which they apply. They must learn expected and acceptable behavior and how to monitor and control their own behavior. In addition, they must learn how to read the social cues of others and how to compromise and negotiate, social skills that will remain important throughout their lives. The development of these skills is a gradual process. Although maturation and experience play large roles in the development of behavior and social skills, children are greatly influenced by adult guidance. Therefore, guiding children to work and play cooperatively, feel a sense of responsibility for their actions, and develop other positive behaviors has paramount importance in the teaching of young children. For this reason, the focus of this chapter is on strategies teachers can use to guide and teach young children to develop positive behaviors and social skills.

DEVELOPMENTALLY APPROPRIATE BEHAVIOR GUIDANCE

The developmentally appropriate classroom should be viewed as a "laboratory of social relations where children explore values and learn rules of social living and respect for individual differences through experience" (Bredekamp, 1987, p. 71). The teacher facilitates the development of positive behaviors through carefully considered support and guidance. Children are given many opportunities throughout the day to practice cooperation, sharing, conflict resolution, problem solving, and peer and adult interaction. The teacher provides clear behavioral expectations and encourages and compliments children for their positive behaviors.

Like all developmentally appropriate practices, developmentally appropriate behavior guidance should be age appropriate and individually appropriate. This means that knowledge of typical behaviors of young children and how children learn positive behaviors is balanced by a recognition of individual differences among children. The combination of these two considerations provides the basis for setting realistic expectations for the behavior of young children.

Age Appropriate: Considering Behavior from a Developmental Perspective

When developing strategies for the guidance of behavior in young children, knowledge of typical child development and learning is essential for several reasons:

1. Knowledge of child development provides an understanding of behaviors common to various developmental levels. Using this knowledge, teachers know which behaviors to expect and understand that young children are gradually developing more mature social and behavioral skills. Many behaviors termed "misbehaviors" actually reflect the child's level of social maturity rather than problem behavior. For example, the unwillingness of a 2-year-old to share his favorite toy is typical for a child this age and should not be viewed as a problem behavior. Instead, the teacher should use his or her knowledge of child development to plan opportunities for the child to share toys that are less precious to him—perhaps even sharing one of a set of duplicate toys. In this manner, the teacher is guiding the child to develop more mature sharing skills but is doing so within his present level of capability.

2. Knowledge of child development provides a basis for setting realistic behavioral expectations. The teacher's expectations for child behavior should match the developmental maturity, cognitive readiness, typical developmental level, and individual uniqueness of the children in the class. For example, young children typically have a limited attention span and are very motor oriented. Requiring a group of 3-year-olds to sit quietly during an hour-long activity would not be an appropriate behavioral expectation and could set the stage for misbehaviors to occur. A wise teacher plans for brief activities that are highly motivating and engaging and include as much hands-on and movement-oriented learning as possible.

3. Knowledge of how children develop and learn gives teachers a basis for designing instructional activities and selecting strategies to teach children increasingly more mature, positive social behaviors. Young children learn from their experiences, from opportunities to practice, from observing others, and from the "teaching" that important adults in their lives provide. Therefore, teachers should provide opportunities for children to practice positive social skills such as being helpers, sharing, taking turns, and resolving conflicts. Instructional procedures such as role-playing, turn-taking games, the use of positive reinforcement, discussions, and peer modeling can be used by teachers to base their teaching methods on knowledge of how young children learn positive behaviors.

Individually Appropriate: Considering Individual Differences among Children

When developing behavior guidance strategies, teachers not only need to understand typical child development, but must also consider the uniqueness of each child. It is widely recognized that enormous variance exists in the developmental growth of individual children of the same age. Additionally, children have many different experiences at home and in their communities that may affect their social and behavioral development. The uniqueness of each family and its cultural or ethnic background must also be considered because different styles of behavior may be expected or valued. For example, some children may come from homes in which there is little tolerance of misbehavior and a child is given few choices. Children are expected to obey or face firm consequences. Others may come from homes in which parents impose few rules and are inconsistent in their response to misbehaviors. These differences in home settings can affect the behaviors displayed by children in the classroom.

The importance of considering individual learning styles to set appropriate behavioral expectations and guide teaching methods is well documented by Dunn, Dunn, and Perrin (1994). They found that some children learn best when allowed flexible seating arrangements rather than a rigid requirement to sit at a desk with feet on the floor, facing the front. Some children learn best when given a careful explanation of why a certain behavior is not allowed, while another child may need added visual cues as reminders. Because there is such variance in learning styles, teachers must consider each child individually.

The principle of individual appropriateness is especially essential when behavioral expectations and guidance strategies are developed for children with disabilities. There is evidence that children with disabilities exhibit more problem behaviors than do children without disabilities (Hunt, Johnson, Owen, Ormerod, & Babbitt, 1990). Several factors could be responsible for this. Disabilities that involve impaired language comprehension or expression may lead to inappropriate behaviors because the child lacks skills that enable him or her to communicate wants, needs, and frustrations. Cognitive delays or limitations may also influence the child's ability to understand and respond to behavioral expectations. Further, children with disabilities may have limited exposure to group social experiences and few opportunities to interact with nondisabled peers. Because many social and behavioral skills such as sharing, turn-taking, and negotiating are learned through interactions with others and through observing others, children with few experiences in typical group settings may be lacking appropriate interaction skills.

The presence of behavior problems can be one of the greatest obstacles for the inclusion of a child with special needs in general early childhood programs. In a study of the attitudes of parents of nondisabled children toward integrating preschool children with disabilities, Green and Stoneman (1989) found that behavior was a frequently named area of concern. In a national survey, parents and directors of child care, Head Start, and special education services expressed concern that children with disabilities would be too disruptive in the classroom and would pull resources from the typically developing children (Rose & Smith, 1993). For this reason, it is essential that teachers help children with disabilities develop positive behaviors that will help them be successful in regular classroom settings.

In general, principles of good behavior guidance and management can be applied to all behavioral concerns, and children with disabilities do not require "special" techniques. However, teachers should consider how a child's disability may be influencing behavior and determine whether modified expectations are appropriate or special instructional adaptations are necessary. For example, a child with limited receptive language skills may need added visual cues to understand what the teacher is asking him to do. To help the child understand that it is time to pick up the blocks, the teacher could play a "clean up game" by shining a flashlight beam on each toy to be picked up. The added visual cue of the flashlight beam would provide the necessary adaptation and structure for this child.

To use the principle of individual appropriateness, it is essential that teachers consider each child to determine his or her developmental level and readiness, understand the family influences, address learning styles, and develop necessary adaptations in selecting behavior guidance strategies. Strategies teachers select to guide children toward positive behavior and social skill development must be flexible enough to adapt to individual concerns and needs. No one method of behavior guidance is appropriate for all children. Therefore, it is important for teachers to learn a variety of strategies for guiding behavior and, in addition, how to make decisions regarding which techniques to use in a given situation. The rest of this chapter provides information that helps teachers make professional decisions in the selection and use of behavior guidance strategies.

WHAT IS CHALLENGING BEHAVIOR?

Many terms have been used to describe misbehavior: inappropriate behavior: difficult behavior, negative behavior, problem behavior, maladaptive behavior, aberrant behavior, and others. The use of the term *challenging behavior* in this chapter emphasizes that misbehaviors challenge teachers to develop strategies that help children develop more positive behaviors and social skills. This term serves as a reminder that the child is not the problem and puts the major responsibility for changing and guiding behaviors on the teacher.

It is important to note that not all challenging behaviors are the same. Various levels or intensities can be identified. First, there are developmentally typical challenging behaviors. These are behaviors that, although common to stages of child development, are not viewed as positive. Children exhibiting this level of challenging behavior need adult support and guidance to help them develop more mature, positive behavior. Tantrums, for example, are quite typical of preschool-age children; yet understanding principles of behavior guidance can assist adults in selecting responses that help the child learn more appropriate ways to express frustration and refusals.

The second level of challenging behaviors are typical, yet problematic behaviors. These behaviors may also be considered as within the behavioral norms of young children, but they are inappropriate and require adult intervention. Hitting and other physical aggression are examples of this level.

The third level of challenging behaviors consists of intensely challenging behaviors or maladaptive behaviors. Such behaviors include typical behaviors taken to an extreme, nontypical behaviors, and extreme behaviors associated with a disability or disorder (e.g., self-abusive behaviors, extreme noncompliance, extreme hyperactivity, and extreme aggression). These behaviors are of great concern to families, teachers, and caregivers. They may endanger others, interfere with learning, and have serious impact on the social acceptance of the child.

Understanding that there are different levels of challenging behaviors is important because it may be necessary for behavior guidance strategies to vary with the severity of the behavior. More intensely challenging behaviors require more intense guidance strategies. For example, although redirecting a child to another activity may be an appropriate behavior guidance strategy for a child who is trying to take away his peer's toy truck, it may not be enough to manage the extreme aggressive behavior of another child. The teacher of an extremely aggressive child may have to plan a behavior guidance plan that includes systematic reinforcement schedules, shaping strategies, and planned responses to the aggressive behaviors. It is essential for teachers to understand a variety of behavior guidance intervention strategies of varying intensity and be able to make professional decisions regarding the most appropriate strategy in various situations. This chapter offers a practical summary of many proven strategies of behavior guidance. Teachers must decide which strategy will work best for each child in each situation.

New Questions: What Can I Do for a Child Who Exhibits Challenging Behaviors?

Applying principles of developmentally appropriate practices to the guidance of child behavior provides a focus that is child centered and promotes the development of positive social and behavioral skills rather than a focus on the "elimination" of "negative" behaviors. Rather than using traditional disciplinary approaches to challenging behavior, which often rely on punitive strategies, developmentally appropriate behavior guidance teaches children positive behaviors. Behavior guidance leads children to solve problems in socially acceptable ways (Gartrell, 1994). Adults working with children are challenged to think of each child's need for assistance in becoming a socially competent person. To do this, teachers must ask new questions about challenging behaviors. Instead of asking, "What can I do about this problem child?" teachers must begin to ask "What can I do for this child?" Table 8.1 summarizes the questions that teachers should ask.

TABLE 8.1   Questions Teachers Should Ask When Considering a Child Who Exhibits Challenging Behavior

- How can I help this child develop positive behaviors that will lead to life-long social competencies?
- How can I expand and deepen this child's relationships with peers and help him develop friendships?
- How can I help this child give a positive impression to others and provide him/her opportunities to contribute and be valued?
- How can I help this child gain more self-control and a sense of responsibility for actions?
- How can I help this child learn to work and play cooperatively?
- How can I help this child learn to negotiate and resolve conflicts peacefully?
- How can I help this child learn to like and respect himself/herself?
- How can I support this child's family and other caregivers?

- How can I help this child develop positive behaviors that lead to lifelong social competencies?

  The positive social behaviors that a young child develops will help throughout life in interactions with others and adjustment to societal norms of expected behaviors. Children who develop effective social interaction skills are more likely as adults to be socially at ease with others and to have the skills necessary to get along in their personal and work-related lives. The skills children learn related to conflict resolution, sharing, taking turns, being kind and polite, self-discipline, and so on will be essential in their adult lives. Teachers should ask themselves what it is that they should be teaching about getting along with others and how they can help children learn and use these skills consistently?

- How can I expand and deepen this child's relationships with peers and help him or her develop friendships?

  Is this child unable to make or keep friends because he or she does not know how to be a good friend? What behaviors could this child develop that would help him or her make friends? Sharing? Taking turns? Appropriate play skills? Asking a peer to play? Keeping a conversation going? Peaceful conflict resolution? These are all skills that teachers can facilitate with planned intervention. Having and being a friend can add much joy to a child's life and provide essential feelings of being liked and accepted.

- How can I help this child give a positive impression to others and provide opportunities for him or her to contribute and be valued?

  Too often a child who exhibits challenging behaviors is viewed as a bad or difficult child. Teachers can change the way the child is viewed by systematically planning ways for the child to be seen as the "nice guy." For example, the teacher can have the child take a flower to the secretary in the school office or deliver a kind note to the teacher down the hall. In the classroom, the teacher can give the child "helping" jobs such as passing out the juice to the other children or giving out the stickers at the end of the day. In social contexts with peers, the teacher may actually have to guide the child to do "nice" things for friends and compliment the child openly.

- How can I help this child gain more self-control and a sense of responsibility for actions?

  A child may require assistance in determining whether behaviors are acceptable and understanding the effects of behaviors. The teacher may have to help the child evaluate his or her own behavior and discuss the ramifications of the behaviors. Role-playing can help children develop a repertoire of positive responses to conflict situations. Sometimes it is necessary for the teacher to take a very systematic approach and teach the children to use techniques such as self-monitoring to evaluate and control their own behaviors. This technique is described later in this chapter.

- How can I help this child learn to work and play cooperatively?

    Cooperation in work and play involves learning to give and take, viewing situations from other people's perspectives, and working with others for a common outcome. Teachers can facilitate cooperative work and play by establishing small cooperative groups for various activities, modeling and discussing appropriate methods of group work, and complimenting children for observed cooperation.

- How can I help this child learn to negotiate and resolve conflicts peacefully?

    A young child tends to see conflict situations from his or her own personal viewpoint, but teachers can provide guidance and experiences that help the child begin to empathize with another person's point of view and construct positive methods of dealing with problems. These skills enable him or her to feel capable of solving problems (Carlsson-Paige & Levin, 1992).

- How can I help this child learn to like and respect himself or herself?

    The self-esteem of a child who exhibits inappropriate behaviors can be gravely diminished. Peers may avoid interacting and playing with a child who exhibits aggressive behaviors, who will not take turns, or who is always demanding. The child may be viewed as the "mean," "bad," or "difficult" child by both children and adults. Teachers must find ways to point out the child's positive traits and skills, give the child a sense of accomplishment and importance, and help the child build an identity he or she can be proud of. Encouraging children to praise themselves helps them develop a lifelong trait of finding value in what they do and feeling good about who they are and what they have accomplished.

- How can I support this child's family and other caregivers?

    Families often experience increased stress related to the challenging behaviors of children. Severe problem behavior can restrict family social activities, strain marital relationships, and decrease the amount of assistance families can expect from relatives and the community (e.g., child care). Therefore it is important to communicate with families, determine their concerns and priorities, and work jointly in developing guidance strategies. Some families may choose to be very involved in implementing and monitoring the behavior guidance strategies, while others may not. Whatever level of involvement a family chooses should be respected, and teachers should make a continuous effort to keep families informed of the strategies being used, progress that is made, and any concerns that emerge.

GUIDING BEHAVIOR

In the classroom, teachers must consider how they will guide the behavior of their entire class in general and then, on an individual basis, what strategies they will use to respond to behavioral concerns. No one strategy works for all situations, so it is essential that teachers understand a variety of behavior guidance strategies that can be applied to overall classroom management and to individual situations as they arise. Guiding behavior involves helping children develop positive behavioral skills, using techniques that prevent challenging behavior, and responding to challenging behavior appropriately.

Helping Children Develop Positive Behavioral Skills

Behavior guidance should be considered an integral part of the early childhood curriculum and equally as important as other curricular domains (McAllister, 1991). Teachers should plan and use many strategies to teach appropriate group and individual behavior. Part of the art of child guidance is helping children learn by giving them enough information and practice so that they are able to learn and use appropriate behavior in various situations (Marion, 1991). A number of strategies can be used to do this including embedding learning into activities and routines, modeling, direct teaching, role-playing, peer-mediated interventions, providing feedback and reinforcement, and shaping behavior. The next sections describe each of these strategies.

Embedding Learning into Activities and Routines
The development of positive behaviors can be integrated into daily routines and activities. For example, lessons in sharing and cooperation, with ample opportunities to practice these skills, can be a part of many activities. At the art table, materials can be distributed in such a way as to necessitate sharing of glue, scissors, and so on. Children can be paired or assigned to small groups and given a cooperative outcome to accomplish. They can be encouraged to say "please" and "thank you" as they receive materials or toys from their teacher or friends, and they can be given "helping" jobs that promote a sense of responsibility and self-value. As children interact with adults and other children, the teacher can encourage and praise acts of kindness. Embedding the teaching of positive behaviors into the daily curriculum can be done through planning specific opportunities to directly instruct and guide children and through incidental teaching. Planning specific opportunities for teaching positive behaviors involves thinking through daily activities and including teacher-facilitated activities that focus on teaching positive behaviors. An example is the planning of a large group activity to teach children to

follow directions. As they do when playing "Simon Says," the children practice listening to and following the teacher's directions. This can be done as a circle-time game, an outdoor game, a transition from one activity to the next, or in many other contexts.

Many games, activities, and toys can be used to foster cooperation and positive social interactions. Teachers should be sure to include in their classrooms toys and activities that require group work toward a common goal. Some good examples include block building, dramatic play and dolls, group art projects, cooking activities, parachute play, and puppets.

Incidental teaching is the use of naturally arising situations to teach skills. A typical day includes many situations that can become the impetus for a lesson in positive behavior. The teacher must develop skill in seeing situations as teachable moments and quickly formulating strategies for turning everyday occurrences into opportunities for learning positive social skills. For example, if Stuart and Monique are fighting over the pitcher at the water table, the teacher may use this opportunity to help them develop skills in conflict resolution appropriate to their developmental level by asking each child to suggest a way that each can have a turn playing with the pitcher. At first the teacher may have to provide young children with examples of ways to resolve their conflicts, role-play, and carefully monitor the situation until resolution is reached, but as the children have more practice they will be able to create solutions for their own problems.

Modeling

Much learning takes place simply by watching someone else. Bandura's research (1971) demonstrated how influential adult models can be and how effectively children learn a behavior just by watching someone else. Adults, other children, or even puppets can model good listening, appropriate language, polite behaviors, sharing and caring behaviors, and a genuine respect for everyone in the classroom. Planned modeling can be effective in teaching specific actions or behaviors. For example, a teacher may plan to encourage saying nice things to friends during a small-group activity by making a point to say something nice to each child. Other examples include modeling turn-taking, following directions, using a quiet voice, and many other positive behaviors.

Direct Teaching

Direct teaching involves deciding on the behavior to be taught, selecting a specific time, and teaching the behavior directly to the children through discussion, provision of instructions, demonstration, prompting, and practice opportunities. For example, a teacher who wants to teach the children to raise their hands to be called on can use this strategy by focusing a large-group activity on a discussion of raising hands to be called on, telling children when and how to raise their hands, showing them how to raise their hands, and providing a practice session during which children are prompted and complimented for raising their hands to answer questions.

Role-Playing

Sometimes it is helpful to have children explore solutions to problems or conflicts in practice situations. In role-playing, children are given a particular role to play in a situation described by the teacher. Children benefit from formulating exactly what might be said or done in a situation. For example, one child may be playing the role of a child building a block tower, and a second child is given the role of a child who knocks down the tower. Other children in the class are observers and discuss how they might feel in the situation, what more appropriate behavior might have been, and possible peaceful resolutions to the situation. Role-playing provides children with the opportunity to experiment with various solutions and helps them to view the situation from multiple perspectives. It also gives them actual practice in positive ways to interact with peers and adults. Role-playing can be used not only for practicing solutions to problem situations, but also for practicing positive social skills such as asking a friend to play with you.

Child-directed role-playing often occurs spontaneously in various centers in an early childhood classroom, but especially in the dramatic play area. In the dramatic play center, children naturally negotiate roles and experiment with interactions and solutions to problems such as whose turn is it to wear the fireman's hat. Teachers can facilitate this child-directed learning by creating a center area that promotes cooperative play. For example, a teacher may place items in the dramatic play area to encourage children to play "pretend restaurant." Materials can be available for a customer, someone who sets the table, a server who takes the order, a cook, a dishwasher, and so on. Children should have many opportunities to practice cooperative play as they negotiate the various roles and actions in the pretend restaurant. Other enjoyable center ideas are a fast-food restaurant, a bakery, a pet store and care shop, or a doctor's office.

Peer-Mediated Interventions

Peer-mediated interventions involve teaching a peer to interact with a particular child and to provide reinforcement to that child for targeted positive behaviors. The teacher gives specific instructions and training to the peer and then prompts and reinforces the peer for successfully interacting with and reinforcing the targeted child. Teachers can make good use of peers to teach appropriate behaviors by arranging activities that involve the children in cooperative groups that have a joint purpose. The teacher can set up the activity and define the outcome for the children. For example, during a co-operative group art activity, the teacher can provide appropriate supplies and suggest that the children make a picture to hang outside the classroom door. The teacher can prompt peers to model cooperative behaviors such as sharing materials, requesting materials, complimenting other children, and making suggestions to the group.

Feedback and Reinforcement

One variable that is critical to learning is feedback. Feedback provides children with information about how they are doing and guidance about changes to improve their behavior (Marion, 1991). One type of feedback, positive reinforcement, can be a powerful teaching strategy. The primary principle of reinforcement is that if a behavior is consistently paired with a pleasant or positive consequence, that behavior is likely to reoccur. For example, if the teacher praises the children for walking down the hall quietly, they are likely to repeat this good behavior the next time they go down the hall. Although there may be some controversy about the exact strategies to be used, most experts agree that reinforcement is among the most effective teaching techniques. By using reinforcement strategies, the teacher can greatly influence the behavior of children in his or her classroom. The vital principle of this strategy is noticing appropriate behaviors and conscientiously reinforcing them.

Many reinforcers occur naturally. For example, if a child enjoys the creative art activity planned by the teacher, this enjoyment of the activity reinforces the child's cooperative and appropriate behavior during the activity. The ultimate goal is to have children develop an internal system of reinforcement. That is, to feel good about themselves and behave positively because they know it is the right thing to do and it gives them a sense of value and "goodness." Young children need help in developing this internal sense of motivation and appropriateness. They rely on feedback from adults and from their peers as they learn the merits of appropriate social behavior (Watkins & Durant, 1992).

Sometimes it is necessary to use more systematic, formalized reinforcement strategies to guide behavior. In this case, the teacher must carefully select reinforcers that will be viewed as positive by the children. Teachers must remember to consider individual preferences; because some children may not be motivated by what the teacher thinks is positive. For example, Billy may love to be tickled, while Sara finds tickling annoying. The most important consideration when deciding on a reinforcer is whether it will be effective in motivating the child to repeat the positive behavior. Observations of child preferences, including insights from family members and the children themselves, will lead to a selection of reinforcers that are truly positive. Reinforcement can include social rewards such as praise, smiles, or positive attention; tangible rewards such as toys or food; and token or symbolic reinforcers such as stickers, stars, or teacher-made tokens. Examples of reinforcers that are often viewed as positive by young children include enthusiastic praise, "high fives," tickles, hugs, "swing-arounds," stickers, happy faces on a chart, edible treats, earned computer time or time with a small hand-held electronic toy, a special piece of jewelry to wear, free time, and a walk down the hall. Providing a variety of reinforcers avoids satiation or boredom with overuse.

Reinforcement should be paired with specific positive behaviors that can be described to the child. For example, a teacher may enthusiastically praise a child for following through on a directive by saying, "Thomas, give me five. You did such a nice job of cleaning up those blocks when I asked you to." Describing specifically what the child did is critical for ensuring that the child knows exactly what behavior is desired. Reinforcement should be given immediately after the behavior and usually is most effective when it is delivered within five to ten seconds (Marion, 1991). Effective teachers use reinforcement strategies naturally throughout the day as they praise and respond to children's positive behaviors. Reinforcing positive behaviors need not take more than a second or two as the teacher enthusiastically praises "quiet listeners," or "sharing nicely with a friend."

There are many motivating, enjoyable ways to provide positive feedback and reinforcement to a large group. Having a plan for consistent, continuous reinforcement of positive behaviors creates a positive classroom focus—one in which noticing and complimenting positive behaviors is emphasized rather than reacting to misbehaviors. It is important that the children have a clear understanding of specific behaviors that the teacher will be looking for and how they can earn the reinforcers. The teacher should strive to reinforce everyone in the class regularly. Reinforcement principles work only if children have success and, therefore, earn the reinforcers. It is the teacher's obligation to ensure that every child can be successful. The following is an example of using a group method of reinforcement in an early childhood classroom.

The Hungry Hippo. "Harriet" is a very hungry hippopotamus whose face with open mouth has been drawn and placed on the classroom wall. "Hippo food" is earned by the children for positive behaviors throughout the day. Each child should have a cup with his or her name on it into which the teacher (or other adults working in the classroom) can drop a piece of "hippo food" as they praise a child for positive behaviors. Hippo food can be construction paper circles, plastic chips, hamster pellet food . . . anything that is simple and inexpensive. Because "Harriet" is *very hungry*, she can eat a lot of food. So the teacher can, and should, feel free to reinforce positive behaviors frequently throughout the day. The teacher should always tell the children why they are being given the hippo food. For example, the teacher might say, "Chris, you are keeping the sand in the sand table so well. I'm going to add a piece of hippo food to your cup!" At the end of the day, the children can feed their food to "Harriet" by placing the food that is in their cup into a special hippo food bowl near Harriet's picture.

This group reinforcement can be adapted easily to include an emphasis on a particular child who requires a more intense behavior guidance plan. For example, if a child is acting aggressively toward peers, the teacher may use the hippo food more intensely and systematically to reinforce "nice playing" for this child while continuing to reinforce general positive behaviors with the rest of the class. In this manner, the child with the more challenging behavior is not singled out, but the teacher can modify the strategies for administering the reinforcement to address specific challenging behaviors. Other group reinforcement ideas that have been observed in early childhood programs are listed in Table 8.2.

Positive reinforcement should be an ongoing part of early childhood programs (Watkins & Durant, 1992). However, as children learn and use new behaviors, teachers should gradually begin to fade external reinforcement. This can be done by fading the frequency of the positive reinforcement, which helps children develop their own intrinsic motivation and assists in strengthening the positive behavior in the absence of reinforcers. This fading of planned reinforcement should be gradual, not abrupt. Many studies have shown that the gradual fading of reinforcement can help with generalization (that is, learning to use the positive behaviors in a variety of settings) and maintenance of the positive skills over time.

Shaping Behavior

Effective reinforcement should reward the small steps and improvement that occur. Of critical importance is finding a point of success for each child. Teachers should ask themselves "How can I be sure this child will receive positive feedback and reinforcement for appropriate behaviors? What level of

TABLE 8.2   Group Reinforcement Ideas

Have children earn construction paper strips that are added to a "loop chain" that can be strung around the classroom as it grows in length.

Have children earn buttons that are placed in a jar. When the jar is full the class gets a special treat like popsicles.

Make a "window chart" using one large piece of construction paper on top of another. Windows are cut in the top piece of paper much like an Advent Calendar. Behind each "window" is a letter of the alphabet. Good behavior earns the right to open a window. When all the windows have been opened the revealed letters spell out a special class reward such as P-O-P-C-O-R-N P-A-R-T-Y.

Have children color a picture of a gum-ball machine—one gum ball at a time—for good behavior. When all the gum-balls are colored, the class gets a special treat.

expectation should I select that will guarantee that the child will be success-ful, earn the reinforcement, and, therefore be encouraged to exhibit more of this reinforced, positive behavior?" At first, a teacher may have to accept small steps in the right direction and give a child some special assistance such as additional verbal prompts, or even physically guide the child to ex-hibit the desired behavior. Shaping behavior is a strategy that calls for sys-tematically reinforcing successive approximations of the desired behavior. That is, the teacher must start out small and build from there, first accepting less-than-perfect behavior, and then gradually increasing the expectations. The two examples that follow illustrate the importance of finding a point of success for each child and gradually shaping behavior.

Mary was extremely hyperactive and, although she would sit momentar-ily, she never remained in her seat during circle time. The teacher decided to set a timer for five minutes and reinforce Mary when the timer went off if she had remained in her seat during that time interval. During the first three days after this behavior guidance plan was started, Mary never sat for the required five minutes; therefore the teacher was never able to reinforce her. As might be expected, Mary's behavior did not improve as the teacher had hoped.

The mistake Mary's teacher made was that she should have determined a point of success and selected a level of expectation that Mary could meet eas-ily to earn the reinforcement. This might have meant setting the initial re-quired sitting time at a much shorter interval and increasing it gradually over time. The teacher could also have helped Mary succeed by providing an ex-citing motivation for her to sit, such as time with a favorite toy or a high-in-terest activity. Physically guiding Mary to sit may have been necessary at first. Reinforcement could work only if Mary was successful and could be rein-forced. Ultimately, it was the teacher's obligation to find this point of success.

Clara is a 4-year-old with multiple disabilities. She refused to comply with the teacher's requests most of the day and usually did not engage in any class activities. One afternoon Clara's teacher was having the children in her preschool class paint tepees. For most of the children it was an enjoyable, en-gaging activity, but Clara refused even to pick up the paintbrush and resisted any hand-over-hand prompting. The teacher decided to use shaping strate-gies to encourage Clara to paint the tepee. At first, the teacher started by re-inforcing Clara for simply looking toward the tepee: "Clara, look at you; you are really looking at that tepee; that's great!!" The teacher knew that Clara loved attention and loved to be tickled. So the teacher would give Clara a little tickle and tell her how happy she was that Clara had looked at the tepee. The reinforcement was so powerful for Clara that immediately she made the con-nection between her behavior and the "reward" (i.e., praise and tickling). The teacher was then able to increase her demands on the required behavior grad-ually. The teacher gave Clara's arm a gentle nudge in the direction of the paintbrush, immediately said, "Look at you reaching for that paintbrush;

that's wonderful!" and gave Clara a tickle. Next, Clara had to reach toward the paintbrush before receiving reinforcement; then touch the paintbrush; then hold on to the paintbrush while the teacher guided the brush to make a mark of paint on the tepee. Finally she had to make her own paint marks on the tepee. The teacher had found a point of success for Clara and had built upon it, moving from complete refusal to making paint marks on the tepee in less than ten minutes. The teacher considered Clara's individual needs, found her point of success, and used systematic shaping strategies to help her develop new skills.

PREVENTIVE STRATEGIES

Everyone is familiar with that old adage, "an ounce of prevention is worth a pound of cure." How true it is when discussing the guidance of young children's behavior. Researchers observing successful teachers noted that the most effective classroom managers are skilled in effective preventive actions. Kounin (1970) is a frequently noted researcher who conducted studies of orderly and disorderly classrooms. He found that a significant difference between effective classroom managers and poor classroom managers is the strategies that teachers use to prevent misbehavior.

Kounin concluded that effective classroom managers are aware of what is happening in all parts of the classroom and communicate this awareness to the children. He labeled this skill *withitness*. He described the teachers as being "tuned in" to the children and recognizing signals that predict behavioral problems, correcting any misbehaviors before they intensify or spread. In the early childhood classroom, this means that the teacher should monitor all of the children constantly. The classroom should be arranged so that the teacher can see all areas in order to respond quickly to situations that may lead to escalating problem behaviors. For example, if the teacher notices that one child is taking blocks away from other children, a quick redirection of this child to another area of the classroom can prevent bigger problems.

Kounin also found that effective teachers are able to manage multiple tasks at the same time (*overlapping*). In the early childhood classroom, this may mean responding to a crying child while continuing to direct a small group activity at the art table. The teacher who is able to organize and monitor multiple activities can prevent disruption to the classroom flow and prevent behavior problems that occur as a result of the distraction.

Effective teachers also keep activities moving at a brisk pace so that students are less likely to become inattentive and disruptive. The short attention spans of young children make this an especially important skill for early childhood teachers. They must plan brief activities with enough variety to keep children attending and engaged. Designing a classroom schedule that reflects the need for a briskly paced day with smooth transitions between activities is essential.

Another indicator of effective classroom managers is the evidence of clear rules and expectations. Effective teachers have stated expectations for desired behavior and spend significant time, particularly at the beginning of the year, teaching children the classroom rules and expectations (McLaughlin, 1988).

Specific examples of preventive strategies that effective teachers can use in their classrooms include the following:

1. Establishing the teacher as someone the children want to please by developing a trusting and warm relationship. This type of relationship requires consistent and predictable caring behavior on the part of the teacher and often evolves over time.

2. Knowing children well enough to predict when problems will arise. Skilled teachers are able to redirect children before the misbehavior occurs or intervene quickly to stop the behavior and prevent further difficulties. For example, if Bobby is headed toward the block area, where he often knocks down other children's structures, the teacher may intervene and suggest an alternative activity.

3. A high level of planning that includes motivating activities that are engaging (child reads this as "F-U-N") and developmentally appropriate. Simply put, teachers should strive to make learning interesting! Planning is essential, and studies have shown that the most effective teachers engage in high levels of planning (Rosenberg, O'Shea, & O'Shea, 1991). This should include a daily written lesson or activity plan with necessary individualized adaptations.

4. Advance preparation of activity materials. Materials for each activity should be organized and then gathered and distributed easily. This minimizes the disruptions between activities caused by children having to wait for materials to be located and distributed and allows teachers to move briskly from one activity to another.

5. Appropriate schedules that reflect the children's ability to attend and remain interested and include a mixture of quiet and more energetic activities. Schedules should include snack and rest times as appropriate for the age group. Consistency and knowing what to expect are important to children and can eliminate some problem behaviors.

6. Plans for transitions between activities. Teachers should provide specific guidance to children about which activity comes next and how they are to make the transition to that activity. Cleanup time can be an especially troublesome transition if not adequately planned. Table 8.3 lists some creative ways of guiding transitions.

7. Avoidance of downtime and the potential behavior problems that may go with inactivity and boredom. Wait time should be minimized. Teachers should plan enrichment or self-directed activities for children who complete one activity and have extra time before the next planned activity.

8. Planned adaptations to activities to accommodate individual differences and special needs of children. By carefully analyzing each activity, the teacher can make necessary adaptations to ensure success for each child. This is especially critical for children with disabilities. By ensuring a way for each child to participate, much misbehavior can be avoided.

9. Setting limits that are clearly stated and appropriate to the age level of the children. Good rules reflect appropriate developmental expectations, protect the children's safety, are meaningful, and help teach self-control (Marion, 1991). Whenever possible, the children should be involved in deciding upon the classroom rules. Black and Puckett (1996) suggest that rules should be few in number and focus on the most crucial behaviors first. They suggest the "Three D's" of discipline as a good starting point: "Set rules that help children recognize

TABLE 8.3   Smooth Moves: Ideas to Help Children Transition from One Activity to the Next

- Plan transition activities that are related to the daily theme. For example, if the theme is rain have the children jump over paper puddles on the floor to get to the next activity location or have them carry an umbrella to the gathering spot near the door in preparation for an outside activity.
- Give each child special instructions about how they are to get to the next activity location. For example, "Sarah, touch your toes, then go and sit on a carpet square." There are lots of ways that this could be modified to work on individual objectives as well.
- Have something new, novel, or exciting waiting at the next activity location.
- Have children line up like a "sandwich." Two children are the bread, the rest are the bologna, cheese, lettuce, tomato, mustard, etc.
- Whisper instructions in each child's ear about where to go.
- Use a flashlight beam and have children follow the beam to the next activity location.
- Have a tub that contains objects that pertain to the theme of the day or the next activity. Have each child pick one object out of the tub and carry it to the location of the next activity.
- Give instructions using pretend phones or "walkie talkies." (A rectangular board with a pipe cleaner antenna makes a great "walkie talkie").
- Use pretend binoculars (toilet paper tubes) to look towards where the children are to go next.
- Have children take clothespins and clip on a chart as they transition to the next activity.
- Gather children around a hula hoop.
- Use props such as HATS to make the transition fun.

things that are Dangerous, Destructive, and/or Disturbing or hurtful to others" (Black & Puckett, 1996, p. 312). Rules should describe what children should do rather than state what they should not do. For example, a more positive way to state that children are not allowed to yell in the classroom is to say that the classroom rule is to use quiet voices in the classroom. Five to eight classroom rules should be sufficient (Evertson, Emmer, Clements, & Worsham, 1994). Teachers should communicate expectations for appropriate behaviors and give ample reminders of classroom rules. They should also explain to children why certain behaviors are expected and the reasons for each classroom rule.

10. Clear consequences. The preventive aspect of this strategy is letting children know ahead of time the consequences for appropriate and inappropriate behavior. Being consistent about consequences helps children learn that the teacher means what he or she says. An effective teacher has a classroom plan emphasizing positive consequences for positive behaviors.

11. Setting up contingencies. That is, setting up an "If you do _____, then _____ will happen" situation. For example, "When you sit on your carpet square, I will let you look in my 'surprise' bag." Once again, setting up clear expectations and consequences right from the beginning prevents many misbehaviors.

12. Opportunities for children to make age-appropriate choices throughout the day. For example, the teacher lets the children select the colors they would like to use for their art work, the activity center in which they would like to play or work, the friend with whom they would like to work, and so on. Giving children opportunities to make choices and exert some control in their lives fosters self-discipline, problem solving, and positive self-esteem.

13. Using high-interest activities and novelty. High-interest activities that excite children can prevent many behavior problems. Introducing something new to the class or selecting activities that build on observed interests are great ways to encourage participation, spark new interest, and prevent misbehavior. Boredom and short attention spans are the culprits behind much misbehavior in young children.

14. Arrangement of the classroom environment to promote positive social skill development (interaction with peers) and discourage misbehaviors. For example, if there is a large open space, some children will use it for running or for rowdy play. Rearranging the furniture can prevent this behavior. For more information on preparing the room for learning refer to Chapter 6.

15. Providing enough materials and toys. Children should have ample choices, and duplicates of highly desired items should be available. In this way, disputes over materials and toys may be avoided. Teachers can also promote many positive social behaviors through the selection of toys. For example, providing multiple toy telephones may facilitate peer communicative interactions.

16. Use of proximity. The teacher should position himself or herself close to students and should even reach out and touch children on the shoulder at times to send the message, "I am here and I am watching what you are doing ... I see all." It is especially important to use this strategy when you know that misbehaviors are likely to occur in certain situations.

17. Use of correspondence training. Correspondence training involves reinforcing the correspondence between what a child says he or she is going to do and what he or she actually does. That is, a child is praised or rewarded for actually following through. Once this pattern is established, the teacher can ask the child leading questions that relate to specific positive behaviors. For example, the teacher may ask, "What are you going to do when the cleanup song comes on?"

RESPONDING TO CHALLENGING BEHAVIORS

Even if all of the listed preventive strategies are used, there are still times when teachers must respond to challenging behaviors. Responding to misbehavior involves careful consideration of the individual child and the application of responses that treat children with respect and dignity. Teachers should always be aware of how their responses may affect a child's self-esteem. A teacher's response to challenging behaviors should be viewed as feedback that helps the children learn from their mistakes. All early childhood professionals should be committed to using positive approaches in responding to challenging behaviors and should avoid using punitive methods of controlling children's behavior.

It is important that responses to challenging behaviors keep children safe and secure while demonstrating that the teacher is firm in setting appropriate limits. Young children need to have adults set boundaries and guide them toward more responsible behavior. Methods teachers use to respond to challenging behaviors should be only one part of a teacher's strategy for guiding children toward more appropriate behavior. In other words, teachers must always consider an approach that includes teaching children what to do rather than telling them only what not to do.

In the following examples, responses to challenging behaviors demonstrate respect for the child while setting firm limits.

1. Showing empathy. The teacher can respond by letting the child know that he or she understands how the child must feel. Then the teacher should help the child brainstorm alternative ways to behave in that situation. For example, if Leon hit Christopher because Christopher grabbed his toy, the teacher can say to Leon, "I understand how you must have felt when Christopher took your toy, but can you think of a better way to let Christopher know you don't like it when he takes your toy?"

2. Distracting and redirecting to an appropriate activity. Sometimes a simple response is best, drawing as little attention as possible to the misbehavior. For example, Sam and Jane are fighting over the policeman's hat in the dramatic play center. The teacher may go over to Sam and say, "I see Michael is building a castle in the block area. Let's go over there and see if we can help him build a moat."

3. Prompting or giving reminders. An initial response to a misbehavior may be a reminder to the child about classroom rules or appropriate behavior. The teacher may even prompt the positive behavior orally, with a gesture, or physically. For example, a child who is dumping a bucket of sand on the sliding board may need an oral reminder of the rule that the sand stays in the sandbox. The teacher may even have to guide the child physically to return the bucket to the sandbox area. Even when prompts or reminders are given, the teacher should follow through with positive reinforcement when the child engages in the appropriate behavior.

4. Giving choices instead of demands. When possible, provide choices for children instead of placing demands on them. For example, if Jennifer refuses to leave the block area and come to circle time, the teacher may say to her, "Right now, Jennifer; we all need to sit for circle time. You can take a blue block or a red block to the circle area with you." Or, "You can crawl like a tiger or jump like a bunny to the circle area."

5. Ignoring. Providing no response to a behavior can be a very powerful reaction to certain misbehaviors, especially those that seem to be done for attention-seeking purposes. Planned ignoring is done systematically and consistently. For example, Tomika cries whenever she does not get her way. Using planned ignoring, the teacher may respond by saying, "I'm sorry, Tomika, I can't pay attention to you while you are crying." As soon as Tomika stops crying, the teacher should immediately say, "Great Tomika. I can listen to you now that you are not crying. What did you want to tell me?" *Special note: Teachers should never ignore behavior that can be dangerous or unsafe for the child or others!*

6. Role-playing. The teacher may ask a child who is misbehaving to practice an appropriate alternative. For example, a child who grabs a toy from his peer may be guided to practice a more appropriate way of asking a child for a turn with the toy. The teacher should prompt and reinforce the positive behavior.

7. Using relaxation or "calming down" techniques. This includes teaching children to calm themselves by counting to ten, for example, or taking deep breaths. Students can be directed to a special quiet area designated as the place for getting behaviors under control before returning to classroom activities. Children as young as two years of age can learn that they need to sit and "take a break for a couple of minutes."

8. Using the "talk-it-over place." Dinkmeyer, McKay, Dinkmeyer, and Dinkmeyer (1992) describe a special place in the classroom where children can talk over their disputes. It should be a small area used only for this purpose. The goal is to increase the children's responsibility for solving their own problems. When a conflict arises, the teacher sends the children to the talk-it-over place with instructions to talk over their problem and come to a decision about how to solve it. They can return to play when they are ready to cooperate. The teacher casually monitors the children in the talk-it-over place, intervening only if necessary.

9. Signaling interference. This involves using something concrete to signal that a change in behavior is required. An example is the use of a red poster board stop sign as a signal for the class needs to stop talking. Other signals often used in the classroom include blinking the lights, putting a finger to our lips to signal "quiet," and clapping hands.

10. Self-monitoring. Self-monitoring is a systematic method of providing reinforcement. It is based on the child's ability to determine whether he or she is behaving appropriately. The child is taught to self-monitor, that is, he or she considers his or her own behavior and decides whether he or she has acted appropriately. For example, a child who has difficulty attending to the teacher may be asked at specific intervals to determine whether he or she is "looking at the teacher." Either the teacher or an audible signal such as a kitchen timer prompts the child to stop and reflect on whether he or she is engaged in the predetermined behavior. The child is reinforced for monitoring his or her own behavior correctly as well as for engaging in the target positive behavior.

11. Employing natural and logical consequences. *Natural consequences* are natural results of a behavior. Natural consequences can, of course, be positive or negative. In the case of using natural consequences to respond to a child's misbehavior, the teacher should consider the situation carefully and determine whether allowing the child to learn from the natural consequence of his or her action will safely allow the child to learn from mistakes. The natural consequence of Lena's refusal to put her coat on for playground time is that she will probably get cold. The teacher must always consider the impact the natural consequences may have on the child as well as on his or her behavior. For example, it would be highly inappropriate to let a child learn from the natural consequence of touching a hot stove.

A teacher can fabricate logical consequences when natural consequences are dangerous or impractical. The term *logical* consequence implies that the selected consequence has a clear relationship to the misbehavior. For example, a teacher may tell a child that if he or she is unable to pick up the blocks, the teacher will put them away in the closet for awhile. By using natural or logical consequences to respond to misbehaviors, children learn that their own actions can cause very clear results, enabling them to develop a sense of responsibility for their own actions.

12. Mild oral reprimanding or "let's have a talk." Sometimes it is necessary to express to a child that what he or she has done is inappropriate. Gentle reprimands are a mild form of punishment designed to help children understand the impact their behavior has on others, which may then lead to greater self-control. An example of a mild oral reprimand in the classroom is a quick response to a child who is calling names, telling him or her to stop and explaining that name-calling is not nice because it hurts others' feelings.

13. Using time-out or "let's take a little break." Time-out involves removing the child to a location away from any reinforcing conditions in response to a misbehavior. Time-out can be viewed as a chance for the child to calm down and collect his or her composure before returning to the ongoing activity, ready to participate in an appropriate manner. Time-out can be an effective immediate response to a misbehavior, but care should be taken to avoid the overuse of time-out in early childhood classrooms. By itself, time-out does not teach appropriate behaviors and should always be paired with more positive approaches to guiding and teaching positive behaviors. See Table 8.4 for guidelines for using time-out.

14. Using response cost or "let's try again." This technique involves the loss of privileges or rewards for inappropriate behavior. Examples include taking away privileges such as on the playground or the opportunity to play with a special toy. Response cost is really a punishment and should be used only if the child is given the opportunity to earn back his lost privilege. Remember that using response cost as a punishment teaches the child only what not to do. Letting the child earn back the privilege or token by behaving appropriately provides a better opportunity to learn and practice what to do.

Including Families

Teachers must always view families as partners in the educational process (Bredekamp, 1987). Any intervention, including strategies to guide and change behaviors, is most likely to be effective if it is consistent with family goals and priorities (Wolery, Strain, & Bailey, 1992). Behavioral issues are of special concern to families and require continuous open communication between home and school. Teachers should always let families know that they are interested in helping the child develop important social competencies and skills that will enable the child to develop self-control, self-esteem, and the ability to develop positive relationships with peers and adults.

Daily demands in a family's home life are often very different from those in the school environment, and families may experience behaviors at home that are either similar to or very different from those the child exhibits at school. Family or cultural traditions may offer a competing opinion on a child's behavior when compared to that which is expected in school. Families should be asked to share their concerns, goals, and ideas concerning behavior. They can

TABLE 8.4   Guidelines for Using Time-Out

- List the behaviors that will result in time-out
- When the misbehavior specified occurs, follow this plan:

  1. Immediately go to the child and say (calmly), "You were _____ (Tell the child what he/she did that was a misbehavior — hitting for example). That is not allowed. You must go to time-out."

  2. Don't say any more. Don't get into the conversation trap!
     Take the child to time-out. Use a timer!! Set the timer for no longer than two minutes. Do not talk or even make eye-contact with the child during time-out! In some cases it may be necessary the first few times to use a gentle arm across the child's lap to keep him/her in time-out. Providing a time-out location near to the continuing class activities can sometimes be effective in allowing the child to observe the other children engaging in appropriate behavior.

  3. When the timer goes off, immediately say to the child, "Time-out is over. You can go _____ (direct child to appropriate activity). Remember that (*the misbehavior*) is not allowed."

  4. Quickly help the child engage in positive behavior that you can praise and reinforce!

POINTS TO REMEMBER

  1. Time-out should not be the major behavior management strategy you use. It is only a supplement to a plan that is positive.

  2. Remember, time-out only teaches the child what not to do. It is essential to teach and reinforce positive behaviors.

  3. Always have a plan.

  4. Always keep records. Something is wrong if time-outs are not becoming less frequent.

often share insights, pertinent history, and possible strategies for helping their child develop more appropriate behaviors. Family members should be invited to provide feedback as to how the behavior guidance plan is working by reporting on progress at home and in other settings outside of school.

Family members should be allowed to choose the level of involvement with which they feel most comfortable. For example, some families may choose to have close, ongoing involvement in behavior guidance strategies, while others may elect to have the teacher update them periodically on the progress their child is making. Some may want to work with teachers by volunteering at school or by following through on the behavior guidance strategies at home. Families may also want suggestions for dealing with behaviors exhibited only in the home. To whatever degree a family chooses, teachers should invite their involvement and provide honest, regular feedback. Communicating with parents can be done through notes, phone calls, progress reports, teacher conferences, home visits, or parent visits to the classroom. Teachers should communicate their philosophy regarding behavior guidance by explaining the general classroom guidance strategies to families at the beginning of the school year. A brief written summary describing a teacher's goals for developing positive social behaviors, appropriate classroom behavioral expectations, and the teacher's general behavior guidance strategies is helpful. Figure 8.1 contains a sample format for a letter to be sent to families at the beginning of the year.

Sample Letter

Dear Families,

Developing good behavior skills is an important part of childhood. During childhood, children learn to make friends and get along together. They learn to listen to their teachers and other adults. They learn that being kind and helpful, respectful and caring are skills which will help them as they grow up and even as adults. In our classroom we work very hard to help children learn these skills.

We let our children know how proud we are of all of their good behavior by:

_____

_____

_____

We have a few classroom rules. They are:

_____

_____

_____

If a child forgets one of our classroom rules, we:

_____

_____

_____

We have a commitment to focusing on positive behaviors and on helping each child develop behaviors they can be proud of. If you have any questions or concerns please do not hesitate to call us.

FIGURE 8.1   Communicating with Families

A DECISION-MAKING MODEL FOR DETERMINING AN APPROPRIATE BEHAVIOR CHANGE PLAN

Because no one strategy works for all behavioral concerns or for all children, following a basic six-step process helps guide responsible professionals in developing a systematic plan of action for individual children. This planning process leads to a behavior guidance plan that includes methods of teaching new, more appropriate skills; systematic reinforcement of positive behaviors; preventive actions; and planned responses to the challenging behaviors. As this six-step process is discussed, practical examples are given relative to the case of Jerome, a 4-year-old child with significant language delays who is exhibiting some very challenging behavior. Table 8.5 contains the six steps in developing a behavior guidance plan.

The first step is to clearly identify and define the challenging behavior. The behavior must be described in specific terms so that everyone involved understands exactly what behavior is being addressed. Nonspecific descriptions will not provide a clear target or goal. For example, just to say that the child never listens is too vague. The description does not provide a clear understanding of the problem behavior. In contrast, describing the child's refusal to comply with the teacher's requests provides a much clearer picture of the problem behavior. The left column in Table 8.6 lists examples of vaguely defined behaviors. The right column shows ways that behaviors can be described more clearly. Describing a challenging behavior in this well-defined manner is an important first step in planning a consistent approach to changing and guiding behavior. Narrowing down problematic behavior to concrete and clearly described behaviors relieves the sense of enormity that some teachers feel. When a teacher has a clear picture of exactly what behavior needs to be addressed, it becomes easier to develop strategies to address the specific concerns. In our example case, the teacher is concerned because Jerome frequently leaves the classroom without supervision and runs throughout the school. He

---

TABLE 8.5   Steps in Developing a Behavior Guidance Plan

1. Identify and define the challenging behavior.
2. Look for causes or reasons the child is engaging in the challenging behavior.
3. Decide . . . should the behavior be changed? Why?
4. Plan the intervention strategy. Think positively!!
5. Implement the plan. Think consistency!!
6. Evaluate the effectiveness of the plan. Make adjustments!!

TABLE 8.6   Identify and Define Challenging Behaviors Clearly

These statements are too vague.	These statements describe the behavior more clearly.
Phillip doesn't play nicely.	Phillip uses both hands to push his peers when they try to join him at the sand tables.
Chante never pays attention.	Chante is able to participate in an activity for no more than 1 minute before losing interest and leaving the activity area.
Cary is stubborn.	Cary does not comply with requests made by the teacher.
Dale is hyperactive.	Dale does not remain in his seat during circle time.

has even run out of the building on occasion. Jerome does not respond when the teacher calls out for him to stop. So that a clear goal can be set for changing this challenging behavior, the teacher has defined the behavior as any time that Jerome leaves the classroom without an adult or adult's permission.

The second step is to look for causes or reasons for the child's challenging behavior. Looking for clues can provide insights that help the teacher (1) select strategies to prevent the behavior, (2) decide what positive behaviors can be taught to replace the function of the challenging behavior, and (3) select strategies to best respond to the challenging behavior. Often termed a *functional analysis*, this step in the process calls for an examination of the context in which the behavior occurs and a reflection on the child's perspective (i.e., what purpose this behavior may be serving for the child). It is during this step that the teacher should consider the impact that antecedents may be having on this behavior and what, if any, consequences may be reinforcing this behavior. *Antecedents* are anything that exists or occurs before the behavior is exhibited. Antecedents include the setting or environment, any requirements or requests made of the child, the presentation of certain activities or tasks, the perception the child has of the activities or requests, the degree to which the child is tired or hungry, the presence of particular people, and anything else that exists before the behavior occurs that may influence the behavior. The teacher should ask, "What events or conditions seem to precede the behavior? When is the child most likely to engage in this challenging behavior?" In the case of Jerome, the teacher notices that he is most likely to leave the classroom when he is asked to stop playing and join a more structured, teacher-directed activity. This request to stop playing and join the group could be an important clue regarding a possible antecedent cause. The teacher can use this clue to develop strategies for helping prepare Jerome for transitions, and to decide when to use proximity or other preventive strategies to avoid the challenging behavior.

A *consequence* is anything that follows a behavior and may influence whether that behavior is likely to occur again. Consequences can be naturally occurring in the environment or initiated by the teacher, and they can be positive (pleasant) or negative (unpleasant). Positive consequences reinforce the behavior and increase the likelihood that the child will engage in that behavior again. The teacher should ask, "What consequences may be reinforcing this behavior?" Often, unintended consequences may reinforce a behavior. For example, Jerome periodically looks back to see whether the teacher is following him. The teacher feels that Jerome views this as fun, as a cat-and-mouse chasing game, and enjoys the attention. The attention and chasing may be inadvertently reinforcing Jerome's inappropriate behavior of running from the classroom.

Along with looking for clues regarding possible antecedents and consequences, the teacher should confer with other people who have frequent contact with the child to obtain their thoughts on possible causes of the behavior. In some cases, the teacher may even ask the child why he is engaging in the challenging behavior. Finally the teacher develops a hypothesis about why the behavior is occurring. This hypothesis is the teacher's "best guess" based on his or her professional opinion and the information gathered. The teacher cannot absolutely know with all certainty that the hypothesis is correct, but a professionally based judgment provides many clues as to how the behavior guidance intervention should be developed. In the example of Jerome, the teacher may conclude that Jerome does not like to stop playing and leaves the classroom to express his anger at being asked to join a group activity. The teacher may also decide that this behavior has been reinforced because of the attention Jerome receives as his teacher runs after him. The hypothesis provides the basis for the selection of appropriate intervention strategies in step four of the decision making process.

In step three, the teacher decides whether the behavior should be changed and, if so, why. This step requires a decision as to the reasonableness of expectations and the seriousness of the challenging behavior. The teacher should consider age appropriateness and individual appropriateness. Further, the teacher should consider what impact the behavior is having on the child and the likely impact on the child's future learning and social development if it is allowed to continue. Will the behavior influence this child's ability to make and have friends? Will it impact on his success in general educational programs? Is the behavior likely to continue if not treated, or is this just a temporary behavior of short duration? Is the behavior dangerous to the child or others? It is possible at this stage in the decision-making process that the teacher will decide that the behavior is not of a serious enough level or duration to warrant special intervention, that the expectations were unrealistic, or that there is a justifiable rationale for developing a behavior change plan at this time. If the latter is determined, the teacher will proceed to step 4. In Jerome's case, the teacher decides that it is important to intervene because of concern for his safety, the disruption the behavior is causing in the class, and the impact the behavior has or could have on Jerome's present and future learning opportunities.

Step four is to plan the intervention strategy. The teacher should state the goal of the behavior guidance plan carefully and develop appropriate intervention strategies. The behavior guidance plan usually requires a three-pronged approach. That is, all aspects of the challenging behavior must be considered and a strategy developed to address each aspect.

First, the teacher should consider what positive skills can be taught or encouraged to replace the function of the challenging behavior. Is there some other, positive way that the child can accomplish the same purpose? The new behavior must serve the function of the challenging behavior at least as well or the child may revert to the former behavior. A common example of challenging behavior that has an important function is that of children with delayed or limited expressive language skills who use inappropriate behaviors to express their desires, frustration, or anger (e.g., tantrums, crying, and aggression). In this case, teachers should consider alternative or augmentative methods of communication (e.g., sign language, communication boards, or electronic communication devices) that can provide a more appropriate way of expression. The new method of communicating must be as effective as the previous behaviors were at letting people know what the child wants. Returning to the example of Jerome, because the teacher feels that leaving the classroom is his way of communicating anger at being told to stop playing, she might role-play with Jerome to teach him how to use words to express that he is not ready to stop playing. Initially, so that the new, positive behavior will serve the function as well as or better than running out of the class, the teacher should praise Jerome for telling her he was not ready to stop playing and give him a minute or two more to play. Later the teacher can use gradual shaping to teach Jerome that when the teacher gives the signal for the end of play time, he must begin to clean up and move to the next activity.

Second, a proactive strategy for reinforcing positive behaviors should be planned. Reinforcement should be frequent and systematic to provide the intense level necessary to improve challenging behaviors. A kitchen timer may be used to signal reminders to "catch the child being good" and reinforce. In the case of Jerome, the teacher observed that his leaving the classroom was reinforced by the attention he got as the teacher ran after him. The teacher can use this clue and decide to provide lots of attention, praise, and other reinforcement for positive behaviors throughout the day. For example, the teacher can make an effort to notice Jerome playing nicely with his friend, following directions, and sitting quietly. Receiving attention for these positive behaviors, Jerome will be less likely to seek out the teacher's attention by running from the classroom.

Finally, the teacher must decide on an immediate response to the challenging behavior should it occur. Although the primary emphasis on any behavior guidance plan should be on teaching more appropriate skills and reinforcing positive behaviors, the teacher must have a plan for responding when necessary. In Jerome's case, the teacher may decide to respond first by going after Jerome because of a concern for his safety. Ignoring Jerome when he leaves the classroom is not an alternative, because he may endanger himself or others if allowed to run. However, the teacher should not talk to or make eye contact with Jerome but should take him by the hand and walk back to the classroom. The teacher should show as little reaction and expression as possible. When Jerome is back in the room he should be directed to the ongoing activity, prompted if necessary, and then immediately praised for participating in the ongoing activity.

The fifth step is to implement the plan. It is important that the teacher decide exactly when the planned intervention will be implemented and who will be responsible. Then the plan should be implemented in a consistent manner. Jerome's teacher may decide that the paraprofessional in the class will be responsible for going after him and that all adults working or volunteering in the class will look for ways to praise and give attention to Jerome for positive behaviors. The teacher will be responsible for the direct teaching of more appropriate ways for Jerome to communicate to others that he is not ready to stop playing, and for using shaping procedures to guide Jerome toward complying with requests to clean up and move to the next activity center.

Step six of the decision-making process is to evaluate the success of the plan and make any necessary adjustments. From the moment the teacher decides that a behavior is problematic, records should be kept of every occurrence as well as any notations as to possible antecedents, causes, functions, or inadvertent reinforcement. Families and other people who work closely with the child should be consulted to determine whether the behavior is improving in other settings. Records can be kept using checklists, a count of the number of times the behavior occurs, the amount of time a child engages in the behavior, and ongoing anecdotal records. More than one method may be used, but the method(s) selected should be easily managed by the teacher or other adults and should provide enough information to determine progress. The teacher should review these records regularly to gauge improvement and to determine whether any side effects are occurring. If the plan is working, the teacher should consider ways to diminish the intensity of the strategies gradually, including fading the level of reinforcement. If the behavior is not improving, the teacher may have to develop a new plan by determining which aspects of the behavior guidance plan appear to be ineffective.

Jerome's teacher could keep a simple running list of how many times he leaves the classroom each day, with brief anecdotal notes recording any antecedent events or consequences that may be influencing the behavior. After noticing improvement, the teacher can begin to reduce the intensity of the reinforcement and start to use shaping strategies to guide Jerome's behavior toward a more appropriate compliance with requests to end play time, clean up, and move to the next activity.

For many mild or transient misbehaviors, the use of preventive strategies, direct teaching of positive behaviors, and one-time responses to the misbehavior are enough to correct the problem. However, when a child exhibits challenging behaviors with great frequency or of a more serious nature, it is necessary to develop a systematic intervention plan. The six-step decision-making process provides a method of determining appropriate strategies for individual children in specific situations. It guides teachers as they develop a plan that focuses on teaching positive behaviors to replace the function of the challenging behaviors, while at the same time intervening to decrease the inappropriate behavior.

SUMMARY

Early childhood is a time of tremendous growth and development for children. Along with development in the domains of language, cognition, and motor skills, children are learning to get along with others and to behave according to society's expectations of appropriate behavior. As with other skill domains, developmental growth and experience play an important role in the formation of positive behaviors and social skills. However, adults greatly influence children's social skill development and can do much to guide and teach children to work and play cooperatively, resolve conflicts peacefully, be good friends, use self-control, follow important rules, be responsible for their actions, and develop other positive social behaviors. Families should be viewed as partners in the planning, implementation, and evaluation of the behavior guidance plan. Open communication allows families to stay informed and select the level of involvement that they desire.

Developmentally appropriate behavior guidance incorporates the principles of age appropriateness and individual appropriateness by matching behavioral expectations to the developing capabilities of the children, using intervention strategies based on the ways young children learn and considering each child's uniqueness. The focus of behavior guidance strategies is on assisting children who exhibit challenging behaviors in developing identities and behaviors that they can be proud of and on guiding children to develop positive behaviors that can lead to lifelong social competencies.

ACTIVITIES AND RESOURCES

Case Study: Brad

Review the case of Brad, and apply the principles and strategies of developmentally appropriate behavior guidance to the following discussion questions.

1. Based on the assessment information noted for Brad, list possible purposes of the hitting and tantrum behaviors described.
2. Based on the information presented, what are possible reinforcers for Brad?
3. What are some positive skills that the teacher could target as instructional goals that would help Brad in group settings?
4. Using the six-step decision-making process, develop a behavior guidance plan to encourage Brad to keep his glasses on for longer periods of time.

Activities

1. Observe a classroom and make note of any strategies the teacher uses to guide the behavior of the children in her class. Is the teacher teaching a positive behavior, preventing misbehaviors, or responding to misbehaviors?
2. Develop a hypothetical behavior change plan for a child who bites other children to communicate that he does not want them to play at the water table with him.
3. Develop a letter to families that reflects your philosophy of developmentally appropriate behavior guidance and the strategies you will use in your classroom to promote positive social and behavioral skills.

Class Discussion Questions

1. Studies have shown that children with disabilities exhibit more challenging, inappropriate behaviors. Why do you think this is so?
2. How are age appropriateness and individual appropriateness reflected in behavior guidance strategies?
3. Provide an example of embedding behavior guidance into routines and activities.
4. Why is it important to find a "point of success" when using positive reinforcement techniques with young children?
5. Why is it important to develop a hypothesis about the function of a severely challenging behavior?
6. Why is it important to include families in the development and implementation of behavior guidance strategies for young children? How would you accomplish this?

Resources

Charney, R.S. (1991). *Teaching children to care: Management in the responsive classroom.* Greenfield, MA: Northeast Foundation for Children.

Dinkmeyer, D., McKay, G., Dinkmeyer, J., & Dinkmeyer, D., Jr. (1992). *Teaching and leading children: Training for supportive guidance of children under six.* Circle Pines, MN: American Guidance Service, Inc.

Dunlap, L.K., Dunlap, G., Koegel, L K., & Koegel, R.L. (1991). Using self-monitoring to increase independence. *Teaching Exceptional Children, 23*(3), 17–22.

Dunn, R., Dunn, K., & Perrin J. (1994). *Teaching young children through their individual learning styles.* Boston: Allyn and Bacon.

Gartrell, D. J. (1994). *A guidance approach to discipline.* Albany: Delmar.

Marion, M. (1991). *Guidance of young children* (3rd ed.). New York: Macmillan.

REFERENCES

Bandura, A. (1971). Analysis of modeling processes. In A. Bandura (Ed.), *Psychological modeling?* Chicago: Aldine-Asherton.

Black, J., & Puckett, M. (1996). *The young child: Development from prebirth through age eight.* Englewood Cliffs, NJ: Merrill.

Bredekamp, S. (Ed.). (1987). *Developmentally appropriate practice in early childhood programs serving children from birth through age 8.* Washington, DC: National Association for the Education of Young Children.

Carlsson-Paige, N., & Levin, D. (1992). Making peace in violent times: A constructivist approach to conflict resolution. *Young Children, 48*(1), 4–13.

Dinkmeyer, D., McKay, G., Dinkmeyer, J., & Dinkmeyer, D., Jr. (1992). *Teaching & leading children: Training for supportive guidance of children under six.* Circle Pines, MN: American Guidance Service, Inc.

Dunn, R., Dunn, K., & Perrin, J. (1994). *Teaching young children through their individual learning styles.* Boston: Allyn and Bacon.

Evertson, C.M., Emmer, E.T., Clements, B.S., & Worsham, M.E. (1994). *Classroom management for elementary teachers* (3rd ed.). Boston: Allyn and Bacon.

Gartrell, D.J. (1994). *A guidance approach to discipline.* Albany: Delmar.

Green, A.L., & Stoneman, Z. (1989). Attitudes of mothers and fathers of nonhandicapped children. *Journal of Early Intervention, 13*(4), 292–304.

Hunt, F., Johnson, C., Owen, G., Ormerod, A., & Babbitt, R. (1990). Early intervention for severe behavior problems: The use of judgment based assessment procedures. *Topics in Early Childhood Special Education, 10*(3), 111–121.

Kounin, J. (1970). *Discipline and group management in classrooms.* New York: Holt, Rinehart, & Winston.

Marion, M. (1991). *Guidance of young children* (3rd ed.). New York: Macmillan.

McAllister, J.R., Jr. (1991). Curriculum-based behavioral interventions for preschool children with handicaps. *Topics in Early Childhood Special Education, 11*(2), 48–58.

McLaughlin, R.A. (1988). Consistent rules. In R. McNergney (Ed.), *Guide to classroom teaching* (pp. 67–79). Boston: Allyn and Bacon.

Rose, D., & Smith, B. (1993). Preschool mainstreaming: Attitude barriers and strategies for addressing them. *Young Children, 48*(4), 59–62.

Rosenberg, M., O'Shea, I., & O'Shea, D. (1991). *Student teacher to master teacher.* New York: Macmillan.

Watkins, K.P. & Durant, L., Jr. (1992). *Complete early childhood behavior management guide*. West Nyack, NY: Center for Applied Research in Education.

Wolery, M., Strain, P., & Bailey, D., Jr. (1992). Reaching potentials of children with special needs. In S. Bredekamp & T. Rosegrant (Eds.), *Reaching potentials: Appropriate curriculum and assessment for young children, Vol. 1* (pp. 92–111). Washington, DC: National Association for the Education of Young Children.

9

SUMMATIVE ASSESSMENT: EVALUATING THE PROGRESS OF CHILDREN

OBJECTIVES

As a result of studying this chapter, readers should be able to perform the following:

- Describe summative assessment and its purposes.
- Identify and use strategies that document a child's progress, and evaluate whether or not stated objectives have been achieved,
- Describe methods for including families and children in the summative assessment process.

In this chapter readers examine procedures for collecting summative assessment information that focuses on children, teachers, and the curriculum.

SUMMATIVE ASSESSMENT FOR CHILDREN

As stated in Chapter 4, *assessment* is the process of collecting information in order to make a decision (Salvia & Ysseldyke, 1995). Collecting information about a child's skills and behaviors, the family's priorities and concerns, and the demands of the settings in which the child spends time is partially a formative assessment process. This information assists the child's teacher and family as they formulate a hypothesis about the needs of the child and the program strategies to be used to address those needs. Formative assessment procedures help us make decisions about goals or outcomes, program plans, and methods to achieve those outcomes. The decisions made using formative assessment information are those that a teacher or other professional must make to enable a child to enter a program and to determine the activities, materials, and experiences that should be provided in the curriculum (Campbell, 1991).

Other decisions include how to adapt the curricula, how to respond to major events in a child's life (e.g., a new sibling or moving to a new house or apartment), and how to enhance curricular approaches as the child learns new skills. These decisions illustrate the importance of ongoing, continuous assessment so that programs change as the child develops (Bailey & Wolery, 1989; Bagnato, Neisworth, & Munson, 1989). They are based on formative assessment information, which teachers continually collected in order to make daily decisions about the best way to provide services for young children.

Just as important, teachers and other professionals ask whether children are achieving the goals and outcomes identified in their program plans (Herman, Aschbacker, & Winter, 1992; Hill & Ruptic, 1994; Meisels, Jablon, Marsden, Dichtelmiller, & Dorfman, 1994). These questions are asked at regular intervals (e.g., quarterly, semiannually, or annually) so that teachers can systematically examine the progress of children, report to families about their children's progress, identify possible problems that may go undetected on a day-to-day basis, and determine how teachers and other professionals should focus their overall intervention strategies during the upcoming weeks and months. Further, answers to these questions are the basis of summative decisions. In sound, developmentally appropriate early childhood programs, teachers participate in summative assessment because it helps them answer questions about the effectiveness of their interactions, the efficacy of their curriculum decisions, and whether or not student goals have been achieved (Meisels et al., 1994).

Although summative assessment should take place in all developmentally appropriate early childhood programs (Hills, 1992), it is particularly important for young children with known or suspected disabilities. The IEP or IFSP for a young child with a disability is a legal document that must be reviewed at regular intervals to determine how the child is progressing and to make necessary curricular and instructional modifications to meet emerging needs (Congressional Record, 1991). The dynamic nature of child development is such that children are continuously changing. Child-child, child-material, and child-adult interactions affect knowledge, skills, and understanding. The classroom environment, teacher attitude, accessibility, prior experience, and child's family interact to help the child grow. Sometimes the growth is subtle; at other times it explodes with excitement when the lightbulb goes on as the result of a new activity. Summative evaluation enables teachers and other professionals to assess the sum total of all the child has learned over an extended period of time and then to plan for the future.

PROCESS FOR DETERMINING CHILDREN'S PROGRESS

All assessment procedures require that teachers and other professionals know why they are collecting information before they collect it. Program eligibility decisions call for assessment procedures that allow professionals to compare an individual child's development to the development of other, similar children. Initial programming decisions call for assessment information that helps them determine what skills and competencies a child currently possesses. Summative assessment information is collected to determine children's developmental progress as well as progress toward attaining goals or outcomes (Bailey & Wolery, 1989; McLoughlin & Lewis, 1994). The professionals must use procedures that help them make comparisons of where a child is today with where he or she was in the not-too-distant past.

Achievement of Children's Program Plan Goals, Objectives, and Outcomes

Determining the extent to which a child's program plan goals, objectives, or outcomes have been achieved depends upon the way they were written for the IEP or IFSP. If general case objectives have clear conditions and criteria (see Chapter 5), determining the extent to which the child has achieved the objectives requires collecting the appropriate information. For example, if an IEP objective is to "orally request assistance from adults when materials or equipment are inaccessible to the child," the conditions (when materials or equipment are inaccessible to the child) and the criteria (orally request) are clearly stated. When the criteria and conditions are clear, a second task is to decide how to collect and record information that provides evidence of the child's progress.

As can be seen in Table 9.1, the summative assessment process, much like the formative assessment process, is ongoing. It differs, however, in that it is conducted when teachers, family, administrators, and other service providers step back from daily programming and ask whether and how the child is progressing. In some programs or schools, these occur at regular intervals called *grading periods* or *marking periods*. For children with IFSPs or IEPs, this process must occur every six or twelve months, respectively. For other programs, it may occur quarterly at parent–teacher conferences. However, no matter what the interval, summative assessment gives everyone involved with a child's program the opportunity to review the stated objectives and to determine the extent to which the child has made progress. (Table 9.1 outlines a process for summative assessment. The eight steps can be worked into the daily procedures of any early childhood program.)

TABLE 9.1   Process for Collecting Summative Assessment Information for Determining Individual Children's Progress

1. Identify the child's objectives with criteria and conditions. Determine which objectives must be documented.
2. Identify the best method or combination of methods for documenting each of the skills or behaviors.
3. Identify the opportunities for the child to exhibit or use each of the skills or behaviors. Include multiple settings and situations.
4. Identify a schedule for documenting the skills and/or behaviors.
5. Identify which staff member will be responsible for documenting the skills and behaviors.
6. Record the information and store it in a confidential manner.
7. Share the information with the child's family/caregivers, authorized professionals, and classroom staff.
8. Review summative assessment information and use to determine children's progress, necessary curriculum changes, and teacher interaction adaptations.

Step 1: Identify children's objectives. With well-constructed IEP or IFSP objectives or outcome statements, the teacher begins by examining the objectives for each child. Because children's program plans are often written for six months to a year, only those objectives that have been addressed by the program since the last reporting period should be included for evaluation. The teacher should make a comprehensive list of objectives so that the staff members and families will know which skills and behaviors are being assessed. The list should be constructed in collaboration with the child's family and service providers shortly after the last reporting period, whether that be a report card, a parent conference, or a semiannual review of the child's IEP or IFSP. This list of objectives guides the summative assessment process.

Step 2: Identify the best method or combination of methods for documenting each skill or behavior. This is a crucial step in the accurate and efficient documentation of children's progress. Each objective, depending upon the skill being assessed, can be measured in one or more ways. Discrete skills such as using writing utensils or placing objects, as in block building, can be documented through the use of work samples and anecdotal narratives describing the process of the work produced by the child. Behaviors and skills that occur often or continuously, such as a child's attention to task or sitting in a group, can be measured through a time-sampling technique. Infrequently occurring skills and behaviors can be documented through event-sampling strategies. Specific documentation methods are described in the next section of this chapter.

Step 3: Identify opportunities for the child to exhibit the skill or behavior. It is essential that program staff know at what point during the program day it is appropriate to expect a child to exhibit the specified skill or behavior. If the IEP or IFSP objective has been well written, the conditions under which it is appropriate to exhibit the skill will be present. For example, when documenting Brad's ability to ask a peer to play with him, it would not be appropriate to collect evidence of this behavior during a time when talking is not permitted, such as during a group presentation or while walking in the hall.

Identifying opportunities for observing skills is especially important for lower-frequency behaviors such as using a fork or spoon, dressing, or other self-care skills that may occur only once during a program day. Staff must identify the opportunities when those skills may occur and plan to document their presence or absence at those times.

Step 4: Identify a schedule for documenting skills and behaviors. When it has been determined when opportunities for exhibiting a skill exist, a schedule for documenting each child's progress should be developed.

The frequency with which data is to be collected depends upon the specific objective and its criteria. Skills such as talking with peers should be observed in multiple settings, at different times during the day, and across a number of days before a judgment can be made that the child has met the objective. Because a skill such as talking with peers occurs in a variety of settings, it is necessary to document its existence with multiple observations across the program day.

Other skills may not need as many observations. Skills such as placement of blocks may need fewer examples. Two or three photographs with an anecdotal record indicating how the child used his hands to place and release the blocks might suffice for this skill.

Even if relatively few records are needed to document a specific skill, a schedule to observe the opportunity is necessary to ensure that all objectives are addressed. If a child's objective is to use a writing utensil and a program has markers available only once a day, observation for that skill must take place during that time. A schedule such as the one in Table 9.2 may be useful in planning when to document children's progress.

Step 5: Identify which staff will be responsible for documenting skills and behaviors. After a schedule has been identified for observing children's behaviors and skills or for collecting samples of their work, it is important to identify who will be responsible for gathering the information. If staff members are not given specific responsibility to collect the necessary information and periodic checks are not conducted to ensure that data collection is occurring, it is possible that the documentation of progress will be incomplete. In the schedule for collecting information, several individuals should be assigned to observe and record the same skills or behaviors. Documentation by multiple observers in multiple settings increases the reliability that a child has acquired the skill. The schedule in Table 9.2 indicates that different staff members have the responsibility to observe the same skills at different times.

Step 6: Record and store the information. As information about a child's progress is being collected, it must be organized and maintained (Evans, Evans, & Mercer, 1986; Hill & Ruptic, 1994). One particularly useful approach for teachers is a child *portfolio*, which is a collection of evidence that indicates when, under what conditions, and with what environmental and adult support the child exhibits particular skills and behaviors (Darling-Hammond, Ancess, & Falk, 1995). A portfolio usually includes evidence that illustrates a child's abilities in all domains of development and reflects all of the objectives contained in the IEP or IFSP (Grace & Shores, 1991; Paulson, Paulson, & Meyer, 1991).

Each child's portfolio should contain items such as anecdotal records, photographs of work, audiotapes of children's communication, samples

TABLE 9.2 Schedule to Document Progress on Objectives of Brad and Sharon

Objective	Monday	Tuesday	Wednesday	Thursday	Friday
Transition from free-play to group—Brad	Morning Circle—teacher #2 Song Circle—teacher #1 Story Group—aide		Morning Circle—aide Story Group—teacher #2		Song Circle—aide Story Group—teacher #2
Request peers to play—Brad	Early free-play—aide	Morning free-play—teacher #2	Afternoon free-play—teacher #1	Early free-play Afternoon free-play—aide	
Play with manipulatives—Brad		Morning free-play—teacher #1			Morning free-play—discovery center—teacher #2
Wash hands—Sharon	Clean up—teacher #1	Clean up—aide	Clean up—aide	Dramatic play—washing babies—teacher #1	
Talk to adults—Sharon	Arrival—teacher #2	Arrival—teacher #2	Arrival—aide	Arrival—teacher #1	Arrival—teacher #1
Sit independently—Sharon	Morning circle—aide	Song Circle—teacher #2	Story Circle—teacher #1	Lunch—aide	Free-play—arts—teacher #2

of art work and writing, checklists of skills, time-sample and category-sample records, and other evidence that documents development (Puckett & Black, 1994). In the case of children with disabilities, the child's IEP or IFSP can be used to organize the portfolio. Sections can be devoted to major goals or outcomes, and subsections can be made for individual child objectives. Within each subsection, evidence of the child's progress can be included. For example, if a subsection is developed around the objective of isolating the child's index finger, a photograph of the child operating a keyboard, electronic game, or other device for which he would need to push a button with his index finger might be included. Other evidence in this subsection could be a finger-paint work sample with a narrative indicating how the lines were made with an isolated index finger, an anecdotal record describing how the child used his index finger to scoop a small car out of a "box garage," or an observation record describing the child's actions during a fingerplay, including how he isolated his index finger during the song. These examples would be collected over a number of weeks, by teachers, therapists, paraprofessionals, and parents.

Table 9.3 is an abbreviated example of the types of summative evidence that might be included in a child's portfolio. Each piece of evidence was collected to document the child's progress toward a specific objective. To get to this point of the summative assessment process, steps 1 through 5 were used so that a planned, systematic procedure was followed. The collection of evidence represented by Table 9.3 is a small sample of the total collected in the child's portfolio. The sum total of all evidence reveals the child's changes over time and the refinement of skills from the beginning of the assessment period to its conclusion.

For a teacher who is collecting summative information on two or three children with IEPs, as well as information about all other children in her classroom, portfolio collection procedures might be organized by learning centers and scheduling routines as well as by children's individual objectives. One way to do this is to identify a tentative list of skills that can be exhibited during a particular routine or at a specific center. Staff members can then look for these types of skills and collect evidence for all children. By collecting portfolio information in this manner, they can document the skills and behaviors of many children simultaneously. Table 9.4 is an example of the types of skills that might be observed during some classroom routines and at typical learning centers.

Confidentiality is paramount when organizing and storing children's assessment information (Hill & Ruptic, 1994; McLoughlin & Lewis, 1994). Such information should be made available only to individuals indicated by the child's parents or legal guardians as being qualified to have access (American Educational Research Association, American Psychological Association, & National Council on Measurement in Education, 1985).

TABLE 9.3 **Example of Types of Organization of Evidence to Document Progress on Brad's Objectives**

Name: Brad

Major Goal: To increase communication with adults and peers

	Evidence
Objective 1: Brad will verbally request items when needed.	**Event sampling record** for five days at various centers and routine times (snack, circle, blocks, art, dramatic play). **Anecdotal recordings** of events that may occur at times when event sampling is not taking place.
Objective 2: Brad will verbally turn take at least three times with peers.	**Communication sample** (audiotape) of free-play activities in dramatic play, blocks, and art centers for three days. **Partial interval sampling** of free-play activities on three different days in three different situations.
Objective 3: Brad will greet adults and children when he enters a room.	**Event sampling record** for five days at arrival, departure, and centers. **Anecdotal records** from parents of events at home or in other settings.

(continued)

TABLE 9.3 *(Continued)*

Name: Brad

	Evidence
Major Goal: To transition among different routines and events in his daily schedule without hitting or crying	
Objective 1: Brad will transition from home to school without hitting or crying more than once a week.	**Event sampling** for two weeks at the beginning of each school day.
Objective 2: Brad will move from one routine to another with the group during his school day without crying or hitting more than once a day.	**Event sampling** for three days.
Major Goal: To take personal care of himself	
Objective 1: Brad will use a spoon to feed himself cereal and semi-solid foods (e.g., yogurt).	**Observations** at snack time. **Behavior sample** (photograph) of snack and lunch times. **Anecdotal reports** from parents.
Objective 2: Brad will put on and button a loose fitting shirt.	**Observations** in dramatic play corner and art area (dress-up clothes and smocks). **Anecdotal reports** from parents at home.
Objective 3: Brad will use a cup without a lid to drink fluids with spilling once out of every ten uses.	**Event sampling** for two weeks every other day; opportunities will be noted and spilling or non-spilling will be noted. **Observations** at snack time. **Anecdotal recordings** if Brad asks for water at any time during the program day. **Anecdotal reports** from parents.

TABLE 9.4   A Very Limited Example of Skills and Behaviors to Observe during Selected Routines and at a Variety of Learning Centers

Routines	Learning Centers
Arrival Time	**Art Center**
Greeting adults and peers	Using writing utensils
Removing outer garments	Tactile preferences
Choosing an activity	Copying forms and shapes
Requesting assistance	Knowledge of color, shape, texture
Grooming	Use of language
Answering questions from adults	Awareness of personal space
Circle Time	**Books/Listening Center**
Turn-taking	Sequencing stories
Attention to task	Answering questions
Answering questions	Turning pages
Awareness of others	Identifying pictures/symbols
Clean-up Time	**Dramatic Play Center**
Following directions (one or more steps)	Turn-taking
Washing hands	Use of language
Transitioning between activities	Role-playing
Assisting others	Symbolic representation
Outside Time	**Block Center**
Running	Visual-perceptual planning
Jumping	Symbolic representation
Balancing	Grasping and placing
Climbing	Awareness of personal space

Although most of the legal and ethical statements regarding assessment information specifically mention children's test results, information in a child's portfolio and other evidence of child progress also should be treated as confidential.

Step 7: Share the information with the child's family and other authorized individuals. After the summative assessment information has been collected, organized, and stored, it must be shared with individuals who need the information to make educational decisions, including family and staff members (Garbarino, & Stott, 1992; Herman, Aschbacher, & Winters, 1992). As in all effective assessment procedures, information about a child will have been collected through many means and usually by many people. However, perhaps not everyone who will need to use the assessment information will have seen it in its entirety. Family members especially, may not have had the opportunity to review all of the assessment data. Therefore it is important to give family members, authorized teachers, and other service providers an opportunity to review the complete portfolio of summative assessment information so they will have the resources they need to make programmatic decisions.

Step 8: Review summative assessment information and use to determine children's progress and make necessary program changes. After review and discussion, families, teachers and other professionals can make decisions about child progress, adaptations to teacher interactions, materials and equipment, and curricular routines and activities.

One of the most important decisions to be made regards children's objectives. Summative assessment allows families and program personnel to determine whether and how a child has achieved an objective. For instance, one of Brad's communication objectives is to "orally greet adults and children when he enters a room." Summative assessment information enables Brad's family and his teachers to determine whether he has this skill, under what conditions he uses it, and whether or not it is important to continue to address this behavior. Summative assessment information may indicate that Brad consistently greets adults in any setting and is very good about greeting peers except when he comes into the classroom. Through observation records and play preferences, the summative assessment information indicates that when he enters the classroom he does not remove his coat or backpack but goes directly to the block center to play. With input from his teachers and his parents, the group may decide that they want to foster his engagement with materials and that greeting his peers in this situation is not a high priority.

This eight-step summative assessment process fulfills the legal mandate of the Individuals with Disabilities Education Act (IDEA) that a systematic, periodic review of the IEP take place (Congressional Record, 1991). The process, however, maintains a developmentally appropriate assessment procedure that incorporates the needs of the individual child and does not rely on standardized, norm-referenced tests given out of context, and maintains a constructivist approach to children's acquisition of skills (Kamii, 1990). It is an approach that helps teachers and families determine progress, program effectiveness, and the appropriateness of goals and objectives through a systematic, organized method.

METHODS OF COLLECTING AND RECORDING INFORMATION

Like formative assessment information, summative information can be collected and recorded in many ways. Observations, anecdotal records, work samples, communication samples, behavior samples, checklists, activity preference records, and sociograms can all be used to collect both summative and formative information. On one hand, anecdotal records can be used to make formative assessment decisions so that a teacher can decide on the next day's activities for a child. An anecdotal record that documents Tiffany holding a glue stick in an immature writing grasp versus her use of a palmar grasp when using markers, crayons, and other writing utensils tells the teacher to plan activities that incorporate the use of glue sticks to further encourage the development of her writing grasp. On the other hand, a series of anecdotal records, across time and documenting Tiffany's grasp of utensils in various activities, helps her teacher, family, and other service providers make a summative conclusion about her hand use and her grasping skills. This aggregate anecdotal information can be used for summative purposes. In addition to the assessment methods mentioned above, event sampling, time sampling, and category sampling are summative techniques that have proven to be particularly useful to the classroom teacher.

Event Sampling

Event sampling is a technique in which the teacher records each time that a child exhibits a skill or behavior (Bailey & Wolery, 1989). It is important to indicate both the number of opportunities that a child had to exhibit the skill or behavior and the number of times it occurred. For example, with Brad we are interested in knowing whether he comments on activities to peers and adults. During a specified period of time, a staff member keeps track of the number of times that he comments spontaneously about materials, peers, adults, or activities. If comments are recorded, they are evidence of his ability to comment on his surroundings. If they are absent, this is evidence that he is not yet conveying information about his activities to others.

Event sampling is used primarily with skills that occur infrequently or tend to occur at predictable intervals. Greeting adults who come to the classroom may be an important skill for a child, but the opportunity to display such a skill may occur infrequently. When it does occur, an event-sampling strategy can be used. Likewise, skills such as hand washing or putting on a coat are low-frequency skills. Hand washing may occur three or four times during a normal preschool day, before meals and after activities. Children put on a coat only when they go outside or participate in dramatic play. These events are predictable, and teachers can plan to watch for them. For example, the following might be one of Brad's objectives: *Brad will move from one routine to another with the group during the school day without crying or hitting more than once a day.* This objective has clear criteria and conditions, and progress can be measured by sampling Brad's behavior during each change in the daily routine. As can be seen in Table 9.5, on November 10, Brad cried once and hit once during eleven transition opportunities. In addition to recording that Brad was successful during nine of the eleven routine changes, the form

TABLE 9.5   Brad's Event Sampling Record

Student: Brad W.   Date of Observations: 11/10/95

Objective: Brad will move from one routine to another with the group during the preschool day without crying or hitting more than once a day.

Routine Transition	Crying (Yes/No)	Hitting (Yes/No)	Comments
Arrival to Free-Play	N	N	took off coat
Free-Play to Circle	N	N	sat next to Jamie
Circle to Free-Play	N	N	went to Art table
Free-Play to Song Circle	N	Y	hit Jamie when could not sit next to him
Song Circle to Outside	N	N	put on coat
Outside to Lunch	Y	N	did not want to come inside
Lunch to Rest Time	N	N	restless on cot
Rest Time to Story Group	N	N	had to wake up
Story Group to Free-Play	N	N	
Free-Play to Movement Group	N	N	asked for twirling sticks
Movement Group to Dismissal	N	N	asked for mother

also provides situational information about his other behaviors during those transition periods. Situational information might include children or adults present at the time of the observation, the activity taking place, the time of day, or an event that occurred immediately before the observed behavior. Recording antecedent or concurrent behaviors can often provide a teacher with ideas about how to improve the child's skills or behavior. In Brad's case, we can tell that he is making smooth transitions to group situations when he is able to sit next to a friend, but that he has some difficulty otherwise.

Time Sampling

Time sampling is a recording and documentation strategy that tracks the occurrence or absence of a skill that a child may exhibit frequently or continuously during a specified time period (Bailey & Wolery, 1989; Puckett & Black, 1994). Such behaviors include attending to a task, talking, or interacting with peers. Some time-sampling strategies require that staff observe the child dur-

TABLE 9.6 **Example of Momentary Time Sample of Brad's Sitting Behavior during Group**

Name: Brad W.										Date: 11/15/95
Objective: Brad will remain seated during group times when appropriate for the activity being conducted.										
Instructions: At 2, 4, 6, 8 and 10 minutes into group time, circle whether Brad is sitting (Y) or not (N).										

Moment	2 min.		4 mins.		6 mins.		8 mins.		10 mins.		Comments
Morning Circle	Y	N	Y	N	Y	N	Y	N	Y	N	
Song Circle	Y	N	Y	N	Y	N	Y	N	Y	N	
Story Group	Y	N	Y	N	Y	N	Y	N	Y	N	
Other :_____	Y	N	Y	N	Y	N	Y	N	Y	N	

ing specific moments when the behavior might be present. Table 9.6 shows a momentary time-sample recording sheet of Brad's sitting behavior during group. This strategy asks that a program staff member observe Brad at two-minute intervals during group to determine whether or not he is sitting. An electronic timer set to ring every two minutes or a tape recorder that plays a tape that sounds every two minutes can be used to alert the staff member that it is time to record Brad's behavior.

Partial interval sampling is another form of time sampling. This recording strategy can be used to document the occurrence of a moderately to frequently occurring behavior that is not predictable. Partial interval sampling requires that a staff person observe the child for a brief but continuous period of time and record the number of occurrences of the skill or behavior. Positive behaviors such as play or communication turn-taking, as well as inappropriate behaviors such as hitting, can be documented in this manner. In Table 9.7, Brad's communication turn-taking is being observed. During six different intervals throughout the day, Brad is observed for ten continuous minutes. Each time he continues a conversation by responding to a peer's communication, the behavior is recorded in the frequency column. The comments column is for recording the specific situation and possible circumstances that may have affected Brad's behavior.

Like event sampling, both momentary time sampling and partial interval time sampling are employed when there is opportunity for the skill to be observed. It is important to designate the criteria for the behavior or skill and to indicate the conditions under which it must occur. If Brad receives an *N*, indicating that he was not sitting at the four-minute mark during song group, the conditions must be present for him to be able to be sitting. If the teacher were leading a song in which the children were expected to stand and march,

TABLE 9.7   Example of Partial Interval Record for Brad's Communication Turn-Taking Skill

Name: Brad W.   Date: 11/21/95

Objective: Brad will respond verbally to other children's communication and continue the conversation.

	Activity	Frequency	Comments
8:45 - 8:55	Early free-play	IIII	Played with Ginny; quiet
9:45 - 9:55	Morning free-play #1	IIII IIII III	Active play in the block corner with Jamie
10:30 - 10:40	Morning free-play #2	III	Working with one other child at the art table
11:50 - 12:00	Lunch	II	Sat at the end of the table and watched a first grade eat pizza they had won
2:15 - 2:25	Afternoon free-play #1	II	Still tired from nap
3:15 - 3:25	Afternoon free-play #2	IIII IIII IIII IIII	Worked with Jamie in both block corner and at the easel

sitting would not be expected, and the moment should not be recorded, because it does not meet the conditions necessary for the skill to be exhibited.

Category Sampling

A final sampling strategy that can be used to document children's progress is category sampling (Bailey & Wolery, 1994; Wolery, 1992). *Category sampling* is a variation of time sampling and utilizes either the momentary or interval sampling technique. It is used when professionals are concerned with variations in a skill or behavior. For example, we are interested in how a child grasps a marker or pencil, but there are a variety of grasping methods. A *pincer grasp* (using the thumb and forefinger), *palmar grasp* (using all four fingers against the palm), or *radial grasp* (using the index and middle finger against the pad of the palm or thumb) might be the categories developed to record how the child grasps.

When category sampling is used to document a child's behaviors or skills, it is important to create exhaustive categories. In other words, teachers and other professionals should try to anticipate all possible variations of the skill or behavior being documented (Bailey & Wolery, 1989). Because this is difficult to do, most category sampling records have an "other" category or a "comments" category to explain behaviors or variations of the skill that might not have been anticipated. It is also important to develop categories that are mutually exclusive (Bailey & Wolery, 1989). A teacher should not be able to indicate that the child is simultaneously exhibiting two variations of the same behavior or skill being observed. Table 9.8 is an example of a category sampling record that shows five mutually exclusive group behavior categories.

TABLE 9.8   Example of Brad's Category Sampling Record for Sitting Behavior

Name: Brad W.   Date: 12/6/95

Objective: Brad will remain seated during group times when appropriate for the activity being conducted.

	Sitting and attending	Sitting and responding to the teacher	Sitting and talking with a peer	Standing in the group	Away from the group	Comments
Morning Circle 9:20						
Morning Circle 9:25						
Song Circle 11:05						
Song Circle 11:10						
Story Group 1:45						
Story Group 1:50						
Other Time: _____						
Other Time: _____						

CHOOSING A SAMPLING STRATEGY

Deciding which sampling strategy to use to collect information about a child's skills or behaviors is often difficult. One factor that assists in this determination is the frequency with which the skill or behavior is displayed or may potentially be displayed. "Communicating," for instance, whether a child does it through oral language, gestures, sign language, or other modes, is potentially a frequently occurring behavior that a time-sampling strategy might be used to document.

Self-care skills, such as hand washing and eating, are generally infrequently occurring behaviors. Because the number of times a child uses these skills during the program day can be counted easily, an event-sampling system might be used to document their occurrence. Table 9.9 lists a number of

TABLE 9.9   Examples of Frequent, Moderate, and Infrequent Behaviors or Skills

Frequency of Behavior/Skill	Possible Sampling Strategy
Continuously or Frequently Occuring Behaviors/Skills	
Talking	Momentary time, partial interval or event sampling
Attending to task	
Listening in group	
Sitting at story circle	
Moderately Occurring Behaviors/Skills	
Requesting assistance	Event sampling
Turn-taking	Momentary time or partial interval sampling
Commenting to peers/adults	Event sampling
Using a pincer grasp	Momentary time or partial interval sampling
Infrequently Occurring Behaviors/Skills	
Washing hands	Event sampling or other* assessment stategies
Greeting strangers	
Using scissors	
Saying "yes" or "no"	

*Other assessment strategies might include observations, anecdotal records, or work samples. In the case of using scissors, a work sample with a note could provide evidence of the child's ability to cut with scissors.

common skills and behaviors found in children's IEPs or IFSPs, the general frequency of the skills, and the sampling method or methods that might be used to document them.

Sometimes the context of the skill, in addition to the frequency with which it is used, determines the sampling method most appropriate for documentation. For example, if a teacher wants to document a child's use of a pincer grasp she might use an event-sampling method throughout the day. However, if she is concerned about the child's use of a pincer grasp during the time the child is performing an art or manipulative activity, a category or momentary time-sampling procedure might be appropriate because of the increased opportunities to use a pincer grasp during those activities.

Whether one of these sampling procedures or one of the assessment strategies presented in Chapter 3 are used, it is important that the strategy match the skill or behavior identified by the objective. If it does not, inaccurate information will have been collected, staff time will have been wasted, and, most importantly, teachers and family members will not be able to determine the child's progress.

ADDITIONAL SUGGESTIONS FOR COLLECTING SUMMATIVE ASSESSMENT INFORMATION

Although the primary concern in conducting summative assessments is with children's progress toward achieving their IEP or IFSP objectives, collecting additional information is beneficial to the children, their families, and their teachers. When observing children for skills or behaviors that indicate acquisition of objectives, program staff should also note other skills and behaviors that the children exhibit. Consulting developmental checklists such as those found in Allen and Marotz (1989) helps teachers determine the appropriate skills and behaviors to note. For example, the language of a 4-year-old typically includes the use of prepositions such as *on, under,* and *in,* as well as possessives such as *his, momma's,* and *their.* Documentation of these skills, in addition to the objectives found in the child's IEP or IFSP, provides everyone with a more well-rounded view of the child's abilities.

Whether focusing on children's IEP or IFSP skills, classroom interactions, or general development, it is most important that observations be recorded across settings, situations, and times. In this way, we can be assured that behaviors or skills have been generalized across both the school day and the child's day outside school.

Summative assessment information about a child's skills and behavior should be collected from multiple settings. A skill exhibited in one setting may not easily transfer to another. Even skills that a child should be able to transfer easily, such as using a fork, may not occur at home, in restaurants, or at a relative's house. Professionals should work with family members and other caregivers to identify instances at home, with relatives, at church, or in other settings during which the skills may be used. For example, if the concern is with Brad requesting his peers play with him, staff members might ask his parents to keep track of whether and how he requests that his siblings, parents, or playmates play with him at home.

Family members are important members of the summative assessment process and can provide many sources of assessment information. At least three strategies can be used to include family members in the summative assessment of their children.

Collect Information at Home

Professionals can ask family members to review the objectives from their children's program plans and to note or record any evidence of those skills. In addition, talking informally or by conducting an interview with family members, evidence can be gathered about children's abilities. A large body of recent research has indicated that family members' identification of their children's skills are as accurate as those of professionals (Bricker & Squires, 1989; Diamond & Squires, 1993). These findings reinforce the efficacy of including parents in the data collection process.

Collect Information in Other Settings

Teachers often do not have the opportunity to observe children in other settings. Parents and primary caregivers see them in settings such as at church, the grocery store, neighborhood parks, relatives' houses, and restaurants. Asking parents to report evidence of their children's skills in various settings adds to the validity and accuracy of the summative assessment process. This is especially true for skills used across settings such as eating with utensils, talking with adults, or going to the bathroom.

Rate the Importance of Skills

Family members can be asked about the relative importance of a skill or behavior that may be present or absent from their child's repertoire. Skills included on a child's IEP may be very important in school settings, but less so in other areas of the child's life. For instance, it is important for preschoolers to learn to place pegs in a board because of the fine motor and pincer grasp implications of that skill. Family members may not, however, consider this an important skill and may indicate that a child's lack of progress in this area is not critical to them. Parents and caregivers can indicate the importance of a skill relative to all of the settings in which the child spends time.

Summative assessment information should be collected across various social situations. The presence of a group of peers, strange adults, no adults, or one trusted adult may greatly influence a child's ability or willingness to use or exhibit a skill or behavior. Brad may be able to greet his teacher when he arrives at school. However, when his father takes him to the grocery store, Brad may not be able to say "hello" to the cashier. Brad's ability to use this skill in different social situations is important to know for his family, his teachers, and other staff members.

Finally, summative assessment information should be collected at various times of the day. Whether they have had enough sleep, eaten recently, or just awakened from a nap may influence children's ability to use a skill or exhibit a behavior. A skill that a teacher believes to be absent from a child at 3:00 P.M. may be present at 9:30 A.M., or it may be exhibited after lunch but not after outside play.

As an example of the importance of collecting information across times, settings, and social situations, consider the process for documenting Brad's ability to request help. The teacher needs to know whether he has the skills during meal times, when playing independently, and when in a large group. Each of these situations contains slightly different but equally important social dynamics, occurs at different times of the day, and is demonstrated in different settings. Knowing that Brad can or cannot use the skill under a specific circumstance provides his family and the program staff with information they can use to determine whether he needs further work on the skill, when it is appropriate to expect the skill, and when not to press him to use it.

Involving Children in Their Own Summative Assessment

Finally, it is important to include children in their own summative assessment process. By including them, teachers can begin to tap into what they value, enjoy, and find interesting. Following are four questions to ask of young children about their work and skills.

1. Ask whether they want to save something. When collecting work samples, teachers can ask children whether they want to save something special to share with adults and also ask them to describe their work and record their responses in a note. This can be done with art work, photographs of block and manipulative structures, and even dramatic play scenarios.
2. Ask children what skills or behaviors they are proud that they can accomplish. When collecting information from children, teachers can ask what children think they do best and ask them to perform the work or behavior. If it is a finger play, it can be recorded on audiotape. If it is a Leggo

structure, take an instant photograph of the building when it is complete or as it is being built. Again, ask the children to talk about their work, recording what they say in an accompanying note.

3. Ask what children think of the work that has been collected. Teachers can share with children the work samples, communication samples, videotapes, or audiotapes of their skills and behaviors and ask them what they think of their productions. Children's comments can be included as part of the summative assessment process.

4. Ask children how they completed their work. When teachers collect a work, communication, or behavior sample, they can ask children to talk about the process they went through to complete the task. Asking them "why" and "how" questions can provide insight into their thinking, decision making, and planning.

When teachers ask children to comment on their skills and behaviors they should explain why they are interested in the children's thoughts. Children should be assured that the questions are asked so that others will be able to learn about them and know the positive skills that they possess. Children thus begin to learn about privacy, confidentiality, and respect for information about others.

SUMMARY

By creating a systematic summative assessment process for the children in their programs, teachers document progress toward their objectives and can communicate that information to the children's families and other staff members. Including summative assessment information from both family members and the children adds to the richness of the data and enables teachers to make decisions about both the effectiveness of the program and individual children's accomplishments. The summative assessment process may occur either toward the end of a marking period or at the end of a program, but the information gained from the process enables professionals to continue to serve young children with disabilities effectively within a developmentally appropriate context.

ACTIVITIES AND RESOURCES

Activities

1. Review the objectives or outcomes from an IEP or IFSP and determine which method(s) should be used to collect information about the child's progress related to specific skills and/or behaviors.

2. Select three objectives from a child's IEP. Determine when, by whom, and how often evidence should be collected to determine the child's progress.
3. Using two of the objectives in Brad's IEP, create recording forms to document his progress for each required skill.
4. Review the objectives in Brad's IEP. For which of these objectives can his parents collect information? What type of information will be collected for each of the objectives you have identified?

Class Discussion Questions

1. Using your classroom or one that you have observed, select two learning centers and list the methods you can use to collect summative information about children's skills.
2. How can you make summative information readily accessible to those who must use it to determine children's progress and make decisions about curricular changes, yet also ensure that the information is secure and kept confidential?
3. Review Tiffany's case. We know that she has cerebral palsy and that she cannot grasp objects well with her hands. Through continued observation, we learn that she especially enjoys creating pictures. At the art center you have paints, glue, collage materials, brushes, and Popsicle sticks. How can you determine whether these materials meet Tiffany's needs and interests? What type of information will you collect so that you can better adapt the center to meet her needs?
4. Children's portfolios can contain large amounts of information. How can you share the information with the children's family in a meaningful manner?

REFERENCES

Allen, K.E., & Marotz, L. (1989). *Developmental profiles: Birth to six.* Albany, NY: Delmar Publishers.

American Educational Research Association, American Psychological Association, & National Council on Measurement in Education. (1985). *Standards for educational and psychological testing.* Washington, DC: American Psychological Association.

Bagnato, S., Neisworth, J., & Munson, S. (1989). *Linking developmental assessment and early intervention: Curriculum based prescriptions.* (2nd ed.). Rockville, MD: Aspen Publishers.

Bailey, D., & Wolery, M. (1989). *Assessing infants and preschoolers with handicaps.* Columbus, OH: Merrill.

Bricker, D., & Squires, J. (1989). The effectiveness of parental screening of at-risk infants: The infant monitoring questionnaires. *Topics in Early Childhood Special Education, 9* (3), 67–85.

Campbell, P. (1991). Evaluation and assessment in early intervention for infants and toddlers. *Journal of Early Intervention, 15*(1), 36–45.

Congressional Record. (October 7, 1991). *Public Law 102-119: Individuals with Disabilities Education Act.* Washington, DC: U.S. Government Printing Office.

Darling-Hammond, L., Ancess, J., & Falk, B. (1995). *Authentic assessment in action: Studies of schools and students at work.* New York: Teachers College Press.

Diamond, K., & Squires, J. (1993). The role of parental report in the screening and assessment of young children. *Journal of Early Intervention, 17* (2), 107–115.

Evans, S., Evans, W., & Mercer, C. (1986). *Assessment for instruction.* Boston: Allyn and Bacon.

Garbarino, J., & Stott, F. (1992). *What children can tell us: Eliciting, interpreting, and evaluating critical information from children.* San Francisco: Jossey-Bass Publishers.

Grace, C., & Shores, E. (1991). *The portfolio and its use: Developmentally appropriate assessment of young children.* Little Rock, AR: Southern Association for Children under Six.

Herman, J., Aschbacker, P., & Winters, L. (1992). *A practical guide to alternative assessment.* Alexandria, VA: Association for Supervision and Curriculum Development.

Hill, B., & Ruptic, C. (1994). *Practical aspects of authentic assessment: Putting the pieces together.* Norwood, MA: Christopher-Gordon Publishers.

Hills, T. (1992). Reaching potentials through appropriate assessment. In S. Bredekamp & T. Rosegrant (Eds.). *Reaching potentials: Appropriate curriculum and assessment for young children: Volume 1* (pp. 43–63). Washington, DC: National Association for the Education of Young Children (NAEYC).

Kamii, C. (1990). *Achievement testing in the early grades: The games grown-ups play.* Washington, DC: National Association for the Education of Young Children (NAEYC).

McLoughlin, J., & Lewis, R. (1994). *Assessing special students.* (4th ed.). New York: Merrill.

Meisels, S., Jablon, J., Marsden, D., Dichtelmiller, M., & Dorfman, A. (1994). *The work sampling system: An overview.* (3rd ed.). Ann Arbor, MI: Rebus Planning Associates.

Paulson, F., Paulson, P., & Meyer, C. (1991). What makes a portfolio a portfolio? *Educational leadership, 48*(5), 60–63.

Puckett, M., & Black, J. (1994). *Authentic assessment of the young child: Celebrating development and learning.* New York: Merrill.

Salvia, J., & Ysseldyke, J. (1995). *Assessment.* (6th ed.). Boston: Houghton Mifflin.

Wolery, M. (1992). *Teaching students with moderate to severe disabilities: Use of response prompting strategies.* White Plains, NY: Longman.

INDEX